£3
M

NEW WRITINGS
by SWINBURNE

NEW WRITINGS *by SWINBURNE*

or MISCELLANEA NOVA ET CURIOSA

Being A Medley of Poems, Critical Essays, Hoaxes and Burlesques

EDITED BY CECIL Y. LANG

AND PUBLISHED BY SYRACUSE UNIVERSITY PRESS 1964

Manufactured in the United States of America
by The Heffernan Press of Worcester, Massachusetts
and Vail-Ballou Press of Binghamton, New York

FOR

VIOLETTE
(without whom this book
would never have been
finished at all)

AND

FRANÇOIS-MICHEL
(without whom it would
have been finished
much sooner)

CONTENTS

PREFACE

I have never measured, even approximately, the total quantity of Swinburne's unpublished writings. It is enormous, and may approach, if it does not equal, what he published. By comparison with what might have been, then, my aim here has been modest—to bring together in one volume those works that have not before appeared in hard covers and that, at the present stage of Swinburne studies, seem to me to have a clear, unequivocal claim to attention.

In a slightly different form, this book was originally begun nearly ten years ago. When well over half completed, it had to be shelved indefinitely because, contrary to my expectations, certain essential parts of several manuscripts were not, after all, available. To the limit of my resources, I have long observed and recorded the appearance and disappearance, the advance and withdrawal, the transfer from hand to hand, the ultimate apotheosis in a public or academic library of the Swinburne manuscripts that come on the market, much as the great auction houses, librarians and collectors, directors of museums and galleries keep tabs on the choicer incunabula, Old (and modern) Masters, the manuscripts, and even typescripts, of seminal poems; so when I became aware, not long ago, that the several texts, one by one, and for various reasons, had at long last become accessible, I took my work down from the shelf, and this volume is the result.

Spanning Swinburne's entire productive life, it consists of a largish body of verse, some criticism, and a considerable quantity of what I have grouped together as "Hoax and Burlesque." The title is a punctilious epitome of the contents, and, except for the odor of waggery or preciosity, could have been prolonged, in the manner of the old miscellanies, to read:

Entertainments for the Ingenious of Both Sexes
and
An Antidote against Melancholy
Calculated for the Diversion of the Country

—though not, alas, "For the Profit of the Publisher."

Swinburne has lain so long in limbo already that I would scruple to repel anyone by excessive enthusiasm, but I am bound to say, nonetheless, that "Duriesdyke," "Roundel," "The Ballad of Villon and Fat Madge," "Father Garasse," "Les Amours Etiques. Par Félicien Cossu," and "Les Abîmes. Par Ernest Clouët" all seem to me, in their several ways, little masterpieces of balladry, lyric, translation, obloquy, and satiric burlesque, that "La Fille du policeman," if only Swinburne could have taken his comedy seriously, *ought* to have been an achievement comparable, in kind and quality, to *Les Liaisons dangereuses*, to *Der Rosenkavalier*, to Byron's *Don Juan* or even (one ventures to hint) the great opera centering on the same superb antihero. But, though a robust comic gift was stifled, his imitative and assimilative powers were so astonishing that they win the admiration even of those hordes immune to his other charms and achievements. The ballad "Duriesdyke" is a triumph in its own right, but inevitably, in this fallen world, part of the "virtue" of a literary ballad consists in its very imperfections, part of our pleasure arises from being able to isolate what is too modern or too obviously contrived. A mastersinger like Swinburne, latter-day Northumbrian minstrel without peer, plays the game with such finesse and sophistication that it is almost refined out of existence: "One cannot help feeling that Swinburne's modern touches in 'Bonnie Bahome' are perfectly deliberate," writes Mrs. Ehrenpreis ("Swinburne's Edition of Popular Ballads," *PMLA*, Dec. 1963, p. 571), "that he could have mimicked the ballad style even more precisely if he chose. . . . But when he does choose, Swinburne can recreate to perfection the true ballad note, something which has always been said to be impossible for a 'literary' artist." Obviously, a comparable response sharpens one's relish of the translations, the French poems, and the hoaxes and burlesques.

Swinburne shares with Dryden, Coleridge, Poe, Arnold, and T. S. Eliot the distinction of being a great poet who was also a practicing critic, a galaxy in which he is neither least nor the least versatile, and despite the limitations of subject matter, tone, mood of the pieces printed here, I believe the volume will both enlarge and deepen critical appreciation of his whole achievement. I think it might alter fundamentally the general view of his whole personality. I am myself, of course, a fierce Swinburnian—my very handwriting is becoming like his—and I respect and admire, in some

important way, all the works included here and believe my pleasure
in them will be shared by others. To some extent, their appeal is
no doubt to the jaded palate, but, apart from that perhaps too rare
enjoyment reserved for connoisseurs, the selections, one and another,
tell us much about Swinburne's conception of the poet's role and of
the nature of poetry, they extend our knowledge of the creative
process, his working habits, critical opinions, critical assumptions,
and of their evolution, they unmask more effectively than anything
else I know the provinciality of English literature, the insularity of
English criticism, the priggish humbuggery of the journalism, the
vulgarity of popular morality, the often infirmities of received repu-
tations. And they are one and all, whatever else they may or may
not be, readable.

I am not, however, so blinded by partisanship that I consider
every single piece here a masterwork, and I believe the book has a
value that is not strictly literary. Whatever future study of Swinburne is not to be exclusively or primarily esthetic will have to be
(I am persuaded) psychological, even psychoanalytical, before it
can properly be biographical—that one shudders to imagine what
will be perpetrated in the name of all this cannot fairly alter one's
conviction—and it is surely significant that every piece in this
volume, late as well as early, will contribute to such an investigation. This claim may be of course either a truism or a fallacy, for
any piece of writing, given a key or sufficient authority or a short
supply of tact, can be used as some kind of index to its creator's
mind, and in the process negative evidence or no evidence at all
may seem as valuable as "fact." Nevertheless, hardly anyone would
deny that Swinburne's preoccupation (as revealed in this volume
alone) with Sade and Villon, Webster and Marlowe, "spasmodic"
poetry, Garasse, "The Maiden Tribute of Modern Babylon" and
the hypocrisy of the Parisian press in dealing with it, with the actual
creation of such alter egos as "Félicien Cossu" and "Ernest Clouët"
and of such fantasies (I use the word in its modern psychological
sense) as "La Sœur de la reine" and "La Fille du policeman" sprang
from a single taproot.

And there are other considerations. Why, for instance, did he
collect none of these works for publication in any of his several
dozen volumes? For all the prose it is easy to turn up reasons, and
for most of the verse also (though not for "Duriesdyke" and

"Roundel," the earliest and latest in date). Second, soberer thoughts doubtless led him to withhold most of the critical pieces, and the nimble-witted despair of the human condition seen in the hoaxes and burlesques is glimpsed only fleetingly in his published works.

But something more must be said. It has been suggested that in "La Fille du policeman" Swinburne was motivated by a dissatisfaction with the "Victorianism" of his society. This observation, I suspect, though not inaccurate as far as it goes, finally begs the question. That certain critical stances can be assumed only with certain kinds of masks is no doubt a basic principle of satire—certainly, current fashion would have it so—and all of the hoaxes and burlesques here are, in some degree, satirical. But I think it is true that the satire and burlesque (the satire of English society, for instance, the burlesque of French writers dealing with English settings) are merely vehicles for deeper, more intimate compulsions. What satire, what burlesque can be found in the poems "Messaline au cirque" and "Charenton en 1810," both attributed to "Félicien Cossu"? A thin edge of self-mockery, a hardly visible barrier of ironic distance. Nothing more. The undergraduate who invented Ernest Wheldrake in order to demolish him, the poet who composed his own epigraphs, the critic who, writing his essay "Matthew Arnold's New Poems," created a French observer in order to controvert his elder, the novelist who issued *A Year's Letters* under the name "Mrs. Horace Manners," the mimic whose surgically incisive parodies, in *The Heptalogia*, of Tennyson, the Brownings, Rossetti, Patmore, and Owen Meredith, all anonymous, were so far superior to his parody of himself, also anonymous, was the same strange, brilliant creature whom Lady Trevelyan sketched as "the typical miss anglaise émancipée" to be passed off on George Sand or who, even earlier, had taken the role of "Mrs. Skewton in her Bath chair" in a tableau from *Dombey and Son,* who, as Herbert Seyton in an obvious self-portrait in *Lesbia Brandon,* successfully carries off a masquerade as a young girl, who, as a rising young poet, nearly became the anonymous editor of a new literary review, who had (or thought he had) an agreement with his publisher by which he could send in, as he put it, "without my name and without in any way committing myself to their authorship, MSS which I should wish you to print as though they were avowedly or probably mine" (*Letters,* I, 156). Neither Stendhal, with his hundred-odd pseudonyms, nor Defoe, perpetually surrendering to the first person singular, nor such voluptuous votaries of their own egos as Rousseau and Gide, nor Emily Dickinson, with her unposted letter to the world, is a stranger case in point. The biographer and critic of Swinburne will have to recognize the pattern in all this and deal with its relation to the recurrent themes, in both the poetry and prose, of barrenness and sterility, Lesbianism, incest, the death of love, spiritual withdrawal and isolation ("I will keep my soul in a place out of sight," "I hid my heart in a nest of roses"), all counterpointed in a peculiarly Swinburnian way, with those of growth, fertility, liberty, freedom, and the progress of mind. Every piece in this volume has some obvious bearing on such an approach.

The book is so designed that, for those who prefer it, Swinburne can speak for himself with a minimum of interference by the editor. My conscience as a scholar and whatever vestiges of puritanism remain in me would have been amply satisfied by the formidable, fascinating difficulties encountered in the mere assembling and transcribing of "The Chaotic School" and "La Fille du policeman," but in general Swinburne's work is so little known that a certain amount of commentary and critical apparatus seemed desirable, seemed in some cases indispensable. I love footnotes, and I love them at the foot of the page, but since this is, after all, the first edition of most of the works here, decorum demands that they stand alone. The editorial matter is, therefore, at the end of the book, easy to avoid and (I hope) easy to find. Included in it is a fair amount of additional relevant material—exiled to the notes because it seemed too frail for the first part or because it was already (technically) available in boards.

My commentary deals with "sources" and "influences," which, even in the colleges and universities, are certainly not the mode of the day, but I do not apologize for it any more than I apologize for my love of Swinburne, who (though the wind is shifting) is certainly not a modish poet. He is said to have been much influenced by Hugo, and most of his French verse is Hugolian to the last degree. Everyone says so. But no one has said how or where or precisely in what way. In protest against so much vagueness I have tried to be at least suggestive, and I hope it will be helpful to have some such demonstration on record, once.

For myself personally, though I am undoubtedly guilty of having conducted my education in public, the quest, the demonstration, have been entirely salutary. My wife, having a strictly Continental education, lacked the advantages of being trained, as I had been, to distrust, even to dislike or scorn, long didactic or hortatory poems with great themes, written in the nineteenth century, and she was astonished at the (ignorant) superciliousness with which I viewed Hugo. Nous avons changé tout cela—and so much else! My admiration for Hugo, though not yet Swinburnian—few of us, after all, can aspire to such perfection of surrender—is, as they used to say, utter, and I am heartily ashamed.

One's feelings upon concluding a book are ambivalent. Relief is of course present, however keen the dread of proofreading and indexing, but there is regret as well. One is reluctant to abandon the cherished, bewitching problems, lived with so constantly and so long, recognizing how much less imperfect it all might be after another decade of reading, worrying, burrowing, borrowing, despairing. But as it becomes apparent to me, year by year, that I know less and less and that there are more problems than there are solutions, I begin to realize what wise masters have long reminded us—that art is long, that no life lives forever, that I solicit my thoughts with matters hid, that the gods made me mutable, not perfect, that a good book is indeed precious lifeblood. My melancholy is therefore probably assuageable. It is certainly diminished by the pleasure of being able to acknowledge in print the generous, selfless help I have received. Without Lowell Kerr, who handsomely gave me photostats of his portions of "The Chaotic School," and John S. Mayfield, who made available to me his privately printed issue of "Le Prince prolétaire" and much else, this book would not have been. Henri Peyre, Frank E. Brown, and Talbot Donaldson, more than anyone else, encouraged and aided me from the beginning. Halsted VanderPoel lent me the album of Swinburne manuscripts containing "La Sœur de la reine" and the French poems years before he presented it to the Library of Congress, and I am obliged, further, to David C. Mearns and Carroll Hollis in the Manuscript Division there for drawing my attention to the donation. Whether one can have a love affair with a library is not certain, but everybody who has had the privilege of working in the Yale University Library owes to it more than can decorously be recorded in print, and I am specially indebted to Herman W. Liebert, to Donald Wing and

Roy Watkins for favors as witty and graceful as they were helpful, and, as always, to Barbara Simison and Marjorie Wynne. Herbert Cahoon, at the Pierpont Morgan Library, called my attention to the lovely (and puzzling) "Roundel" printed here. The ballad "Duries-dyke" owes its very survival as a whole poem to Anne Henry Ehren-preis, who generously gave me permission to reprint it and, in addition, helped me in many other ways, strategic, diplomatic, delib-erative, and all Swinburnians are always in the debt of Clyde Kenneth Hyder, who has counseled and steadied me for over a dozen years. Jean Borsch, Donald Gallup, Lachlan Phil Kelley, W. D. Paden, Robert L. Peters, Gordon Ray, James M. Osborn, Herbert C. Schulz, Donald A. Sinclair, Garry Wills, and Edmund Wilson have all been intimately involved, in different ways, with different parts of the several Swinburne manuscripts, and to them all I am indebted, specifically and generally. And Leslie Marchand, Bernard Schilling, David Smith, Mark Reed, and Jerome McGann have contributed much more than I would attempt to define in a preface. The book was begun in the first place during a leave of absence made possible by the Morse Fund at Yale. More recently, a grant from the American Philosophical Society gave me an op-portunity to spend time in England and work with the actual manuscripts in the British Museum, an investigation that made it possible for me to draw certain conclusions and put on record in-formation and documentation that I believe will be helpful for other students.

CECIL Y. LANG

Syracuse, New York
Summer, 1964

POETRY

DURIESDYKE

The rain rains sair on Duriesdyke
    Both the winter through and the spring;
And she that will gang to get broom thereby
    She shall get an ill thing.

The rain rains sair on Duriesdyke
    Both the winter and the summer day;
And he that will steek his sheep thereby
    He shall go sadly away.

"Between Crossmuir and Duriesdyke
10]   The fieldhead is full green;
The shaws are thick in the fair summer,
    And three wellheads between.

"Flower of broom is a fair flower,
    And heather is good to play."
O she went merry to Duriesdyke,
    But she came heavy away.

"It's I have served you, Burd Maisry,
    These three months through and mair;
And the little ae kiss I gat of you,
20]   It pains me aye and sair.

"This is the time of heather-blowing,
    And that was syne in the spring;
And the little ae leaf comes aye to red,
    And the corn to harvesting."

The first kiss their twa mouths had,
    Sae fain she was to greet;
The neist kiss their twa mouths had,
    I wot she laughed fu' sweet.

3

"Cover my head with a silken hood,
　　My feet with a yellow claith;
For to stain my body wi' the dyke-water
　　God wot I were fu' laith."

30]

He's happit her head about wi' silk,
　　Her feet with a gowden claith;
The red sendal that was of price
　　He's laid between them baith.

The grass was low by Duriesdyke,
　　The high heather was red;
And between the grass and the high heather
　　He's tane her maidenhead.

40]

They did not kiss in a noble house,
　　Nor yet in a lordly bed;
But their mouths kissed in the high heather
　　Between the green side and the red.

"I have three sailing ships, Maisry,
　　For red wheat and for wine;
The maintopmast is a bonny mast,
　　Three furlongs off to shine.

"The foremast shines like new lammer,
　　The mizen-mast like steel:
Gin ye wad sail wi' me, Maisry,
　　The warst should carry ye weel."

50]

"Gin I should sail wi' you, Lord John,
　　Out under the rocks red,
It's wha wad be my mither's bower-maiden
　　To hap saft her feet in bed?

"Gin I should sail wi' you, Lord John,
　　Out under the rocks white,
There's nane wad do her a very little ease
　　To hap her left and right."

60]

It fell upon the midwinter
    She gat mickle scaith and blame;
She's bound hersell by the white water
    To see his ships come hame.

She's leaned hersell against the wind,
    To see upon the middle tide;
The faem was fallen in the running wind,
    The wind was fallen in the waves wide.

"There's nae moon by the white water
70]   To do me ony good the day;
And but this wind a little slacken,
    They shall have a sair seaway.

"O stir not for this med, baby,
    O stir not at my side;
Ye'll have the better birth, baby,
    Gin ye wad but a little abide.

"Gin ye winna cease for the pity of him
    O cease for the pity of me;
There was never bairn born of a woman
80]   Between the sea-wind and the sea:
There was never bairn born of a woman
    That was born so bitterly."

The ship drove hard upon the wind,
    I wot it drove full mightily;
But the fair gold sides upon the ship
    They were bursten with the sea.

"O I am sae fain for you, Lord John,
    Gin ye be no sae fain
How shall I bear wi' my body,
90]   It is sae full of pain?"

"O I am sae fain of your body,
    Ye are no sae fain of me;
But the sails are riven wi' the wind
    And the sides are full of sea."

O when she saw the sails riven
    The sair pain bowed her back;
But when she saw the sides bursten
    I wot her very heart brak.

100]

The wind waxed in the sea between,
    The rain waxed in the land;
Lord John was happit wi' saut sea-faem,
    Lady Maisry wi' sea-sand:
And the little bairn between them twa
    That was to her right hand.

The rain rains sair on Duriesdyke
    To the land side and the sea;
There was never bairn born of a woman
    That was born mair bitterly.

CHARENTON EN 1810[1]

En ce temps-là c'était un vieillard grave et fort;[2]
Il avait le front calme et l'œil serein; la Mort
Avait peur à l'aspect du satyre sublime;
Et la Douleur, qui ronge et mord comme une lime,
Se tordait sous son pied comme un chien écrasé.
Parfois il débordait de son cœur évasé
Quelque parole amère, effroyable, cynique;
Tout se courbait devant ce vieillard titanique,
La Haine avec l'Amour, le Mal avec le Bien:
10] On sentait, à le voir rire et songer, que rien,
Ni le Désir dont l'œil éblouissant étonne,
Ni l'Homme qui rugit, ni Dieu qui trompe et tonne,
Ni l'affreuse Vertu, gouge au cœur ulcéré,
N'aurait su mettre un pli sur ce front vénéré.
Il vit le monde énorme et vide où rien ne bouge;
Gomorrhe lui jetait des reflets d'un feu rouge,
Et Capri tout entier s'allumait sous ses yeux;[3]
Il contemple; et sa main semble avoir dans son creux
Tout ce grand siècle éteint qui n'est qu'un brouillard pâle;
20] Sporus couché sanglant près d'Héliogabale,[4]
Et le plaisir caché sous la profonde horreur,
Et les bains effrayants de ce sombre empereur[5]
Qui livrait sa chair nue aux morsures craintives
Des enfants violés et des filles plaintives,
Et saignait des garçons pour sucer les plus beaux;
Le succube qui rôde et rit dans les tombeaux;
Sémiramis pâmée au milieu de l'étable;
Et la Luxure auprès du Meurtre assise à table;
La fauve Lesbienne au corps brûlé de feux;[6]
30] Et l'abîme: et l'amour sans forme et sans aveux,
Ce qu'un faune impudique en ses vêtements cache;
Et cette reine, ayant des appétits de vache,[7]
Haletante, et l'œil plein d'une affreuse douceur,
Mère du Minotaure et de Phèdre sa sœur;

Et Vénus Aphacite,[8] effroi de la nature;
Toute la flamme avec toute la pourriture;[9]
Et de Retz aspirant la cendre avec les chairs
Et la fumée humaine éparse dans les airs;
Cinyras[10]renversé sur les seins de sa fille;
40] Tout ce qui vibre, éclate, émeut, frissonne et brille;
La terre en fièvre, monstre aux ébats furieux;
Le ciel, lupanar fait d'azur luxurieux
Où s'échappe et jaillit le jet d'un Dieu phallique
Qui laisse aller sa gourme en un flot métallique;
Où la lune erre et cherche un assouvissement;
Où le grand soleil entre au lit cyniquement[11]
Et répand, rouge et nu, sans pudeur et sans trêve,
Le débordement vaste et vermeil de sa sève;
(Car les rayons sont tous des souillures; l'envers
50] Du ciel, c'est le boyau pourri[12] de l'univers;)
Il marchait l'œil voilé, fauve; et toute Sodôme
Vivait, rêvait, brûlait, hurlait dans ce grand homme.

Il touchait au grand temps, au siècle antique, aux dieux;
À le voir on sentait un frisson aux cheveux;
Sa mâchoire avait l'air d'une faim titanique;
Il avait la candeur superbe et satanique;
Quant il baisait, sa bouche avait la soif du sang;
Son rire était un grand rictus éblouissant,
Son haleine était comme un souffle plein de rage;
60] Il semblait le Priape assis sous le feuillage,
Qui ronge à belles dents sa nymphe au dos bruni;
Cet homme était le noir cadet de l'infini.

Il revoyait, plissant son sourcil plein de rides,
Marseille et la fureur des âpres cantharides,
La tanière d'Arcueil, les onguents, le canif,[13]
La chair trouée et rouge et qu'il taillait à vif.

Un dédain sombre enflait sa poitrine orageuse.
L'empire l'avait pris dans sa griffe fangeuse,
Il souriait. Cet homme avait des dieux à lui.
70] Il vit tout, mais jamais il ne fut ébloui.
Un appétit grouillait dans son âme profonde
Plus grand que Bonaparte et plus grand que le monde.[14]
Or, un soir, un jeune homme âgé de vingt-deux ans

Vit ce front blême et fier chargé de cheveux blancs,
Ces yeux noirs, cette bouche impérieuse et fine;
Il tressaillit. L'enfant lisait ce soir *Justine;*
Il leva le regard, comme on fait en priant,
De la page proscrite au vieillard souriant.
Enfin, pensif, il dit: "Qu'est-ce donc que cet homme?
80]   Je voudrais bien savoir, pardieu, ce qu'il se nomme.
On se rappelle, à voir les gestes de sa main,
Les sublimes ébats du vieux monde romain,
Tous ceux qui furent grands et qu'on appelle infâmes,
Femmes de leurs maris et maris de leurs femmes;
Tout l'éblouissement au sein des nuits rentré;
Le gladiateur nu dans l'arène éventré,
L'empereur qui lui tient son talon sur la nuque,
En flattant de sa lèvre imberbe un glabre eunuque;
Tout ce que la nature abhorre, et ce que Dieu,
90]   Lâche et jaloux, noya dans un grand flot de feu;
Ce qui revit; ce qu'on dérobe à sa colère;
Ce que rêva Socrate et ce que fit Tibère;
La cynique mamelle où boit le monde entier,
Et l'emblème aperçu du côté du sentier;
Ce qu'un satyre errant venait apprendre au pâtre,
Et ce que la vertu funeste efface et châtre;
Ce qu'on entend hennir et rugir dans la nuit;
Et tout ce qui ruisselle et tout ce qui reluit;
L'homme suprême, élan de la nature altière,
100]   Qui prend Dieu par l'oreille et l'appelle compère,
Regarde l'infini, le nargue et lui dit *Tu;*
Qui sent sous ses deux mains sangloter la vertu;
Et le sang jaillissant de la chaude ruelle;
Et l'alcôve, et la femme abominable et belle,
Et le rire de l'homme assouvissant ses dents
Sur l'épaule nacrée[15] et sur les seins ardents.
Tout cela flotte et fuit dans sa prunelle vive,
Dans la crispation de sa bouche lascive.
Qui donc es-tu, vieillard?[16] d'où viens-tu? qui t'a fait
110]   Cet air triste d'un Dieu qui frappe et qui se tait?
Quelle main surhumaine a posé ce sourire
Sur ta lèvre orgueilleuse et blême? que veut dire

Cette flamme allumée au fond noir de tes yeux
Comme un éclair du soir qui passe, et, radieux,
Dore et ravive toute une morne façade?

—Enfant, dit le vieillard, je m'appelle de Sade."[17]

AMARI ALIQUID

Mon Dieu, je ne veux pas vous faire des reproches;
Car vous m'avez donné de l'argent plein mes poches,
De l'amour plein mon âme, et mon jeune cerveau,
Grâce à vous, tous les jours se grise au vin du Beau.
La nuit, quand le sommeil parfume toute chose,
Avec le rossignol j'entends chanter la rose;
Vous avez allumé chez moi comme un fanal
Le désir âpre et doux du superbe Idéal;
Vous m'avez donné l'or, le vin, les vers, la femme;
Ne pouvez-vous me faire aussi cadeau d'une âme?

CAPRICE

Je ne veux pas de jours où Juin brûle et flamboie,
Pas de rayonnement de soleil, pas de joie,
Pas de bruit de chansons écloses çà et là,
Pas d'amour; je ne veux rien de ces choses-là.
Je ne veux pas, ô Dieu, de lumière ni d'ombre,
Du matin rose et fier ni du soir fauve et sombre,
De la femme ayant l'œil au vent et l'âme en feu,
De l'homme; je ne veux pas de vous-même, ô Dieu.
Car j'ai dans mes chansons, moi poète, des mondes,
Des mers où maint navire a sombré sous les ondes,
Des forêts pleins de chants et des champs pleins de blé,
Des amants égarés sur le sentier sablé;
Des couchers de soleil, des batailles, des femmes,
Des roses, des enfants, des arbres et des âmes;
Mon œil vaut plus qu'un astre; et j'ai dans mes vingt ans
Toutes les fleurs avec tous les pleurs du printemps.

THE BALLAD OF VILLON AND FAT MADGE

" 'Tis no sin for a man to labour in his vocation." Falstaff
"The night cometh, when no man can work."

What though the beauty I love and serve be cheap,
    Ought you to take me for a beast or fool?
All things a man could wish are in her keep;
    For her I turn swashbuckler in love's school.
When folk drop in, I take my pot and stool
And fall to drinking with no more ado.
I fetch them bread, fruit, cheese, and water, too;
    I say all's right so long as I'm well paid;
"Look in again when your flesh troubles you,
    Inside this brothel where we drive our trade."

But soon the devil's among us flesh and fell,
    When penniless to bed comes Madge my whore;
I loathe the very sight of her like hell.
    I snatch gown, girdle, surcoat, all she wore,
    And tell her, these shall stand against her score.
She grips her hips with both hands, cursing God,
Swearing by Jesus' body, bones, and blood,
    That they shall not. Then I, no whit dismayed,
Cross her cracked nose with some stray shiver of wood
    Inside this brothel where we drive our trade.

When all's made up she drops me a windy word,
    Bloat like a beetle puffed and poisonous:
Grins, thumps my pate, and calls me dickey-bird,
    And cuffs me with a fist that's ponderous.
    We sleep like logs, being drunken both of us;
Then when we wake her womb begins to stir;
To save her seed she gets me under her

Wheezing and whining, flat as planks are laid:
And thus she spoils me for a whoremonger
Inside this brothel where we drive our trade.

Blow, hail or freeze, I've bread here baked rent free!
Whoring's my trade, and my whore pleases me;
Bad cat, bad rat; we're just the same if weighed.
We that love filth, filth follows us, you see;
Honour flies from us, as from her we flee
Inside this brothel where we drive our trade.*

       *I bequeath likewise to fat Madge
         This little song to learn and study;
      By God's head she's a sweet fat fadge,
         Devout and soft of flesh and ruddy;
         I love her with my soul and body,
      So doth she me, sweet dainty thing.
         If you fall in with such a lady,
      Read it, and give it her to sing.

VILLON

To my good mother that me bore
I leave in laud of Our Lady,
For bitter pain she had of yore,
God knows, and many a grief for me;
Castle or harbour of land or sea
For soul and body I have none other
Save this in time of tyranny,
Nor she, poor woman, mine own mother!

Lady of heaven and governess terrene
And empress of the bitter lake of hell,
Grant me thine humble Christian woman clean
That with thy people chosen I may dwell,
Albeit I be nought worthy, I wot well;
More than my sins, my queen and soul's lady,
More than they all, thine excellences be;
Nor can man's soul win heaven, me lists not lie,
Save through this perfect excellence of thee;
In this belief I think to live and die.

Say to thy son I am his bondwoman;
Bid him blot out my sins who ransomed us,
And heal me like the unclean Egyptian,
Or as he healed the clerk Theophilus,
Who was absolved of thee most piteous
Though to the devil his soul betrothen was;
Preserve me that I go not hence nor pass,
O Virgin bearing in a maid's body
The sacrament men worship in the mass;
In this belief I think to live and die.

A woman am I poor and sad and old,
Nor nought I know, nor never letters read;
I see at church, where I sit in God's fold,
Heaven painted fair with harps and lutes dispread,
And hell where damned folk boil in burning lead;
This frights me sore, that gives me joy and bliss;
Grant me that joy, high goddess, that there is,
Thou to whom sinners all for help must fly,
Filled full of faith, nor slow nor false I wis;
In this belief I think to live and die.

Thou barest, Virgin, holy lady, Mary,
Jesus the King, that cannot die nor vary;
The Almighty, clad in weakness voluntary,
Came to our help down out of heaven most high,
Gave his sweet youth to death at hands unwary;
He is our Lord, and I his tributary,
In this belief I think to live and die.

THE BALLAD OF BULGARIE

The gentle Knight, Sir John de Bright,
    (Of Brummagemme was he)
Forth would he prance with lifted lance
    For love of Bulgarie.
No lance in hand for other land
    Sir Bright would ever take,
For wicked works, save those of Turks,
    No head of man would break;
But that Bulgarie should not be free,
10]   This made his high heart quake.
From spur to plume a star of doom,
    (Few knights be like to him)
How shone from far that stormy star,
    His basnet broad of brim!
'Twas not for love of Cant above
    Nor Cotton's holy call,
But a lance would he break for Bulgary's sake,
    And Termagant should sprawl.
The mother-maid, Our Lady of Trade,
20]   His spurs on heel she bound,
She belted the brand for his knightly hand,
    Full wide this girdle went round;
The brand was bright as his name, to smite
    The spawn of false Mahound.
His basnet broad that all men awed
    No broader was to see
From brim to brim that shadowed him
    As forth to fight rode he,
South-east by south, with his war-cry in mouth—
30]   "St. John for Bulgarie!"
He had not ridden a mile but one
    When loud and loud cried he,
Now who will stand at my right hand

And beard the Turk for me?
Up spake on this guise Sir William the Wise,
 The People's Knight was he,
Lo, I will stand at thy stalwart hand
And beard the Turk with thee.
Gramercy! then quoth Sir Bright—by my troth!
40] If better may not be
Content I were (though I would not swear)
 To slay the Turk with thee:
But who will stand at my left hand
And smite the Turk for me?
Then up spake old Sir Thomas the bold,
 A Chelsea Knight was he;
On earth no knight was hardier wight,
 No man had seen him flee,
A stalwart sight of a grand old knight,
50] As men of old might see.
Lo, I will stand at thy quaking hand
And beard the Turk with thee.
And "Marry Amen!" Sir Bright said then,
 For better none might be;
But grieved I am, or God me—save,
 That I may not ride with thee
For the words thou hast said of fair Free Trade,
 My lady fair and free.
Up then spake him, True Thomas,
60] And a scornful man was he,
Wilt thou bide at the side of thy Bromwichane bride
 Or go to Bulgarie?
But out then spake him, Wise William,
 Right softly then he spake,
I deem it ill man's blood to spill
 Though but for Bulgary's sake;
And meseems it were better ere weather wax wetter
 Our homeward way to take;
I don't mind writing—I do mind fighting,
70] (So spake the bold Sir Bill)
He don't mean outing—he does mean spouting

Like some in Denmark's ill.
We don't mean hitting—we don't mind spitting—
  For Turks have swords to kill
Which I deeply regret should so happen—but yet
  'Tis true though it gives me pain
For the Greek will not fight (which is far from right)
  And the Russian has all to gain
And I think it were vulgar to cheat a poor Bulgar,
80]   With offers to help in vain.
Ha! Beauséant! said Sir Bright, God's bread!
  And by God's mother dear!
By my halidom! nay, I might add, perfay!
  What caitiff wights be here?
Though Sir Thomas look black and Sir William go back
  While tongue is mine to wag
By the help of Our Lady, though matters look shady
  It shall fight for the Red Cross flag;
Shout, gentlemen, for sweet Saint Penn!
90]   Up, gallants, for Saint George!
(His name in his day was Fox, by the way)
  Till the Paynim fiend disgorge
Till he loosen his hold of the shrines of old
  That yet his clutch is on,
Of the Sepulchre Blest, by our arms repossessed
  (As soon as his own shall be gone)
And the Mount of Might that Olivet hight.
98]   Strike, strike for sweet St. John!

The Marquis of Stead[1]

Knaves, kidnappers, forgers and strumpets,
    Thieves, penitents, panders and saints,
They have scared with the blast of their trumpets
    Poor truth till the heart in her faints.
Till, conscious how foul and accurst is
    The brood that in Grubstreet is bred,
She can hardly be sure if the worst is
    The Marquis of Stead.[2]

Obscenity, falsehood, monstrosity,
    Foamed forth from the lips of the beast,
Whose genius, not grown to precocity,
    Suborned not the press and the priest.
But Archbishops and Cardinals, hoary
    In honour—what prayers have they said?
"God bless and receive into glory
    The Marquis of Stead!"

He has erred—we can hardly deny it:
    It is painful to say he has erred.
Though a lie may be hardly a lie, it
    Is at least an inaccurate word.
Who cares though the mob have its fill of
    Rant, falsehood, and poison for bread,
If it brings but in grist to the mill of
    The Marquis of Stead.

His motives we all must applaud—he
    Endured for the holiest of frauds
To tipple in houses called—gaudy
    With—ladies, whose titles are gauds.
His motives, his deeds, are not plainer!
    Truth smiled at beholding abed
As drunk as a—total abstainer
    The Marquis of Stead.

Not as drunk as a lord, nor as vicious,
 This truth is the plainest of truths
And the savour thereof as delicious
 As the reek and the roar of the Booths—
The Booths of the fair of salvation
 Whom devils and decency dread
Who salute with obscene salutation[3]
 The Marquis of Stead.

With policy fine as the Fabian
 His journal descries at a glance
Offenses that lurk in Arabian
 Or other than London romance.
Justine is as fire that enlightens
 Juliette is a book to be read
But Arabian impurity frightens
 The Marquis of Stead.

RONDEAUX PARISIENS

"Hypocrisy is the homage that France pays to England."

i.

Chaste France is ashamed of such infamies—common elsewhere—
As never, O never, in Paris were dreamt of or named;
At the mention of London, and vices habitual there,
  Chaste France is ashamed.

She covers the maidenly face which herself has proclaimed
As purer and fairer than any most pure and most fair,
And averts from corruption her eyes with abhorrence inflamed.

How well it becomes her, that virginal innocent air!
How shameful it seems that such virtue was ever defamed!
For now at a whisper of evil, her children declare,
  Chaste France is ashamed.

ii.

Pure Paris is shocked. France, matronly maiden of nations,
Shrieks huskily, "Shocking! And these are the wretches that mocked
Chaste France as immoral!" Now—witness her shrill proclamations—
  Pure Paris is shocked.

Chaste France never heard of such horrors as here are unlocked.
Louis Quinze and his deer-park have left to remote generations
Successors—but ah, not in Paris such cattle are stocked!

Hypocritical Albion, abashed at her self-commendations,
Now grovels unmasked, and we see what corruptions are rocked
In that cradle of virtue. At sight of such strange revelations
  Pure Paris is shocked.

iii.

Not in Paris—ah no! is a taint or a touch of pollution
So rank as in London the leprous: and well may she crow,
"What! girlhood abused? Can it be? Premature prostitution?
        Not in Paris—ah no!

"Those loathsome, disgusting, unspeakable Englishmen—oh!"
Lutetia, the daughter of dirt, is in need of ablution—
She has taken their money and fawned on the givers, you know!

But she spits on them now—from behind—if a slight diminution
Occurs in their tribute: if money should ebb, or not flow,
She bethinks her that vice is the child of obscene destitution
        Not in Paris—ah no!

iv.

Sweet innocent French little moralists, born in a land
Where vice never entered and reigned and expired in a stench,
Are shocked if they hear of misconduct they scarce understand,
        Sweet innocent French!

Those infamous English! a cutthroat and thief, with his wench,
Might reign and be worshipped in London for years; they might stand
As Emperor and Empress—the Church at their feet, and the Bench!

No marvel if girlhood and boyhood enlist in a band
Whose banner is infamy, there: but the hand that we clench
Is unsullied; and Europe exclaims, as she looks on that hand,
        "Sweet innocent French!"

v.

Love, purity, shame, are unknown to the rascally Briton.
Mendacity, malice, rapacity—ever the same—
Are the marks of a nation accustomed to spurn and to spit on
    Love, purity, shame.

The sign of the track of its children is bloodshed and flame.
Madagascar, Algeria, Tonquin—not a place can they hit on
But disgrace, in success or defeat, has ensued where they came.

But at least we believed that their clime was a bridle and bit on
The passions—that Albion the virtuous was worthy her fame!
And we find that her virtues are cushions for vices to sit on—
    Love, purity, shame.

vi.

The country of cant, if the plea that a Frenchman advances
Be valid, is England: the world that she looks on askant
May rebuke and deride her, beholding how proudly she prances—
    The country of cant.

France, France is the virgin and matron, who mocks at the rant
That acclaims any country but France: and her scorn but enhances
The gust of the sense of her virtue, though shrivelled and scant.

Though the scream of Parisian morality thrills and entrances
The sense with a rapture of laughter, we feel—as we pant,
And subside into smiling—that England was never what France is—
    The country of cant.

vii.

Fair France shall arise from the sepulchre: anguish and pain
Have purged her of shame and of falsehood: enfranchised and wise,
From the dunghill she sat on, and smiled at the clank of her chain,
    Fair France shall arise.

So said we, and trusted, and dreamed, and averted our eyes
From the fires and the filth of her communal convicts: in vain.
The vermin revive, and the reek of them sickens the skies.

No compromise hold they with honour, that bids us disdain
Intransigent reptiles, and rats of the cesspool of lies.
Foul France must be whipped into silence, if ever again
    Fair France shall arise.

viii.

Foul France must be whipped into silence, or never shall fame
Rearise from the pit of dishonour, wherein when she slipped,
For pity we heard not the judgment of justice proclaim—
    Foul France must be whipped.

We too had our days of dishonour arrayed and equipped
In the trappings of treason and empire, when England became
As a galley for slaves and for harlots, with rudder unshipped.

Long since hath she purged her: shall France too not purge her of
      blame?
—So said we: she rails on us now like a strumpet half stripped.
If shame cannot silence the spawn of her sewage for shame,
    Foul France must be whipped.

ix.

Obscure and obscene as the dense animalcules impure
Which gnawed at a king till from Naples—that felt him unseen
As a leprosy fouler than fire or than iron could cure,
    Obscure and obscene—

He passed into darkness, and was not; as abject of mien,
As noisome of nature are these that insist and endure,
These insects that gnaw the republic and leave it unclean.

Bite England at heel, if they might—were her strengths not secure,—
Fain would they: but France have they gnawed to the heart: and
    between
The folds of her journals we scent them, obscene and obscure,
    Obscure and obscene.

x.

Shame, where is thy blush? Not on cheeks that a Frenchman may
    claim
As Parisian, beholding the manly or maidenly flush
Make answer when honour demands, if dishonour defame,
    "Shame, where is thy blush?"

Throats yelling with rancour, lips frothing with lies as they gush
From the venomous hearts of the railer, attest and proclaim
The soul of the serpent that scorn condescends not to crush.

Cry curs, till the scourge overtake you: denounce and declaim:
There are whips for such hides as the whips were accustomed to
    brush.
But we ask not of man or of woman that shrinks not at shame,
    Shame, where is thy blush?

August, 1885

ROUNDEL

Let us forget; and yet we may not,
　　And yet we would not: yet
We know not surely why we pray not
　　"Let us forget."

　　Is yestersun not set?
The thoughts that swayed our souls and sway not
　　Should fade from hearts they fret.

Ah, yet we watch their ghosts, and weigh not
　　The worth of wan regret,
But sleep, and wake, and sigh, and say not
　　"Let us forget."

CRITICISM

THE EARLY ENGLISH DRAMATISTS
Christopher Marlowe and John Webster.*

In the dramatists of the Elizabethan period and their immediate successors, there are certain salient points of resemblance which no imitation has been able to reproduce, except in a faint and faded mimicry. From the mighty line[1] of Marlowe to the glitter and point of Shirley, a sort of unity may be discerned in all the productions of those old writers, among whom Shakespeare moved only as greatest of many great. Unity in variety; for there is no servile adherence to one standard, no blind conformity to one stock of rules. Still, all the plays of this era are coloured by the same influences, and modelled by the same tone of national thought and feeling. Till the siren-like music of Beaumont and Fletcher, nothing of artificial sentiment or frost-work ornament overlaid the power and purity which clothed in words the lofty actions and profound passions of their drama. The writers above-named, with all their varied and brilliant merit, were the first to mix with the very sources of poetry that faint, false sweetness which enervates the mind and cloys the taste of the reader. In this perhaps, as much as by their more glaring errors, the influence of their plays did much to weaken and lower the tone of the generation which followed and worshipped them. It is with earlier poets, with minds more strong and fresh, from which the stamp of a stern and glorious age was not yet outworn, that we have now to do. I propose to-day[2] to give as fair an account as will come within a range so limited, of two among these whom I consider worthiest of attention, Marlowe and Webster. The latter, indeed, in strict chronology, might perhaps be classed with writers of the second period; his works are as certainly later in date than Marlowe's, as prior to those of Beaumont and Fletcher: but the tone of his writings would be enough to rank him as a dramatist of the earlier class, if indeed a remarkable testimony of his preference for the school of Shakespeare did not remain under

*The Works of Christopher Marlowe, 3 vols. Pickering, 1850.
The Works of John Webster, 4 vols. Pickering, 1830.

his own hand, in the preface to the first of his great tragedies. I shall, therefore, without scruple assign him a place among the poets of the first era, rather than with those of whom Beaumont and Fletcher were the chief leaders, and among whom we may class Shirley, Massinger, and their followers.

Between the two great writers whom I have chosen for examination, there are many points of likeness and many of diversity. Both have a more subtle and profound power of analyzing the nature of man in its height and depth, in its strength and weakness, than (with one exception) was possessed by any of their contemporaries. Both have a fondness for gloom and shadow, which in less powerful minds would have sunk into a morbid lust of horror and pain. Their scenes, as it is, inflict no base emotion of shallow terror or mean suffering, such as weak writers who would fain be strong endeavour to excite, that so, while concealing their inherent weakness and want of faith in art they may at least harrow the nerves and crush the feelings of readers feeble as themselves.

Both have a perfect and facile command of language; it obeys them as a willing slave; each thought is married to a fit expression. To each of these poets it is always an aim to strip naked every passion of all its form and circumstances and hold it up, bad or good, as it is in very truth. Neither has the slightest respect for anything like a sham, poetical or otherwise: another material difference between their writings and the elaborate luxuriance of the later school. Their style has the simple and noble outlines of the great early painters of Italy and Flanders: Fletcher's is ornate and melodious, artificial in its very effusion, coloured and toned down in its very passion, with all the calculated effects and measured theatricalism of the eclectics.

Marlowe has more of pure unmingled poetry in his composition than Webster; he is glad of any chance that allows him to indulge in musical expression and a certain tender glory of description which makes every line a picture and a song in itself: in his fellow-dramatist, the poetry of expression only appears when forced forth by passion—never as an ornamental adjunct, always as a necessary part of the situation: a great and rare merit, which makes it hopeless to give an idea of his power unless by excerpts of considerable length. Throughout Marlowe's works there is a passionate love and worship of beauty, which in Webster gleams out by comparatively

dim and scanty indications. Not indeed that the latter is deficient
in the sense of enjoyment; he reposes now and then in sweet inter-
vals as of music; and we meet with such harmonious touches of expression as in the following lines:—

> "Untie your folded thoughts,
> And let them dangle loose as a bride's hair."
> [*The White Devil,* III.ii.1-2]

> "O, thou soft natural death, that art joint twin
> To sweetest slumber! no rough bearded comet
> Stares on thy mild departure; the dull owl
> Beats not against thy casement; the hoarse wolf
> Scents not thy carrion; pity winds thy corpse,
> Whilst horror waits on princes."
> [*The White Devil,* V.iii.30-35]

> "One whose mind
> Appears more like a ceremonious chapel,
> Full of sweet music, than a thronging presence."
> [*Appius and Virginia,* I.ii.12-14]

Such passages might be easily multiplied, had I space for a
complete analysis; but these may suffice to show the tender grace
and earnest harmony of style with which a poet of true dramatic
genius finds time to soften the tragedy of any subject. He will never
urge terror beyond its due limits, or forget in the hurry and passion
of circumstance the beauty which should ever move as naturally
round his thoughts as its splendour round the motion of a star.

It remains to consider in what measure each of these writers
has fulfilled the main requisitions of the dramatic art. And here I
must notice the chief defect of Marlowe. His dramas usually lag
in the action; sometimes the original interest is dropped midway,
and the artistic significance of the whole work destroyed. Into no
such error does Webster ever fall: but it is fair to remember that
he had lived to study the most perfect models of the dramatic art.
The latter's pathos is, in my opinion, more subtle and intense than
has been attained by any other of our dramatists but Shakespeare
and Shelley: a quality in which I cannot but think Marlowe comparatively deficient. None ever went beyond him in power and

beauty of words; no one could have drawn in firmer outline the scenes of suffering which he loved to lay bare before his readers; but any one of the three dramatists I have mentioned would have steeped them in a deeper pathos and glorified them with a purer compassion. There is a divine pity and love in some great poets which crowns their completed art as with a halo of sacred sorrow. This is not in Marlowe; scorn, and a fierce delight in his own power and skill, have driven out all mercy; others may pity the agony he exhibits, but in him is no compassion. His is the strength that cannot pardon weakness; the realism that will veil nothing, explain nothing away. There is something terrible in his quiet, pitiless dissection of character, his silent scrutiny into all dark and dubious points of circumstance, his steady self-confidence in handling the forbidden and the fearful; his foot slips not, his eye falters not, on the narrow verge of life; where all darkest questions meet and mingle, in religious and ethical speculation, in moral and spiritual doubts, there has he been, a cold and keen enquirer; the sensuous passion of his temperament subdued and subservient to the judicial will. All these questions has he faced without wavering: no influence has bowed him this way or that; and he returns unable, perhaps undesirous, to settle the perplexities of faith and conduct. Such at least seems to me the moral underlying his life and works.

And yet, with all his faults of speculation and action—for this confusion of moral boundaries and hard contempt of human wants is a grave error enough—how did he keep unaltered and unsoiled his name and rank as a poet! In his tragedies, as before stated, we find no less of that "sensuous and passionate"[3] beauty which lies at the very inmost core of his power, than in the rapid rhythms and gorgeous luxuries of his *Hero and Leander.* In that poem, indeed, he seems to have put off all other claims to praise, only to abandon himself in utter freedom to the enjoyments of music and colour. The passion of the lovers is a thin veil for that of the poet; it goes no deeper than external delight; but by a beautiful use of his realizing and analytic style he has done justice once for all to that much misused and belied thing, the purely sensuous and outward side of love. And from the very excess of pleasurable emotion, which burns and trembles through the verse as a flower trembles open to the air, the whole poem is thrown back into some remote visionary land, which cannot affect or alter any human relation. It is not the love that we are conscious of, but the enjoyment only. The same, in a modified degree, may be said of Shakespeare's Venus and Adonis,—a poem of the same character as the present, but so tempered by the peculiar properties of its author as to rank far above all others of the same school.

Another point of contrast requires notice: the terrors of Webster's drama are, for the most part, purely spiritual; those of Marlowe's, often tainted by the intrusion of mere physical endurance: which latter, when lifted by no sentiment beyond its own relations, it is of itself unfit for dramatic treatment. There is a truth in the old Greek theories which bade poets avoid all horrible exposure in their writings, and be careful of turning the exceptional into the repulsive. This dogma, pushed to the extreme, leaves us a tragedy bound in grave-clothes, with a nerveless whine for voice and a draped lay-figure for study; the clear eyes blinded with a fool's bandage, the mighty music and measured thunder as of the choral heavens, changed for an emasculated and sickly drawl. But poets far above the so-called "classic" school, have erred as gravely on the other hand. Art is not dissection: nothing is more offensive than bare and sensuous horror. Spiritual suffering in every detail and symptom belongs to the large dowry of art; but not the details of the slaughter-house. The noble censure passed by Mr. Ruskin[4] on the painters of foul and bloody scenes, the art whose place is in the kennel or the shambles, applies equally to the poet who defiles his power in the same way. I do not accuse either Marlowe or Webster of this hideous lust of pain; I have already expressed my belief in their healthy and vigorous purity of purpose, and I desire here to assert it again. Nevertheless, there is in Marlowe a suspicion of this fatal tendency; had he been a weaker man, it might have widened into a serious defect. Compare, for specimens of different treatment, the death-scene of Marlowe's Edward II with that of Webster's Duchess of Malfi.

To atone for all this inadequate praise and presumptuous censure take two specimens of Marlowe's power of subtle thought and delicate expression; the first pure speculation, as the second is pure description:—

Theory of Beauty.

    "If *all* the pens that *ever* poets held
    Had fed the feeling of their masters' thoughts,
    And every sweetness that inspired their hearts,
    Their minds, and muses on admired themes;
    If all the heavenly quintessence they still
    From their immortal flowers of poesy,
    Wherein as in a mirror we perceive
    The highest reaches of a human wit;
    If these had made one poems's period,
    And all combined in beauty's worthiness,
    Yet should there *hover* in their restless heads
    One thought, one grace, one wonder, at the least,
    Which into words no virtue can digest."
                  [*Tamburlaine the Great,* V.ii.98-110]

Faust evokes the shape of Helen.

    "Was this *the face that launched a thousand ships*
    And burnt the topless towers of Ilium?
    Sweet Helen, *make me immortal with a kiss.*
    Her lips suck forth my soul, see where it flies!
    Come, Helen, come, *give me my soul again.*
    Here will I dwell, for Heaven is in these lips,
    And all is dross that is not Helena.
    I will be Paris, and for love of thee
    Instead of Troy shall Wurtemberg be sacked
    And *I* will combat with weak Menelaus,
    And wear thy colours on my plumed crest:
    Yea, *I* will wound Achilles in the heel,
    And then return to Helen for a kiss.
    O, thou art fairer than the evening air,
    Clad in the beauty of a thousand stars:*
    Brighter art thou than flaming Jupiter
    When he appeared to hapless Semele;

---

*Compare an earlier passage in the same tragedy:
        Spirits—like women or unwedded maids,
        Shadowing more beauty in their airy brows
        Than have the white breasts of the Queen of love.
              [*Doctor Faustus,* sc. 5, 11. 125-27]

More lovely than the monarch of the sky
In wanton Arethusa's azured** arms;
And none but thou shall be my paramour!"
[*Doctor Faustus,* sc. 13, 11. 92-111]

Observe especially, besides the sensuous perfection of language, the passionate will expressed in this passage by the earnest repetition of the mere words "I" and "thou": as if the sorcerer feared that at the least relaxation of his wilful and potent desire, his influence might cease and the vision foil him after all. He is afraid to believe her a mere creature of his will, and half dreams that the spells which evoked may retain her for ever as a real and breathing woman at his side.

A few words more of Webster, to whom alone far more than all my space should be given to do justice; what remains, must be comprised in a few brief remarks. His two great works, Vittoria Corombona and the Duchess of Malfi, are unlike any other plays in composition and in style. There is perhaps more art in the character of Vittoria than we elsewhere find in Webster; the often quoted scene of her trial is the finest instance but one of the author's dramatic power. The guilty woman wears her sin so lightly that it grows an ornament; there is a triumph as of innocence in her fearless bearing, her varied and ready eloquence, her facile turns of phrase, her scornful argument and passionate rhetoric. It is not like innocence, but it supplies the place of conviction with admiration; if we do not forget her guilt, we care for it no more than she does, when her calm and final words ring in our ears, making a glory out of her shame, turning her condemnation to a triumph, and her judge into the criminal.* Brachiano, tho' inferior to the heroine, is a vigor-

---

**Compare Shakespeare's,
          "White and azure, laced
With blue of heaven's own tint,"
(Where see Mr. Knight's excellent note,) and
          "Her two blue windows faintly she upheaveth."
                              Venus and Adonis.
     *It shall not be a house of convertites;
     My mind shall make it honester to me
     Than the Pope's palace, and more peaceable
     Than thy soul, though thou art a Cardinal.
                         Vittoria Corombona.
                         [*The White Devil,* III.i]

ous and careful sketch; Flamineo's colder temperament well sets out the impulsive emotion of his sister's; and in reading the last scenes, we hesitate whether to award most praise to the earnest eloquence of the verse or to the subtle touches of character and dramatic passion.

The Duchess of Malfi, on the whole, is the noblest specimen of Webster; it is more complete and definite as a work of art than Vittoria Corombona; and its pathos is wider and deeper. The scenes before and after the murder of the Duchess are the most perfect instances I know of imaginative realism. Webster would have been a great poet had he never written anything but that ghastly dirge, where the murderer bids a living woman perform for herself the offices done for the newly dead; the sweet and holy words that close as with music the dark scene of pain and evil; or that dialogue between the Duke Ferdinand and his sullen, subtle follower, slow to repent as to sin:—

> "Ferd.   Cover her face: mine eyes dazzle. She died young.
> Bos.   I think not so: her infelicity
>   Seemed to have years too many.
> Ferd.   She and I were twins;
>   And should I die this instant, I had lived
>   Her time to a minute.
> Bos.   It seems she was born first."

There is somewhat in the man's clear, sad insight into sorrow and sin, which makes one shrink. The eyes that had seen this, how did they look on the common day? the ears that had taken those quiet, brief words, how did they listen to the usual converse of men? One thinks of what he knew and of what he has told us, till it seems as though one might almost say, what had this man done, that he should see such things? The prophet who beheld Pallas unveiled, went away blind for ever. Is there no retribution for the poet who has gone so deep into the dark places, where the sun is silent.

As this imperfect analysis draws to a close, its writer sees how much has been left unsaid—how much tacit injustice done to the subject. Much more might worthily be said of either poet: and will be, when the study of our noble literature is fully re-opened to all. There has been enough of neglect and ignorance;* it is time we

---

*See for a comment on this, the insolent and silly "notices" of these poets in Lardner's Cyclopædia. The minor dramatists may take comfort, seeing that the same

should know our own wealth. The earnest reverence and affectionate study of a few should not be all that we can spare the mighty dead.[5] More than this must be given; and it will be. Wise enjoyment, noble and healthy teaching, lies for all in the forgotten writings of our early masters. It was not in vain that such men thought and toiled in the times we affect to praise. Too much honour cannot be given to the brave clear intellect, the earnest and fearless heart of such writers as these. Let us be just at length, and begin to measure reputation simply by merit. We who profess to love the past, and to rate it according to its desert, let us find out what it was and what it has left us. Because justice has not yet been done, shall we perpetuate injustice? Let us remember sometimes that we have heard of

> A lion that dies of an ass's kick,
> The wronged great soul of an ancient Master.

The appeal so well and wisely made in behalf of early art, I would make for our early national poets, and for no dissimilar reasons. Hitherto we have merited the taunt—

> Here, where your praise would yield returns
>   And a handsome word or two give help,
> Here, after your kind, the mastiff girns,
>   And the puppy pack of poodles yelp.

Let us hope that, considering the literary work these men did, all wise students of poetry will come to heed the advice of a later stanza:

> Give these, I say, full honour and glory
>   For daring so much, before they well did it.
> The first of the new, in our race's story,
>   Beats the last of the old, 'tis no idle quiddit.
> The worthies began a revolution
>   Which if on earth we intend to acknowledge,
> Honour them now (ends my allocution)
>   Nor confer our degree when the folks leave college.[6]

In this hope I close the present essay; to be followed as circumstance permits by others, in which the subject of our early drama may be more fully treated.

---

gentleman who crushes them with judicial scorn appears, like the youthful critic of Leech, to "consider Shakespeare a much overrated man."

THE CHAOTIC SCHOOL[1]

There is a story current or adrift somewhere of a certain missionary who went among the savages and there inculcated divine or other truth to such a sensibly insufferable degree that the leading converts, discreetly tempering justice with indulgence, cut off exactly one half of his tongue and sent him back with the other half unextracted. The regrettable result of such untimely mercy was this; that being quite unable to hold the tongue which remained to him he went about talking in a dialect of which no mortal could make anything. Whether or not men in general suffered much loss or expressed much anguish in consequence of this privation, we cannot now say: but the missionary could by no means endure it for them. In the general interest of creation, he went to a surgeon who proved ingenious. This philanthropist, by judicious extirpation of what tongue was left, enabled (it is said) the patient to speak thenceforward in an audible intelligible manner, by a select use of gutturals and labials: to what purpose we can only conjecture.

It has long since been evident to the select and compassionate reader that a poet now living has for his auditor's sins and his own been judicially afflicted by the severe and inscrutable fates with the visitation which human barbarity inflicted on this missionary. With the relic of his tongue chafed perpetually from root to tip with a fruitless irritation or itch for impossible speech, this memorable though mournful example of strenuous human perseverance has now been uttering for the last twenty or thirty years the inarticulate vocal appeal of a tongueless though verbose eloquence. The amount of pure noise produced is really, when one thinks of it, a praiseworthy thing. For a man with organs unimpaired it would indeed be unpardonable; in the case of Mr. Browning, it is more than pitiable—it is commendable. Occasionally too, in a manner interesting and instructive to philanthropic science, some articulate discord produces a qualified variety in the [2] sad monotonous effect; and a sound that pierces and skirrs the agonized human ear becomes to a compassionate mind almost melodious when one reflects that to the tym-

40

panum of the afflictive but innocent being which produced it, it may carry the music of a sweet significance. Moreover, if for no cause that man can tell the singer of inarticulate discords takes pleasure in afflicting men, has not Providence for no cause visible to the sufferer taken pleasure in afflicting *it*? There is even a certain relief to reader as listener in coming upon these audible syllables which do hiss and grind, clash and shriek, in a consecutive manner and to some given tune of meaning. They are indeed too infrequent; and a scientific charity would fain hope that the invaluable surgeon may yet turn up with curative lancet to do all parties a good turn. For a good turn we believe it would be: however incalculably small may be the infinitesimal grain of a message worth delivering which lies presumably latent in the minstrel of Gigadibs and Bombastes,[2] it must be better worth hearing than mere inarticulations jerked up by painful fits out of the noisy verbal whirlpools of a clamorous chaos.

Or perhaps our first pitying illustration was not so applicable as charity yet suggests? and the infliction under which his audience labours is not due to any quite natural affliction on the lecturer's part? Inexcusable, unpardonable, in that case, are the hideous noises which issue, in many a windy gamut of inharmonious sound, from the platform of Paracelsus: shrieks of violated English, groans of grammar undergoing vivisection, gasps of expiring sense and moans of tormented metre. Never surely did any wretched inoffensive dialect of human speech endure such unnatural tortures as those time after time inflicted with diabolical versatility of violence on our patient mother-tongue by the inventive and unsparing author of Sordello. Historic illustration must again be invoked before we can find words to describe them. Either after the St. Bartholomew slaughter or in the time of the *dragonnades*, history asserts, a party of the king's troops destroyed one family of Huguenots or quasi-Huguenots with quite exceptional [3] cruelty; putting the mother in particular through all kind of agonies and brutalities before they made an end of her: hardly one soldier here and there interceding to have her "killed quicker."[3] The simile is horrible; but more horrible is Mr. Browning's treatment of the Queen's innocent English. Read (if you must read to believe) six pages on end, say of Sordello; his biggest book, and accounted his best; which it may be if it please. Count the conjunctions torn out by the roots, the verbs impaled, the nouns crucified, the antecedents broken on the wheel, the relatives cut off by the neck or sawn through the middle, the entire sentences blundering, screaming, plunging, snorting, like harpooned whales or smashed locomotives, through whole horrible paragraphs of mutilation and confusion. The "supplice" of Damiens was a trifle to this. In the hands of her merciless hangman or sworn-tormentor, the miserable English language, garotted, gouged, her jaw broken, and the teeth driven down her throat, howls helplessly for mercy as the lacerating talons of that harpy Muse plunge afresh among her tenderest vital nerves; in vain here and there a stray critic, touching the torturer's elbow, pityingly represents—"Mon ami, tu vois qu'elle n'est plus en état de rien endurer."—"Oh! tant qu'elle saura souffrir —tant qu'il y aura chez la gueuse rien qu'un seul râle, qu'un seul souffle de vie—"[4] and the hideous infliction goes on: apparently to the ineffable and delicious excitement of Mr. Browning: whose supple energy of continuous verbiage it seems impossible to tire out.

To speak without metaphor: no reader could rationally deny that whatever other merit or demerit there may be in this man of letters, here beyond doubt, of all clever and cultivated men, is the one who does absolutely write the worst English. It is not the bad style of ignorance or hurry or patent stupidity. It is not the bad style which comes of bad training; it is not the bad style which comes from bad imitation of good or good imitation of bad models; it is not the bad style which comes of too intense an intricacy of thought or too original a fervour of speech. It is so execrable as to be past all [4] such and all other explanation. The one reason producible or conjecturable for its existence at all is that it does exist. All these books, it is now superfluous to say, have enough of crude thought, of raw talent, of fruitless cunning, of sterile strength, of profitless learning, to furnish forth a whole school of verse. Such a poetic pack has indeed already begun to yelp more or less feebly about the lower slopes and looser fences of our too accessible Parnassus. Justice, long denied, is now at length accorded to what deserts this poet actually has: and there is therefore grave and sufficient reason for pointing out that beyond the limit of those deserts the praise of his adherents should not be permitted to stray. He is ingenious, learned, reflective, retentive, acquisitive, and self-reliant; he has a notable gift of confused and rapid jargon, of copious and chaotic fluency. He has an admirable capacity of compressing as with a vice or screw into the limit of some small monodrame or monologue the representative quality or spiritual essence of a period; such at least as he can conceive it to have been. He has some real humour, forcible and subtle in its way, and well under the command of his imaginative faculty. He has some fitful and erratic sense of violent or ignoble passion in its more obvious and theatrical forms. Being receptive and ruminative, he has matter usually at hand on which to exercise his natural vehemence of spirit. He retains, under an outside show of fresh and vigorous speculation and a manner which gives the idea of depth and subtlety to minds simpler and shallower than his own, a stock of spiritual commonplace, a rag-market of moral old-clothes, always on hand: most acceptable as fairings to the greasy-fingered chapman of intellectual wares. He has a faculty of grave bluster worthy of an ethical Bobadil or philosophic Parolles: a knack of light braggart pretension, when dealing on colloquial terms with his "gentle audience" or "friend,"[5] which would be creditable to Mascarille or Bessus.[6] Having all these excellent gifts, and more which his sectaries may be left to discover and trusted to proclaim, what can he want that a poet or philosopher worth naming should have? Very little. He cannot write a play, he cannot sing a song, [5] he cannot tell a story; contemptible things no doubt, and insignificant enough, but which happen as yet to be about the fairest means of testing the capacity of a dramatic, a lyrical, or a narrative writer. In the huge bulk of his lyrical baggage there is not one good song. In the tight and bulging knapsack of his close-packed dramatic outfit, there is not one good play. In his single attempt at sustained narrative he has erected the most monstrous monument of failure that ever was struck out by the blind concurrence of incongruous and hurtling verbal atoms. He has lavished his irrelevant and valueless praise on Keats, on Shelley, and on Landor; to what end? with what sincerity? under what influence? They are wholly good artists; melodious, spontaneous, perfect at their best; admirable workmen at their worst. A deaf man applauding good music, a blind man praising good colour, would be scarcely so capricious and inconceivable an anomaly as the author of *Sordello* praising the author of *Lamia*—the author of *Colombe's Birthday* praising the author of *The Cenci*—or the author of *Bells and Pomegranates* praising the author of *Hellenics*. It is not a question of different schools and all good in their way. It is not an evidence of liberal genius that can enjoy approving such good work as it cannot hope to enjoy performing. If any of the widely various ways of work pursued by these different poets is even approximately a right way, then are all the many barren tracks down which Mr. Browning gives tongue at every turn wholly and irretrievably wrong.

Take his lyrics. No man "born to greatness"[7] as a lyric writer ever wrote any one line in any one song which on its own ground was actually a bad one. Some must be weaker and worse, some better and stronger, than the others: but nowhere in any such song of any such poet can there be one line like this, from a love-song* in a love-play—*The Blot on the 'Scutcheon;*[8]

Parched the pleasant April herbage, and the *lark's heart's outbreak* tuneless!

[6] The very paper seems to writhe and shriek under the hideous and damnable dissonance of such words. That verse is conclusive; out of the metrical Nazareth which has once produced such a specimen of monstrous, of detestable discord as that, what note of music can come? Find its like in any lyrical poem accepted or acceptable as great, and it may be forgiven. As it is, there is one thing wanting to the vicious perfection of its horror: add one more hiss,—for "outbreak" read "outbreaks," and we may defy the author himself to improve on it.

A little further in the same work—here again we take him at his best, working on ground where he has already won laurels, if laurels they be and not cabbage-garlands or Querno's chaplet[9] of cauliflower —we shall find as choice a sample of the manner in which this dramatist deals with passion and character. A man, supposed to be young, noble, gentle, altogether of the distinct heroic type—accuses his sister (who by the way "is fourteen, remark") of perfidious unchastity

---

*(*Note*) The first two verses of this hideous song are as noticeable for badness of another kind—impotence and impertinence of flaccid language;

> There's a woman like a dew-drop, she's *so purer* than the purest;
> And her noble mind's the noblest, *yes,* and her sure faith's the surest.

The pert emphatic debility of that wretched "yes" is an offence in style akin to the offence in sound noticed in the text. They are twin specimens of feeble violence and flatulent labour. A man who must write thus to seem original had better plagiarize or be dumb. But, his admirers say, he has the "rough energy" of deep-thought and primeval verse. No good verse ever was properly "rough," no bad verse ever properly "smooth." The border ballads are not rough, but written with a perfect loyal sense of metrical law and poetic form. Dekker's dramatic verse is shapely and harmonious in its own way. Rowe's is not in any way.

before their brother and their brother's betrothed wife: thus. The
ancestral house, he says, has held "a thousand Treshams—never one
like her":

> No lighter of the signal lamp her quick
> Foul breath nigh quenches in hot eagerness
> To mix with breath as foul.[10]

No mortal ever wrote anything nastier than that. The foulness
of it is radical and essential; it is no mere fleck of passing coarseness
or hasty casual roughness of speech. It is not an outer speck on the
skin, but a plague-spot or blain in the flesh and core of thought.
There is a baseness of brutality in the choice of words, a dull thick-
hided heavy-headed impudence, a vulgarity of venom, a blushless
bestiality of cruel cowardice, which as attributed to a hero or model
"gentleman" such as this Tresham—this Cloten-Hamlet[11]—it would
be no less impossible to parallel than it would be to cite a more
execrable specimen of lyrical writing than the line before quoted.
Such a passage put into such a speaker's mouth is test enough of the
poet's ability to render the nobler forms of passion or purer types of
character. Any[12] man who was by inherited character and tradition,
one need not suppose especially noble or delicate, but of common tenderness and reserve, capable of the commonest shame or transmitted
reverence for his honour, would have had his tongue burnt out before uttering this speech—which in sentiment and expression is absolutely not human—which tastes of Haynau or Butler[13]—or if he
had uttered it in a mad or drunken fit would afterwards have had
his heart burnt out instead with mere shame; for to read and realize
it must turn such a man hot with disgust. But to whom need one
tell this by way of news? After that one is not surprised to find
throughout the play in hand a laborious sentiment, a violence of
strained [7] and factitious goodness,[14] the repulsive pretence to a
mockery of impossible innocence which utterly drains off and dries
up every chance source of pathos. Lovers who know not what they
are doing—"upon their honour, know it not"—maidens of an intol-
erable virtue which at fourteen does open windows and light lamps
with a skilful silent hand (but "they *were* innocent")[15]—are fit
company for heroic gentlemen of the Tresham pattern. Such incredible brutality on the one hand is well matched with such supra-senti-
mental pseudo-purity on the other: such a man's worship of heredi-

tary honours suits well with such a woman's observance of domestic sanctities. Under all the tinsel of this puerile and ragged frippery of false innocence and incredible[16] virginity of heart, there is latent, as there usually is where we find such cheap verbosity of monstrous morals, an inherent coarseness and dullness of moral imagination which allows a writer to commit such ineffable offences against all good sense, innate feeling, and common taste, as the one we have here too lightly and tenderly stigmatized. Every character, scene, situation, speech in this play is eaten through with a detestable dry rot of falsehood and convention: good and bad are rotten alike; for the mouth of a woman you have the mask of a mime; for the voice of a man the sound of wood and wire.

But he has such force of thought and subtlety of conception? And if he had them? This might be a valid plea to put in on behalf of a rough and ragged prose-writer who really has some great thing to say in fragmentary forms of growing or tentative speech. In his case such nudities and nodosities of style may be condoned. For a man who boasts that "this life allows him this one gift of verse alone"[17] there is no manner of imaginable excuse. Does he fear or blush to look his gift-horse in the mouth? does he apprehend it to be spavined and broken-winded? let him send it to the knacker's. In heaven's name, if it be not a verse-writer's business to write the best verse he may be able, what is he here for at all? What charity would be shewn on such wholly irrelevant grounds to a painter or musician who admittedly could not paint or compose? Does a school-boy who cannot construe escape being put in the bill because he can swim? A man comes forward avowedly to supply us with verse; the metrical ware he offers is palpably bad; what on earth have we to do with his reasons? What can it matter to [8] us that he may possess the genius of a hidebound Milton, the capacity of a costive Newton? He is here to perform a certain thing; not to offer the best possible substitute or suggest the most sufficient reason for its non-performance. Do a bad workman's good qualities as a comrade or moralist find him in good employment? What have we to do with the inarticulate merits of a public speaker? Let him speak well, or go about his praiseworthy private work in silence. His qualities are inexpressible; well and good; then why are we called upon to admire the expression of them? we might admire them on trust if their possessor had reticence enough to let us: but when all we can say of the noisily attempted expression is that beyond doubt *it* is inexpressibly bad, false, harsh, inadequate, insignificant, it is an impertinence to demand our applause for the inexpressible merit of the underlying matter. It is inconceivable that men and critics should require to be taught this—that a form of art is a form of art, no more but no less: should require to have it hammered into their ears and brains as if it were the maddest paradox. They will insist that a form of art is primarily something else; that its casual qualities are its essential properties; that it is first of all either a channel for instruction, a mouthpiece for morals, a speaking-trumpet for thought, a smoking-tube for philosophy, or a call pipe for theories. Works of art have before now done political or social service, proved useful as props for this thing or exponents of that: will you require the same service at the hands of every artist to come? It were as rational to assert that after Othello[18] no tragedy could exist without a spotted handkerchief. Look to the substance of the matter. A man does not do his work: you assert in excuse of him, first,[19] that he can do other things admirably; then, that if he were but a little different—had but something he wants, wanted but something he has—he would do this admirably too: that he has such wealth of capacities in reserve as would delight and amaze one to see, if he could but shew them! Assuredly. If he were not incapable of doing great things, he would be capable. If he were not crooked he would be straight; if he were not dark he would be fair; and so forth. Après? Of a great painter's bad drawing Mr. Browning himself once says, with some force—

> [That arm is wrongly put—and there again—
> A fault to pardon in the drawing's lines,
> Its body, so to speak: its soul is right,
> He means right—that, a child may understand.][20]

[9] We will hope so; but a child also learns pretty soon to understand that right meaning without right doing will not exactly hold water in this world.[21] He will not, if he knows it, sow a crop of false quantities broadcast about his school verses; but for all that, if he does, he must follow his good intentions to the place of torment. False quantities in a hymn deserve as immediate an appeal to the block of judgment as false quantities in a drinking-song. Not in the pupil-room, not in the studio, not on the stage will the plea of

good intentions be held good. A dissonant oratorio designed to elevate the religious sentiment shall incur as swift and sure damnation as a dissonant opera-buffa designed to stimulate the secular sentiment. What you meant to do when you began may signify somewhat to yourself: what you have done now your work is shewn up, this alone signifies anything whatever to us. The boy we spoke of is indeed more excusable, if bad verse can ever be more or less excusable; he was bidden shew up something, and did not work of his own will; but who set you this taskwork to begin upon? who required verse at your hand? who bade you write or speak under pains and penalties if you kept quiet? Look back again at that instance of the painter, always the closest parallel and surest touchstone you can bring for a man's verse. If the limbs are impossibly moulded—if the colour is nearer clay than flesh—if the figures do not stand right and the sun does not shine right—who but some strong clerical or female critic will care for the briefest instant to consider whether the purpose was devout or undevout, whether the man hoped to excite noble or ignoble emotion? Set, as a judicious Academy has done before now, an etching of Mr. Whistler's under or over an etching of Mr. Redgrave's.[22] To what purpose is the latter work tender (as they say) in feeling, innocent in aim, laudable in wish to do well? a finished work of soft English expression representing some domestic grace of country beauty, while the other is but some rapid rendering of a rough interior or sterile mudbank? Good intention has made the one pretty and passable; but the man with eyes to see who looks upon the other is struck through with the strong and delicious sense of absolute genius—of secure and splendid genius that need put forth no feeler of apology, lean on no stay of intention—of great power greatly [10] trained and put to great use. That will give us the thing we want; the sharp swift indefinable inexpressible passion of a liberal and lofty pleasure, which good work must give to all who have eyes to see it: and which nothing else can give to any human creature. Form a contemptible thing? it is the one adorable thing in the world. In the religion of that supreme God of art—in his infallible speech and inspired scripture—no mortal artist can disbelieve if he would. Greatness of form in all art implies excellence of matter. Only the purest metal is capable of taking that visibly divine stamp. Only the most fine gold can be forged or carved to such visibly divine purpose. Where form is, there are all good things; where form is not, there is nothing good. So wide and so unspeakable is the difference between art and ethics. Consider the two meanings of the word design. In morals, it means good or bad intention—which may in effect be assumed as the soul of morality. In art, it means form of work—which must without question be accepted as the soul of art. "Execution is the chariot of genius," said a poet and painter who spoke by right of knowledge.[23] Without form there is no salvation.

We have passed in an instant far out of sight of Mr. Browning; but then we have spoken for an instant of noble and admirable art. Strange as it sounds, the swift utter change of topic was not irrelevant. In judging verse we must begin by finding out what are the grounds of just judgment. Now the formal side of the poetic art is no less predicable and definable[24] than the formal side of the pictorial art. And we have our present writer's word for it, he is nothing if not a poet. If therefore he violates the formal conditions of good poetry—conditions rigorously distinct, wholly indispensable and wholly unalterable—such a sentence as law most justly passes on a thief, painting on a dauber, divinity on a heretic, medicine on a quack, morality on a criminal,[25] philosophy on a sophist, and scholarship on a dunce—such a sentence must be passed upon him. All laws lie in this: that what you do shall be well done. The law of verse is that it shall be good verse; as surely as the law of painting is that it shall be good painting. Capital punishment, though unhappily not always applied, has never as yet been abrogated under this law. It is empty to charge criticism [11] with going hungrily into minute things and paltry questions of verbal or metrical quibbling. Upon these things depends the form of a poem; and upon the form depends the spirit; and upon these two depends the value of a man's work. The technicalities of metre, neither as yet verbally defined nor easily expressible in English without apparent pedantry of detail, are to poetry what the technical minutiae of combined colours are to painting. By the goodness or badness, the failure or success, of an artist's workmanship in these matters his entire achievement must be judged, if judgment be at all worth giving or having. A man in "this life"[26] must at his own peril choose between prose, silence, and good verse. From this rule no good or great workman will shrink; for against it he will not need to appeal. Of course an artist at work does not think of these laws. Of course too he does not infringe them. It is no matter of special praise to him; he cannot but obey them; it would be painful and laborious to him to offend against the conditions of his very life. These laws of liberty and loyalty are current and ingrained in the very flesh and blood with which he works—burnt into his nerves and brain.

Now if there is a small and simple thing in the technical line of metre it is the scheme of English anapæsts. That you shall not count anything but a foot of two long syllables equivalent to a foot of two short and a long, is surely no rigorous, no perverse, no perplexing rule. That you shall not allow the iambic substitute, which the facility of our lax English laws admits on sufferance as tolerable if illegal, to overcharge your verse, is as obvious and as requisite a law of common harmony as can well be conceived. Yet versifiers do continually violate these rules: but at least the run of such metrical Tarquins do not push their brutality beyond this simple crime of violation. Now as one of many specimens, read this line—which the context will show ought to consist of two rhyming anapæsts or their equivalent feet: *Stop veins I'd—have subside.*[27] Actually the writer has made three long heavy full syllables—equivalent properly to a spondee and a half—serve as equivalent to a single anapæst. Let the schools consider that and "devise brave punishments for him"[28] if they can; he has done it, and lives. This is a crime in[29] the sight of any artist equivalent to murder in the sight of any judge: nay, to parricide under aggravating circumstances. This [12] "Metidja" is a "dramatic lyric"—it is brought to the bar under that suspicious and uneuphonious name on the authority of the man who committed it; but the stage-directions are wanting. Let the studious annotator supply one from the original margin of the "Tempest"— (*Sings brutishly.*) But Caliban, under extreme provocation of cramps and pinches, never uttered a sound like that. These are small things, petty holes to pick in the "singing-robe" of a poet? They are not small; and the holes are of no man's picking; they gape there on that ragged and tinselled coat as the tailor left them.[30] These are poor school and slopwork metaphors? true; but we have to deal with "a poor thing in" verse. "A poor thing, sir, but mine own," says the Touchstone of Helicon,[31] as "motley on back and pointing-pole in hand"[32] he introduces to us by way of a Muse this tattered and reeling Audrey. The last words quoted are his own, spoken of himself; in the same paragraph where they occur he tells us that "there's a

realm wherein" Fate "has no right and he has many lovers." Could
a better definition be attained of Chaos? There where there is no
form, where there is no law, where there is no beauty, where there
is no coherence, where there is no order, where there is no significance, where there is no vitality—in that extreme limbo of confounded cloud and clay the few or many "lovers" of bottomless and
shapeless confusion may receive with gratified ears the music of
transcendental Caliban uttered through the organ of mutilated
Gigadibs.

But here on this unlover-like earth where Fate and Form are not
as yet dethroned, the facts of art and law exist and hold control
over the very sons of night and Chaos. Admirably callous to the
implicit scorn of such an one, Art makes bland reply to her clamorous chaotic friend—"So you despise me, Mr. Gigadibs. No depreca-
tion!"[33] She can dispense with the pestle of Paracelsus-Machaon,
with the lyre of Bombastes-Apollo.[34] "If he has no need of her she
has no need of him."[35] The supple splendid English language dies
hard, even in such "hangman's hands."[36] Let the lovers of Chaos go
on their own way and utter their peculiar noises; artists will take
their stand on the "ancient ways" of art, and hold fast the faith
once delivered[37] to all who [13] would do such work as is found
good in her sight. Not porcine or ovine suggestions of sound, but
human and harmonious tunes of just deliberate music—impulsive
and instinctive as any bird's note or any wave's lapse, but with an
impulse and an instinct which is right and beautiful, not lawless
and loathsome—these are what they will find it best to give. Rules
and schools and arts of poetry are superfluous and despicable?
Doubtless: for artists who can achieve; by no means for artisans
who can but pretend. For a man who cannot sin moral law also is
superfluous and worthless; for one who will steal and stab but for
fear of the cart's tail or the gallows, moral law is requisite and
wholesome. To have writers who cannot write or "painters who cannot paint"[38] pulled up and tied down by the laws applicable in such
cases, is an evident and a certain benefit. We need not fear that the
fetter of such laws will be found to gall the hand or foot of any
artist worth his right of liberty.

So much for that mendacious or maniacal plea of mere external
culpability. He has but formal faults, you plead? formal fault is the
gravest crime, and implies all others possible. It is the one thing easy

to detect and illegal to tolerate. You cannot but find it out wherever it does turn up; having found it, you may lay hands on it, secure that there can be no excuse for shewing mercy. One plea may be put forward in such a writer's behalf with some shew of force; that formless chaos is an advance upon false form; that palpable deformity is a step beyond plastered putrescence; that "Dramatic Lyrics" are better than "Irish Melodies." As a choice of horrors, assuredly they are: and assuredly also that is no part of the question. One race of foolish readers will split upon the polished rocks of Moore; another will be absorbed in the muddy whirlpool of Browning.[39] We may prefer whetted dagger to drugged bowl; "but pecks of poison are not pecks of salt."[40] Our business is to keep well clear of either. Not upon us is the choice enforced between pestilence and famine.

Has he formal merit to counterweigh these formal faults? Hardly [14] would the excellence of a supreme poet do that: in no wise will any merit of his. He has given no great special verses that strike and cleave by their perfect beauty to the sense and memory of those who can distinguish and appreciate. Much excellent and ingenious work he has given; copious vigorous matter after its kind, embodied in good strong words after their kind. He has often put forcible and strange things into forcible and strange shapes. Not once in all his volumes of heavy-laden verse has he simply said a simple thing in such a way that no hearer can hear it and forget. Lyrics written on his principle (if a principle it be to hold that the great qualities of a lyric are non-lyrical) cannot of course even appear to aim at this. Everything memorable for excellence can only be memorable for excellence in its own way. But he has not pretended—not at least openly or without some shame—to transmute the conditions of playwriting. To this part of his work then we may look for such effects; and may look long in vain. In no hole or corner, in no guest-chamber or bride-chamber, of this big dramatic building, shall we find anything like the effects of a great dramatist. Likeness does not imply—it rather precludes—identity or imitation. We speak of things like in kind; verses that stand on the same rank; coins of the same metal. Of such there is here not one: nothing like Bosola's "She was born first";[41] no verse like Phraxanor's

I prithee do not fret, my pretty lute;[42]

no word like the *Merci* of Ruy Blas.[43] These good separate points are of course not the first things to look out for in dramatic writing. But all great dramatic writing is full of them, as if they fell into place by some divine law of chance. No poet essentially great ever failed to fall in with such great accidents. The style of dramatic verse generally is here also very vile. It is hooked and welded together as with joists of wooden speech and clamps of iron thought. It creaks rustily, heaves heavily, labours lamely into sense. It never leaps or flows with the fierce sweet impulse of pure or passionate sound; at its best and strongest it spills itself into puddles and spends itself in sputtering. This at its very best: of its very worst what shall be said? If it fare thus with his Ottima, who has a touch of truth and force about her, how does it fare with his Colombes, Constances, Mildreds, Phenes, who are visibly fleshless and senseless? Analyze the doings and sayings of the wife of Jules or the mistress of Norbert;[44] the utter mechanical absurdity of the monstrous parts they have to play is equalled by the tight, hoarse, [15] intermittent, hard, febrile manner of their utterances: as far from emotion as from reason. One unfair charge is often brought against the style of Mr. Browning: that of intense obscurity. Taken all in all, he does not write obscurely; he simply writes bad English. The obscurity of his expression is like the obscurity of a costermonger's spelling. Once understand that his sentences are not to be parsed but to be gulped, and you get on fairly enough: to what purpose is another matter. There goes more to obscure writing than the mere omission of the words "to" and "which" wherever they ought to occur, and the mere inversion or dissection of a couplet till it stands on its head with its middle ripped open, and black in the face. This passage, be it narrative or dramatic, is not properly obscure; what else it may be speaks for itself.

> Ah, Naddo's gone!
> Labours this moonrise what the Master meant—
> "Is Squarcialupo speckled? purulent
> I'd say, but when was Providence put out?
> He carries somehow handily about
> His spite nor fouls himself." (*sic*)[45]

Which is more than can be said of all spiteful "purulent" men and rhymers. "Unfair to detach from the context—'spiteful' and not

'handy' to select this morsel from the wide board of *Sordello"*?
Look at that context. As the best things lose, so do the worst things
gain by being detached from their setting. There is a small foul
piece of hideous jargon; offensive enough to all eyes and nostrils;
but the context it welters in, the chaos it has been plucked out of?
the ugliness of that continent of gasping and spluttering jargon no
speech can express or brain conceive. Besides, these separate lines
are separate crimes. A man may have done but a murder or two in
the course of a quiet life, yet you hang him. This poem of *Sordello*
is not on the whole obscure—is far at least from impenetrable.
Where it seems hardest and toughest to the casual reader, it aims
mainly at giving the rapid subtle gradations of a strong, soft,
nervous nature, passed through strange crucibles of thought and
sensation, cast into strange moulds of action and event. As far as
Mr. Browning's power of conceiving [16] the physical and moral
type of even an imperfect artist can reach, so far and no farther has
he succeeded in embodying that type under the name and shape of
"Sordello." Only a man of some moral vigour, subtlety, learning,
and pliable nerve of intellect, could have undertaken or carried
through the merest sketch or tentative suggestion of such a work:
and this decidedly is the main feather in his cap; a somewhat draggled plume, nodding in a sodden manner over a somewhat dubious
blazon. To give any likeness whatever of such a nature—receptive,
sensitive, impressible by every change of possible aim or actual circumstance, yet invariable in essential strength and consistent in substantial weakness,—is an attempt of itself rather great than not,
and commendable by comparison with the smaller attempts of
smaller men which are equally bad and false in point of art: for
bad and false the design, as conceived by the author of *Sordello*,
undoubtedly is. Thus much of comparative praise the sternest Bishop
of the church of art *in partibus* may concede to a hostile but ingenious Gigadibs. It was better to try at this than to try at singing[46]
meaner things no less unfit for noble art to handle nobly; better to
promulgate on such higher ground a spasmodic evangel of hysterical
failure than to preach from a stagnant level of sincere and tender
cant the gospel of matrimonial Anglicanism as a salve and solution
for the wounds and perplexities of the world. But, comprehensible
as the design and laudable as the ambition may be, the old question
remains prominent: what has been done? Rymer and Phillips in-

tended to supersede Shakespeare and his fellows by writing better
plays than they did; a design and an ambition surely distinct and
laudable enough; and the results were *Edgars* and *Distressed
Mothers*. Ponsard intended to outdo and suppress Hugo; a clear
purpose and a lofty aim beyond doubt; and the outcome was a
Lucrèce.[47] Intention is not final; execution is. And this *Sordello,*
though traceable enough and duly comprehensible by imaginative
readers who will take the trouble to pitch their minds in the proper
key, is, as such readers will see, and as other readers will fail to see,
in every [17] several point on which a work of art can deserve or
can desire to be judged wholly damnable. It has no shape, no scheme,
no hands to paint with, no voice to speak with, no feet to walk, no
wings to mount, no sight to discern, no brain to decide. It is lax,
flaccid, violent, verbose, sterile, sickly, incompetent and incoherent.
It means one thing and does another; it has no steadiness of step,
no sureness of eye, no vigour of wrist. Throughout his work the
writer is perpetually liable to be scared or lured off the matter in
hand. Every stray fowler that comes across his path can dazzle him
with a bit of broken glass, attract him with a bit of scarlet cloth,
stun him with a bit of beaten brass. Into every snare that lies in a
singing-bird's way he falls fluttering, stupefied, impotent and screaming. And the best song-note he has to give you even when not thus
fascinated—even when whole "in the liver-wing"[48]—lapses into
sounds like this: and the thing spoken or sung of is a Roman
sculptor:

> Careful Jove's face be duly fulgurant
> And mother Venus' kiss-creased nipples pant
> Back into pristine pulpiness ere fixed
> Above the walls.[49]

What snake has the man eaten? on what nestful of cloven and
hissing tongues has his foot stumbled? "Venus' kiss-creased nipples"!
It is too unendurable to bear dissection or remark. Caliban's love-
sonnets must have been acceptable, delicate, melodious by the side
of that. What ears, what lips, what fingers can have helped in the
concoction of such a verse? Of its non-metrical qualities—choice of
expression, form of idea, manner of taste—we have nothing adequate to say. Let it pass to the limbo of its "lovers."

There are those extant who aver, with a sensible gust and tang of audacious assertion, very comfortable to minds labouring under the softer or chiller kinds of distemper, that these books are found to give a factitious health, a strenuous pleasure, a virile support, to certain readers—readers presumably deficient in these given qualities—radically diseased, flaccid and dolorous, nerveless and parasitic? Not at all: to world-worn [18] earnest men, somewhat soured by the sad sense of years, grey with the growth of experienced deeds and days: strong men, perhaps (and who [?] can help it?) slightly bitter and cynical. These, we should say, must be men of a most mild acerbity; in whom the asses'-milk of semi-human kindness has been too early curdled by super-asinine agonies of experience. Crosses in love or verse, ambition or not, may conceivably reduce such an one, with the soured milk yet warm in his innocent mouth, to browse on the plenteous thistle-crop of Mr. Browning's pastures. But for any spirit or creature of another sort we cannot suppose that the diet will prove medicinal or palatable. A bat may go higher than a mouse or a rat, but hardly as high as a lark. The melody of "No more dams I'll make for fish"[50] may be heard as it were from a tabernacle of cloud on a declivity invisible to moles and ants of the molehill: the melodist may assume the robes of Prospero or the plumage of Ariel; but despite stolen wand and artificial wing,[51] the voice is[52] the voice of the son of Sycorax. The cloud is mere condensed swamp-fog and reek of the fens; a little more sunlight would burn it well away. Evasion or erasure of the proper word is perversity rather than obscurity. Intricate air and intense fire may combine about the luminous body of a star or sun to weave some veil of pure keen haze, translucent indeed but not transparent; you cannot doubtless have a Faust or Hamlet, a Sophocles or Dante, made naked and patent to all comers at first sight. Between this splendid obscurity of glory and the clotted fog that hardens round a marsh-fire in timely twilight, there is distance enough. Purity, exaltation, beauty of extreme light may seem to make the one unavailable and inaccessible to a mere traveller's eyes; the other its own bad atmosphere muffles and blots out. We may say of Mr. Browning's laudation of such poets as these, as did Blake[53] of Reynolds' praises of Angelo, " 'tis Christian meekness thus to praise a foe; but 'twould be madness, all the world would say," if they were to praise Mr. Browning.

But without reverting to great dead men, it may be asked, what is it that we would have in the way of mere art? It is every poet's business to provide matter of his own and good of its kind without prescription or dictation of others. But in order that after the hateful if useful trouble of detecting false and denouncing faultful work [19] we may take a little final pleasure in reconsidering and returning thanks for work that is just and pure, for verse that is proper and perfect, we will give a specimen or so of the manner of thing we want and expect from an artist. We will cite from no past or present English poet; appeal might be with reason entered against the former method of comparison; the latter might easily come to seem ungraceful. We will quote only from French poets of our own time; and the rather because it is a cherished dogma of English faith that French verse is wanting in the supreme musical and delightful qualities of metre: that the most lyrical of languages (for the English and the Italian are both in comparison over facile and slippery, while in French there is no safe walking for any but a strong and faultless master of sound and form; here a man may do decently and passably, there he must do absolutely well or ill) that this noble and subtle lyric instrument is unfit for lyric use; a doctrine upheld with all that stolidity of sciolism which on points of pure art is the especial appanage of the critical Anglican faculty. In poetry as in painting, the English of our own day can show some men as great perhaps as the French; assuredly they can shew no such great school of men, which is the highest thing for a period of great workmen to shew; as witness England under Shakespeare and Venice under Titian. And now hear this: for we will cite nothing but slight and simple things, when we might range high and wide enough.

      À Saint-Blaise, à la Zuecca,
    Vous étiez, vous étiez bien aise
      À Saint-Blaise.
    À Saint-Blaise, à la Zuecca,
     Nous étions bien là.[54]

Think now of that "lark's heart's outbreak"! But again;

    Menez-moi, dit la belle,
    À la rive fidèle
      Où l'on aime toujours.
    Cette rive, ma chère,
    On ne la connaît guère
      Au pays des amours.[55]

[20] Think now of Mr. Browning's "stopped veins" and "kiss-creased nipples"! Finally hear this and lay the loveliness and greatness of it to heart.

> Nous achèterons de bien belles choses
> En nous promenant le long des faubourgs.
> Les bluets sont bleus, les roses sont roses,
> Les bluets sont bleus, j'aime mes amours.[56]

That is what Mr. Browning has not given. These are the things we desire and receive at the hands of all great poets. These are the gifts of pure gold and perfect light fetched straight and safe from "the chambers of the East, the chambers of the Sun," that have not yet, with leave of the great English lyrist, in any wise "ceased from their ancient melody."[57] Though one take "the wings of the morning" and remain in the uttermost places of thought,[58] unless he started with a poet's especial quality of sight and speech he will bring back no such gifts as these. Mere love-rhymes and cradle-songs? doubtless they are but such. Après? He that is faithful over small things will be safe to deal greatly with great things. No small poet ever succeeded and no great poet ever failed in song-writing.[59] What matter whether the work you are bound to do be little or big, secular or sacred? the question is one of better and worse. Christian art, we will admit, is greater than pagan; but we had better admit also that the divine Bacchus and Venus of Tintoretto is worth more than all the virgins and children of Angelico. Besides, had we chosen to vary our range of citation, what innumerable inestimable wealth of diverse choice was there not at hand in the storehouse of the chief master alone, and to bring in by handfuls and lapfuls—

> Garlands of every hue and every scent
> From vales deflowered and forest-trees branch-rent—[60]

what songs of thought and passion, love and hate, action and sorrow, laughter and aspiration, from the date of the *Ballades* to the date of the *Petites Épopées,* from the tourney of King John to the sea-song of the soldiers of the sea[61]—what colour and music, light and strength, divine depths of speechless passion and holy heights of spoken scorn! What has the great master not done, whither not gone for all men's sake—to all time? Such things has he given us of his great grace and fullness of ability to give. What has your man

given you? Philosophy? let philosophers decide. Lyric verse? but
what "plagal-cadence" or [21] "toccata," what "lute or clavici-
thern"[62] of his handling, shall be set against the music and "mighty
line"[63] of those other lyrics? Dramatic or passionate character? He
has betweenwhiles a King Victor or Salinguerra, a Blougram[64] or
Fra Lippo certainly well worth shewing; but let those who dare or
care to set themselves down beside Dogberry, set Pippa beside Esmeralda,* Phene beside Marion, Mildred beside Catarina, Valence
beside Ruy Blas, Luria beside Gennaro, Bluphocks beside Don
César:[68] and what are these among so many? We speak only of
things which the English author has attempted, forms of verse
which he has done his best to assume. We have matched him against
living writers of song, play, and narrative. The sonnet form, for
example, it appears is beneath or beyond him. That sort of excellence is too cheap for such a poet: requires a smaller man with a
touch of pedantry in him. It is remarkable that artisans and sciolists
never have been able to distinguish between pedants,—who are men
of their own kind,—and artists,—who are not. A deep, subtle, exquisite form of verse in which without "a giant's strength"[69] and a

---

*(Note) Compare for one instant the broken, short-winded, "beggar-on-horseback"
style of Pippa's songs—a style like the gait of a man in rags on stilts—lank and
laborious, draggled and difficult,—with Esmeralda's

> Mon père est oiseau,
> Ma mère est oiselle.
> Je passe l'eau sans nacelle,
> Je passe l'eau sans bateau.
> Ma mère est oiselle,
> Mon père est oiseau.[65]

Not even "Gastibelza" or the "Adieu, patrie!"[66] is more perfect and wonderful than
that is. To the adherents of the other party—to the admirers of spasmodico-dramatic,
pseudo-caco-phrenitico-lyric writing (the form of this compound is taken from Mr.
Browning's lyrico-dramatic poem of "Waring"[67])—to such, nothing will make the
plain fact just now laid down even remotely explicable or comprehensible. They will
see much on the one hand, nothing on the other. They will find the one rich, thoughtful,
capacious; the other naked and bare, a thin nursery jingle. It is unfortunate for these,
but certain for all men, that the facts of art are as stubborn as the facts of science.
No man of any cultivated intellectual competence could write worse songs than Pippa's
(we do not take into account any patent imbecile of the kind which is always prolific
enough); no poet since poets began could have improved upon Esmeralda's. The reason
is clear to such as can see it without having to be taught. An artist's business is never
to do many ingenious things at once that his work may seem wonderful for an hour;
it is always to do the right thing at the right time, that his work may hold good
for ever.

god's command over that strength no man need dream of succeeding—a form which allured the whole desire and taxed the whole
ability of Dante, Shakespeare, Milton, Ronsard, and Keats—is evidently despicable and insufficient to a Browning or a Boileau; so
do the extremes of chaotic disorder and pedantic sham-order meet;
so do the heresies of poetic anarchy and poetic convention combine;
so deep and radical is the absolute bond of union between the worship of no form and the worship of false form. "Le néant, c'est le
mal."[70] Otherwise, we might have taken too ready an advantage
and reaped too facile a triumph by reference to such great masters
of that form now present among us as Théophile Gautier and
Charles Baudelaire. The least among their sonnets is far beyond
Mr. Browning's possible power of execution; but what of that? We
are bound to believe that he is above the conception of their best.

Let not therefore any sectary of his presume to say that we
demand of him to do not his own work, but another man's; that
[22] we require at his hands not the gifts he has to give us, but
the likeness of another man's gifts; that we, in a word, are among
those who, as M. Vacquerie[71] has excellently expressed it, must be
content that each tree should bear its own fruit but must needs go
looking for grapes on peach-trees and cursing the figtree as barren
because it will not grow pine-apples. We require of each man, first,
that he should do his own work; then that the work should be really
good of its kind. We desire the bird to sing well, the flower to
smell sweet,[72] the problem to come right, the poet to do good verse,
the orator to speak, the moralist to be moral, the painter to paint,
the musician to compose, the statesman to govern, the preacher to
preach, the soldier to fight, the philosopher to observe, and the sailor
to handle his ship well; we cannot afford to let one of these go
wrong, though he were ever so able in some alien way, but so
capable of managing another man's office. Let each man enlarge
the field, expand the limits, heighten the aspirations, ennoble the
day's work of his personal duty as much and as far as may be possible; but first let him see that it be done at all; let him look to that
at his peril and its. This one possible and necessary thing we simply
must and will have; and will be put off with nothing else whatever
by way of exchange.

FATHER GARASSE

It is a grievous instance of professional ingratitude that his bastard children of the press have not yet raised altars and offered sacrifice to the blessed memory of Father Garasse. Branded by fact, as Théophile by fiction, with the foulest of charges; mendacious even among reviewers and filthy even among libellers; prurient above the run of the virtuous, and virtuous above the run of the prurient; so blasphemous and so obscene in his hysterical outcries against obscenity and blasphemy that no sample of his style can be cited without a sense of sickness which overpowers even contempt itself; this miserable and shameful creature has surely every possible claim to the regard and reverence of his kind. When I speak of his kind, I speak of neither men nor women; there are things that belong to the anonymous sex. Of these are the children of Zoilus, of Rymer,[1] and of Garasse; a nameless race of mysterious propagation, which yet seems never to fail or intermit. They breed without sex and survive without tradition: they are hatched into form by some impure instinct. Nevertheless they might remember their founders from of old; they might bethink themselves betweenwhiles to praise famous men of their kind, and their fathers that begat them after a sort. In every age, in every country, they seethe and scribble and live and lie: but never was there a completer creature in his way than this Jesuit, nor one worthier of their praise whose labour is to emulate his work. And even they seem to have too generally forgotten him. Is it worth while after all (were it not indeed for the hire's sake) for the meanest parasite of diseased literature to think as a slanderer through a nameless life in print, only to be thus forgotten of his own, thus lost in the loathsome whirlpool which absorbs all things ephemeral and obscene as himself? Let such look back upon Garasse. Him in their own way they can hardly hope to rival. He is their prototype, their archetype; *exemplar Dei*. Wanting the works of the divine Zoilus, we may well accept him as the ideal critic, the absolute reviewer. This great man sufficed to himself; neither gazette nor review in those dark days could expose to his fertilizing compost the congenial hotbed of its columns. He had to dig, to plough, to manure his own land from his own resources. And for the latter office at least he was quite admirably qualified by nature. Witness (as far as we can permit such witness) the style of his arraignment of Théophile. This is how the priest speaks of the poet in hand.

He is an atheist, a beast, a pig, a calf, and a devil. He is— what more than one of his assailants were afterwards proved to be. He is mad, drunk, damned, sexless, and soulless. He writes bestially of women, devilishly of God. He is unmanly and unholy. He wants sanity and virility; he is not like other men: he has a devil. He ought to be spat upon and spurned out of sight. He ought to be scourged. He ought to be hanged. He ought to be burnt. He will be damned. The law must lay hold of him; his poems must be quashed and himself indicted, in the name of God and Man.

And so forth, even to the crack of doom. Vive Garasse! I for one will back him against the whole crew of twopenny gazetteers and sixpenny reviewers now on hire. They cannot beat that; they can only repeat it. The foulest and most vicious among them compared to him is no more than an engine-driver compared to Stephenson.[2] He taught them how to slaver; he gave them tongues to revile. And to this holy father of the church of critics the thankless apostles of his gospel have not yet reared statues and burnt incense! His starting-point was ahead of their goal; his first utterance as rancid with mendacity, as venomous with rancour as their last. And where is now Garasse? in which of "The Eternal Cesspools"?[3] Alas! *nunc a labore requiescentes opera sequuntur.*[4] With a noble and just compassion, Victor Hugo says[5] of the obscure libellers of poets, whom time has cruelly defrauded of the immortal infamy they painfully laboured to earn: "Plaignons ces pauvres insulteurs auxquels le mépris a fait faillite."

And yet, is it in this case too late? Let journalism remember what a journalist was lost in this reverend father. Let all such libellers, let all such scribblers, assemble to pay tribute on his tomb —no libation of wine, no sacrifice of perfumes; let each critic on the press as foolish and as foul as he bring hither his little natural offering; the pyramid will be perfected in a day: and the memory of Garasse, duly embalmed and manured, will be fragrant to all time. Then will a fit and monumental shrine preserve, even as vegetables are preserved, at least the name of this high priest of the incompetent, this patron saint of the envious. Thither will future generations of libellers, and liars yet unborn, flock reverently to praise and pray. Thither will the prurient pastors of the press come daily and nightly to discharge their office of thanksgiving. There every incapable who can insult, every hypocrite who can assail, will be indued with the priestly ephod and anointed with the priestly oil. I seem to see in some Temple of Cloacina the leprous multitude of the faithful assembled in prayer; the communion of hate, the love-feast of lies, is made ready for them; Fréron[6] breaks the bread and Gifford hands the cup; and amid odours and sounds congenial, with hiccup and titter, with bray and whine and howl, goes upward —or downward—one unanimous voice from before and after; *Sancte Garasse, ora pro nobis!*[7]

CHANGES OF ASPECT

The task or the diversion of spiritual or mental autobiography has never seemed to me worthy to attract or to allure a man of any self-respect from the private and untroubled path of reticence and self-seclusion. But even the humblest and obscurest of writers or of men may do some service to letters and to truth by the attempt to refute a fallacy or to expose a sophism. Change of opinion as to particular and minor men or matters is the inevitable benefit of growth from crudity of impression to maturity of perception. Change of principle is possible only to men whom a sufficient number of parliamentary votes or pieces of silver will induce to turn tail and desert their colours. Few studies can be more interesting and should be more profitable than the study of development—of transfiguration rather than transformation—in the views of any man in any way memorable who never was other than a man of transparent honesty and flawless honour; of such a man as Wordsworth or Southey, as Landor or Hugo. The change may seem to us to have been a change for the better or the worse; where the thinker's integrity is indisputable, it is in either case equally interesting as a subject of either grateful or regretful study. Alone among the four great writers whom I have named, Landor never changed his views on general or political questions; the youth of twenty was not a purer and more ardent republican than the veteran of ninety. But no man ever made franker admission of more absolute change from sympathy with certain causes or belief in certain pretences. None but the basest of mankind ever pretended to question the perfect and unselfish integrity which inspired and guided the others in their progress or retrogression from the emotions of youth to the convictions of age. But even those meanest among men of their generation were not so pitifully, so typically, so sublimely idiotic as to tax the man whom they desired to malign with apostasy from the faith of a republican on the score of his refusal to repudiate the radical article, to abjure the central tenet, of republican belief.[1] Union, even without liberty,—even with no more personal independence than was enjoyed by the citizens of ancient Rome,—union, even if enforced

64

by the severities of Cromwell or the atrocities of Robespierre—is the first condition of republican life.

Upon such a point as this there can be no possible discussion, as there can be no possible difference of opinion—no imaginable discordance of sentiment or judgment. It is simply a question of knowledge or ignorance with respect to the rudiments of language and the elements of logic. When we come down from the contemplation of general principles to the consideration of particular persons or disputable points of criticism, we pass from matters of faith to matters of opinion. A writer on whom I have lavished what many judges consider an extravagant exuberance of praise has put on record his verdict that a man who never changes his opinion is like standing water—he breeds reptiles of the mind.[2] Whether this be so or not, it is certain that any honest and competent critic may be justified in assuming at different times the alternate parts of an advocate and a judge. There can be nothing disingenuous or wrong in such a writer's outspoken and straightforward championship of such claims as he will never feel disposed to deny because he may think fit to insist on the heavy deductions which must inevitably be made from them—on the serious qualifications with which all rational advocacy of their value must necessarily be tempered and allayed. This is a point—I might say, a point of honour—so well worth making and establishing that almost any illustration may serve to confirm the importance of the truth of it. Even I, naught that I am, may prove to be of service as an example. I have written much in praise of others, and a little now and then in dispraise. I have never found occasion to recall or to modify one syllable of satire or of blame. And when I have felt impelled to qualify though never to recant my praise, I have had no reason to regret the liberal and loyal excess of its original expression.

Take for instance the case of Byron. It was and it is and it always will be right to applaud what was noble in his life and work: but it would stultify the utterance and nullify the value of such applause if we were to ignore or to condone what was ignoble or absurd. "Nothing in his life became him like the leaving it."[3] But this was the epitaph of a criminal who died bravely. Hardly any praise can be too high, hardly any sympathy too cordial, for his constancy and ardour on behalf of Italy against the Austrian and of Greece against the Turk. It is allowable, when this just due of honour is questioned or refused, to insist on it, and to enlarge on the credit which has not always been accorded to the finer qualities of the writer and the man. Speaking as an advocate, one may and must and should say all that can be said on that side of the question: especially when the man's fame is far more endangered by the advocacy of dunces and poetasters than by the depreciation of poets and of critics. And not the most rigid of rational and competent judges will deny the incomparable power, the indisputable fascination, of a writer whom no such judge will accept as a great writer of poetry or of prose, when engaged on such work as does not pretend to be either good prose or great poetry. It is work well worth doing, and well deserving of thanks: but it can no more suffice to raise a minor poet above his natural rank than any display of physical daring or any generous enterprise on behalf of strangers can efface or extenuate the dishonour of treason to friendship, cowardice in attack, mendacity in reprisal, or vulgarity in retort. But the judge, if just, will never forget what I at least have never been slow to reaffirm: the noble sincerity of sympathy with freedom which should always be admitted to redeem so much that was insincere and ignoble, and the marvellous mastery of tragicomedy in narrative which no one need ever dream of aspiring to approach.

Take the case of a truer poet if not a stronger man or a greater writer than Byron. I should be surprised to find that any man of his generation or of mine had lavished more cordial gratitude or more fervent praise on the work and the genius of Tennyson than I. But it would be strange if this were to be held a sufficient reason to preclude me from dwelling or even from touching on what I find unworthy of that genius or contemptible in that work. Did I wish to dwell on it, as assuredly I do not, there is nothing in the printed record of my honest and unselfish and loyal admiration which need prevent me or give me pause. It is now matter of universal notoriety that the author of *In Memoriam* was pleased to describe the author of *Songs before Sunrise* as "a reed through which all things blow into music."[4] Well, I think it may be contended that some things do not which found more or less musical expression through the Tennysonian flute. Here for example are two or three such things: the courtliness[5] which gave unseemly[6] thanks for the allowance or concession of a laurel by way of grace or favour: the resentment which condescended to retort on a doubtless offensive and absurd but not personally scurrilous attack by personal insult aimed at "the padded man that wears the stays":[7] the infirmity of spirit which found it necessary to make public protestation of indifference to the ineffably imperceptible and inconsiderable outrage of a "spiteful letter"[8] such as other men who are favoured with such tributes would not dream of trying to number, to notice, or to recollect.

It is difficult for a man who has the honour of his calling at heart—and no man should follow any calling in which he does not from the first acknowledge, and is not prepared to maintain to the last, a standard of duty and a principle of honour—to condone the weakness of a leader who discredits[9] the flag. It is not less difficult, at first sight or on a general survey, to understand why the calling of Æschylus, of Sophocles, of Dante, of Shakespeare, of Milton, of Alfieri, of Landor, of Wordsworth, of Shelley, and of Hugo, should be supposed to suggest if not to imply some touch of unmanliness in those who follow it. Every calling that a man should follow requires, I should presume, its particular test of manhood. This test —I must maintain it in spite of such superior persons as Henri Beyle and Thomas Carlyle—is applicable even to the pitiful race of poets. And those who quail and wail and wince and spit and sputter when attacked—who do not hit straight back, and whip their insulters openly out of the course—dishonour the standard with which they must be supposed to wish that their names should be associated. Dryden is a far lesser poet than Tennyson: but Dryden fought his enemies like a man. Tennyson could neither fight his enemies nor ignore them. He was a great poet at his best; a glorious figure among the almost incomparable glories of England; but he was also what Keats was not—an example of a poet who confirms, as far as it lies in him to confirm, the malignant and preposterous tradition that a poet must be something other and weaker if not meaner than a man. And, great as was the charm of his genius, the intelligence which could "hail" a proposition or a definition of a principle common to all arts whatever as "truest lord of hell"[10] was simply putid: stupid is no word for it. It is unimaginable, or at least it is incomprehensible, how any man imbued with so much as a smattering of scholarship in English or in French can have imagined—though it is anything but incomprehensible how fools and knaves may have pretended to imagine—that the law which bids an artist or a workman look first of all to the conditions of his

work, think of nothing more seriously than the rules and the requisites of his art, bids him abstain from consideration of moral or
political, patriotic or polemical subjects. The conception of such a
canon could only be hatched in the diseased and feverish heat of
a clerical or canonical brain-pan. And whenever Tennyson himself
was not serving this lord of hell, the law which compels every
artist to do his very best in his own line, and not allow the very
noblest intention or instinct or emotion to deflect or distort or pervert
his hand, he drivelled: he drivelled as pitifully as in this idiotic
eructation of doggrel.

It will hardly be supposed—I need hardly say so—that I am
fighting for my own hand[11] when I say this; or when I add the all
but inevitable remark that the Tennysonian epigram, if we may
judge by this prominent and notorious example, is just a street-boy's
random discharge from a broken squirt of lukewarm water. Humble
and futile as the attempt may have been, I have written a book of
verse which from beginning to end is devoted to the expression and
inculcation of principle and of faith;[12] a book which above all
others would incur the contemptuous condemnation of those actual
or imaginary creatures who affirm that poetry must never be moral
or didactic—that the poet must put off his singing-robes when he
aspires to become a preacher or a prophet. Be that as it may, I have
done this: the gentle courtier and moralist whom we all admire and
regret has not. It is a far cry from Parnassus to Oxford: and it is a
deep descent from the station of Alfred Tennyson to the station of
Matthew Arnold. The great poet of Cambridge, however influenced
in style by emulation of Keats in early youth and of Milton in mature
manhood, was always himself alone: the little poet of Oxford was[13]
very seldom anything but a sometimes fortunate student and a sometimes unfortunate pupil of far greater and more memorable men.
My early estimate of his best poetry[14] was perhaps—most readers, I
believe, have thought and will think so—exuberant in its cordiality
and extravagant in its generosity. A far greater poet, who could no
more appreciate the good work of Arnold than the minor poet could
appreciate the superiority of his, protested in private at the time,
with his usual straightforward earnestness of expression, against the
magnanimous folly, the uncritical enthusiasm, of my tribute to the
merit and the charm of *Thyrsis* and *The Forsaken Merman:* but even
my regard for the authority of so wonderful a genius and so exquisite

a judgment as Rossetti's did not and does not persuade me or convince me that I was wrong in admiring and enjoying those poems. I cannot pretend or attempt to deny that their author at his worst was actually the very hoarsest frog of the Oxonian frog-concert: that in his controversial style there was usually something of varnished vulgarity: that as a critic his place is with Rymer and Emerson rather than with Jeffrey and Gifford: that the applause or tolerance or sympathy of the Arch-Quack who gabbled and slavered abuse or depreciation of Shakespeare and of Shelley was or would have been hardly too severe a retribution for his oracular follies and his academic impertinences. For these were so pert, so dogmatic, so ignorant and so silly, that even the crushing retribution which befell them was not so severe as to make a rationally religious intelligence entertain a doubt of its justice.

Nemesis was not asleep when he was coupled with Tennyson and Browning by critics whose praise would degrade even them from their place among English poets, if their place were no higher and no surer than is his. It is no small dishonour to be branded as a great poet by the patrons or the champions of every clamorous and petulant subaltern in song, from the would-be laureate and pet poeticule of the sixties to the pet poeticule and would-be laureate of the nineties.[15]

The Celt we have always with us, and never notice him: neither as poet nor as critic can a Macpherson, a Moore, a Mangan, and a Maginn be taken into serious account by the countrymen of Chaucer and Shakespeare, of Milton and Wordsworth, of Coleridge and Landor. The "brutal Saxon"—or Northman—is apt to set his "bloody hoof" on their pretentions with a quiet and good-humoured smile;[16] if he be not disposed rather to pass them by with a silent wave of his bloody hand and a kindly nod of his brutal head. But the amateur or would-be Celt, brutal if not bloody and Saxon if not sane, who pretends to discover a visible vein of Celtic fancy, a tangible thread of Celtic influence, in the masterworks of English inspiration, is almost too absurd a figure to pass underided and unnoticed among the ranks in which he has enlisted or shown himself fain to enlist as a volunteer. And when we remember—I am bound to confess that I cannot understand it, or subdue my astonishment at the fact—that this Oxonian Gallomaniac, to whom the charm of the moors and their winds and their waters should have been as incomprehensible and inapprehensible as was the genius of Shakespeare, of Shelley, and of Hugo, has put on record his admiration of Emily Brontë, we must likewise remember with whose name his critical intelligence found it natural to bracket hers. There had not been her like, he thought, since Byron died.[17] We shall not soon see again such a critic of life, such a judge of character as this. When General Gordon was forsaken and betrayed to his death, no writer on the side of the faction responsible for that immortal infamy thought it decent to remark that there had not been his match on earth since the death of Barnum. The laughter excited by so preposterous a copulation of names is stifled in the source by indignation at such hebetude of moral intelligence and such depravity of critical instinct. Reticence and reserve, austerity and heroism, the purity of fire and the passion of the sea, love of earth and faith in life, scorn of creeds and trust in self—in the inner and spiritual self which turns on death and triumphs—these are the qualities by which we know, and by which all future generations of Englishmen must know, the Stoic poetess of the Yorkshire moors. It would be superfluously ungracious to ask in what imaginable point of character or of style she can be supposed to resemble the most inconstant and ostentatious, the most histrionic and hysterical of mankind—half infidel and half theolator, half rebel and half slave. Her last utterance may seem to dispirited sceptics and critical Oxonicules overbold for a dying hymn:[18] to others—to poets and to thinkers "quite other"[19] than these—it will always seem the very noblest and loftiest farewell ever taken of life by the departing soul of a poet or a hero whose fearless faith and divine defiance of clerical or formal divinity were one and unalterable to the last.

Only the most putid and incurable of dunces will ever imagine that there can be, for any intelligent man or woman, a distinction or partition imaginable between the study of life and the study of such books as have life in them. To certain Norwegian naturalists and their adoring satellites life may mean much about what it meant to the young gentleman in Pickwick who "rather" thought he had seen something of life. "He had looked at it through the dirty panes of glass in a bar door."[20] The prospect can hardly have been duller or narrower or uncleaner than the outlook on life of Dr. Ibsen and his patients. But the life that lives for ever in the work of all great poets has in it the sap, the blood, the seed, derived from the living and everlasting word of their fathers who were before them. From Æschylus to Shakespeare and from Shakespeare to Hugo the transmission of inheritance, direct or indirect, conscious or unconscious, is as certain and as traceable as if Shakespeare could have read Æschylus and Hugo could have read Shakespeare in the original Greek or the original English. But in these and such as these there is no such immediate influence perceptible or imaginable as we find in the greatest Roman poets and their greatest English disciples: and yet we see that Catullus[21] and Virgil and Milton and Landor and Tennyson would have been poets of high rank if the Romans had known nothing of Greek and the Englishmen had known nothing of Latin. These learned and studious poets would assuredly and obviously have done good work, if not so great as the work they have bequeathed us, had they been unlearned in book-lore: they were not wholly and merely, in Shakespearean phrase, moulded out of books.[22] But who can imagine an uneducated or unbookish Matthew Arnold? Take his teachers and his models away from him, and what is left? His tender and kindly sentiment, his tentative and sensitive reflection, his bright and transient fancy, would be left helpless and inadequate to the labour of adequate expression; and the joyous and glorious task of a poet would be but too obviously the burden of an honour to which he was not born—a burden too heavy for a masculine counterpart of Tennyson's hapless heroine.[23] As it is, indeed, his rather pitiful and doleful outlook on youth and age makes one feel that it must be a somewhat sad thing to be born a minor poet and a less than minor critic in an age, to say the least, not wanting in great men, if the condition of such existence involves incurable blindness and deafness and insensibility to the greatness of the greatest of them all. But this is usually the badge of all his tribe.[24] That the first great English poet was Marlowe is a truth which was not more inapprehensible by him than by one of the noblest of their kind—William Morris. He too was artificially and accidentally made a poet: the amazing awkwardness of execution and expression in his first book, full as it is of struggling life and straining energy, would suffice to prove it. To men in many ways so admirable as these we should not refuse the title of poet: neither should we forget that to no other class of men can the sense and perception of what is highest in poetry be more probably if not more inevitably impossible. It is true that they both professed their belief in

Homer: look at their renderings of Homer: I would as soon read
Pope's or Cowper's or Lord Derby's,[25] none of which gives, as none
can possibly give, a feebler or a falser notion of the original text.
Mr. Arnold wrote eloquently and nobly in praise of Sophocles: look
at the skinny and osseous outline, listen to the squeaking and creak-
ing utterance, of his bloodless and spiritless Merope. A poet who
exists only by grace of previous poets may yet deserve to live: he
may do beautiful and delightful work in elegiac or in landscape
poetry. A poet who exists mainly but not wholly on such conditions
may now and then show that he can swim without bladders. I must
confess that I have never been able to understand what pleasure a
swimmer or a singer can take in either exercise if it cannot be taken
without artificial support. Morris could hardly swim a stroke without support from Chaucer,[26] Arnold without support from Wordsworth. Tennyson, a stronger swimmer than either of these, was
somewhat too much given to lay hold on spars or bladders left
floating by Virgil or by Milton: but once and again, when the spirit
of song that presided at his birth had leave to take the lead and
power to impel the stroke, he could pitch them right away and wheel
sharply aside from the usually gentle and idyllic shallows that lay
dimpling and glimmering inshore, and strike straight into such
splendid and stormy water as gave its deathless music to the deathless passion of Rizpah and Boadicea. Where were his freshwater
juniors and his shortwinded competitors then?

"Though it be honest," says Shakespeare's Cleopatra, "it is never
good to bring bad news":[27] and though it be unavoidable it can
never be agreeable to refute the reticent mendacity or to expose the
timorous malevolence of the dead. But, as Mrs. Procter said when
compelled to confute the "malignant lies" of Mr. Carlyle, "he should
beware how he strikes who strikes with a dead hand."[28] No falsehood, no insult, no ingratitude, is so impudent, so cowardly, so contemptible as that which the living man holds carefully and studiously
in reserve for the dead man to utter, to offer, to display. "Sir," said
Dr. Johnson of Lord Bolingbroke, "he was a scoundrel, and a
coward: a scoundrel for charging a blunderbuss against religion and
morality; a coward, because he had not resolution to fire it off himself, but left half-a-crown to a beggarly Scotchman, to draw the
trigger after his death."[29] Far be it from me to say of an old

acquaintance[30] what a man less pigeon-livered, less lacking in gall, might and would say: that he was a scoundrel, or at least a somewhat mean and low-bred malignant, for penning injurious and impertinent falsehoods about men who had always treated him with cordial courtesy, and for whom he had always maintained a profession of affectionate regard; a coward, because he had not resolution enough to make them public while alive, and liable to the personal disgrace of immediate confutation, but left to a brother Scot the task of discharging this unenviable office after his death. It is necessary to notice even such unlovely trivialities, when the offender has been honoured by the offering, however undeserved, of a tribute which cannot be cancelled,[31] and which, for the sake of old times and associations with far other memories than his, I do not regret to remember, or wish that it could be withdrawn.

The genius of William Blake—and his genius is one with his character: at one with it on all points and in every way—has so peculiar and personal a charm that no one not incapable of feeling its fascination can ever outlive his delight in it. While we were able to regard this Londoner born and bred as not only a fellow-citizen of Milton's but a fellow-countryman of Shakespeare's, it did seem an almost insoluble problem to explain or to conjecture how so admirable and adorable a genius could be flawed and vitiated by such unutterable and unimaginable defects. Now that we know him for a Celt by descent we understand whence he derived his amazing capacity for gabble and babble and drivel: his English capacity for occasionally exquisite and noble workmanship we may rationally attribute to his English birth and breeding. Some Hibernian commentator on Blake, if I rightly remember, has somewhere said something to the effect that when writing about some fitfully audacious and fancifully delirious deliverance of his countryman's, and trying to read into it some coherent and imaginative significance, I was innocent of any knowledge of Blake's meaning. Probably I was: for the excellent reason that, being a Celt, he now and then too probably had none worth the labour of deciphering—or at least worth the serious attention of a student belonging to a race in which reason and imagination are the possibly preferable substitutes for fever and fancy. The Celtic tenuity of his sensitive and prehensile intelligence throws into curious relief the occasional flashes of in-

spiration, the casual fits of insight, which raise him here and there
to the momentary level of a deep and a free thinker, a true and an
immortal poet.[32]

No more constant and fervent admirer of Fitzgerald's *Rubáiyát*
can ever be unearthed by any pertinacity or assiduity of research than
I. To me it still seems, as to some at least of my elders and betters
it seemed on its first appearance, one of the noblest, wisest, most
thoughtful, manful, and beautiful works of human intelligence and
genius. But I fail to see why the recognition of this obvious and
glorious fact should preclude me from admission of this other and
lamentable truth—that no more futile outrage was ever offered by
a fribble or a dunce to one of the supreme and inaccessible poems
of all time than he attempted to perpetrate in his metrical para-
phrase of the *Agamemnon* of Æschylus: an offence as gross and
monstrous as the counter outrage offered to the same divine masterpiece by the back-broken and jaw-breaking cacophonies of Browning's literal and lineal version. Nor can I see why my enjoyment of
his great work—as great in merit as little in bulk—should forbid me
to remark that when writing of other and greater poets in such
fashion as provoked from Mr. Browning a somewhat regrettable
rejoinder[33] he cannot but suggest, to readers not so illiterate as to be
unacquainted with Ben Jonson, that his real family name must not
have been Fitzgerald, but Fitzdottrel.[34]

Change of opinion, when perseverance in opinion would involve
change of principle, is the test of sincerity, honesty, and honour:
consistency which takes no regard of this can only be the quality of
a dotard or a knave. When it becomes manifest that loyal sympathy
with the aims, the sufferings, the ambitions of a foreign country is
irreconcilable with loyal devotion to his own, the man whose sympathy remains unaltered and unqualified must clearly be a traitor,
an egotist, or a fool. The selfishness, the hypocrisy, and the rapacity
of the nation which stole Nice and Savoy from Italy by the vilest of
fraudulent rascalities became more amusing than revolting when
compared with the ludicrous horror of its defeated politicians at the
reclamation of Alsace and Lorraine. Love and honour of all that is
amiable and honourable in the French character can hardly be expected or permitted to obscure or to suppress the reluctant recognition of the immedicable malevolence and the ineradicable irrationality
which thoroughly explain and partially justify the belief that it is

essentially servile and unalterably untrustworthy—by its English friends, at least, if not by its German enemies. The fascination of France, for evil or for good, is undeniable and unique: the enthusiasm of servility which flung her down in rapturous abasement at the knees of the Bourbons and the feet of the Bonapartes is a quality so utterly alien from the English character, so hopelessly incomprehensible by the English intelligence, that no wise man will wonder at the undying and unchanging hatred of "a natural slave"[35] for a nation to which acquiescence in servitude has always been as naturally impossible as perfidy in alliance or hypocrisy in profession. To exonerate the English character from the charge of self-complacent Pharisaism may be difficult or may be impossible: but this fault is as different a thing from the crime of hypocrisy as is the self-esteem of a Nelson from the self-worship of a Napoleon.

Returning for a moment from the highlands of history to the lowlands of literature, I may reflect with some confidence and some satisfaction that at least I have never changed my note or trimmed my sail in obedience to the windy fashion of assumed emotion or inculcated expression which varies, and blusters as it varies, from the slang of Thomas Carlyle to the cant of Matthew Arnold: that no serious or fitful sympathy with any apparent aim at reform or at ridicule of social abuses or corruptions has ever degraded or seduced my love of dramatic poetry into tolerance of such gorillas of letters as the squalid Sardou and the fetid Ibsen. On such as these, and in such as their parasites, contempt and loathing and abhorrence of such poets as Marlowe[36] and Shakespeare and Webster must obviously be an ingrained and congenital affection—an eruptive disease in that portion of their organism which they mistake for an intelligence or a soul. A somewhat more highly developed failure or error of nature in the attempt to produce a poet under the most unfavourable conditions did undeniably win my warm and cordial praise for the better qualities of a writer on whose pretentions, as advanced by his disciples, I found it necessary to set my foot when I found myself in danger of being cited as a supporter of their stupidities. I still feel as warm a sympathy as was expressed in my lines addressed to Whitman[37] for the noble enthusiasm, heroism, and faith which rarely but surely found something like adequate expression in his work: but I must be allowed to remark that the foremost place among American poets—I do not pretend or presume to judge whether it be or be not Whitman's—can hardly be higher than that of a little, a very little European. Too few now read even the very finest verse of Southey: yet the author of Roderick is to the author of Evangeline as is the author of Paradise Lost to the author of Roderick. Southey is the moon of Milton as Longfellow is the moon of Southey. The star of our English Longfellow paled and sank because he did not "give himself the trouble to be born"[38] on that side of the Atlantic where the American Tupper was and is and will be a great poet. The stars in their courses fought against him.[39] He wanted varnish: he had all the simple virtue and all the facile fatuity of the amiable American, but the graces of even such culture as Boston or as Oxford could have bestowed were withheld from him by too severe a fate. And so the ungilded Longfellow is remembered only as Eusden[40] or as Pybus or as Pye is remembered, while the gilded Tupper still chirps on across the Atlantic with all the fascinating persistency of an artificial goldfinch.

Such names as these it can hardly be held inconsistent with modesty and self-respect to notice or to remember; others which experience may have found undeserving of such loyal goodwill as once and again found honest expression in the past it would be worse than unnecessary, it would be a ludicrous humiliation, to preserve like flies in amber. It is only a Sporus who breaks a butterfly upon a wheel:[41] a man will leave the little animal to flutter and wriggle on its way—a way that leads towards oblivion and collapse through the inevitable stages of compassion and diversion and contempt. Earth to earth[42] is the motto of some dwarfish minds, the doom of some trivial talents. The kindly error of condescension and benevolence, whether unacknowledged or recanted, has never been remembered against any man deserving of remembrance: it has never been imputed for unrighteousness[43] to any man with any claim on the righteous judgment of his peers in the present or his fellows in the future.

A man who has never been mistaken or deceived must be a cynic, an infidel, or an idiot: a man who shrinks from the avowal of his fallibility, who flinches from the admission of his error, can only be a coward and a cheat. The gift of life would be worse than worthless if it left a boy no stronger than a baby, a man no wiser than a boy.

Short Notes

Ibsen

The celebrity of Ibsen is the very reason why a loyal Shakespearean and Hugoist should and must feel bound—or shall we say free? —to protest, by no means against the recognition of his unquestioned capacity,[44] but against the cult of his iconoclastic idolators who blaspheme and revile the name that is above every name in order to exalt that of a writer who has rivalled or exceeded Wycherley in obscenity of subject: without a touch of the revoltingly irresistible humour and the consummate dramatic power which distinguish the splendidly disgusting author of The Country Wife from the stupidly disgusting author of Ghosts. If Ibsen and Zola may be ranked among men of genius, they must be classed with Swift—but otherwise how far below him!—as men of emetic genius.

Lewes

His work as a novelist and a dramatic poet entitles him to a seat beside Bunn, Fitzball, and Reynolds (G. W. M.).[45] The venomous impertinence of a scribbler[46] who may possibly be for some little time remembered as the morganatic wife of H. S. H. George Eliot, towards the dead Dickens would be bad enough if he had never fawned on the living man—as Forster, in his dull but honest and industrious biography, assures us that he did.

M. A.

To the merits of Matthew Arnold I have before now borne witness with such extravagance of generosity as drew down the serious expostulation and remonstrance of a writer[47] immeasurably greater in every way than he. But it must not be forgotten, if he is to be remembered, that the poor man was not more blind to the glory of Dickens than to the glory of Shakespeare, of Shelley, of Coleridge, of Tennyson, and of Hugo. There have been worse poets—though

77

assuredly there cannot have been many—than Matthew Arnold at his worst: there can hardly have been worse critics than Matthew Arnold at his best. Even in his master Wordsworth he could not see what was really great.

Servile, spectral, bloodless, colourless, tuneless, the Merope of M. A. is worthier of its admirers than of its author. Duller than Euripides at his worst it is not: but only because that has never been and never will be possible for any human dullard.

HOAX and BURLESQUE

THE MONOMANIAC'S TRAGEDY, AND OTHER POEMS
By Ernest Wheldrake, Author of Eve, A Mystery. London, 1858.

Nothing is so tenacious of life as a bad poet. The opossum, we are credibly informed, survives for hours after its brains are blown out by a pistol. The author of "The Monomaniac's Tragedy" lives, writes, and finds a publisher; nay, it should appear, admirers also. Nevertheless, the chastisement inflicted for his first offence was severe enough to have killed a dozen rising prose writers. *Eve, a Mystery,* was anatomized "with a bitter and severe delight" by all the critics who noticed it, with the exception (we believe) of Mr. Wheldrake himself. But neither as poet nor as critic was the world worthy of that gentleman. Emboldened, however, by this very questionable success, he has dropped the anonymous veil which his modesty at first compelled him to assume. The reader of his new volume will not be agonized by doubts of the author's personality. It is indeed rumoured that he has adopted a pseudonym; from what we know of his modesty we might conceive it possible; but we ask our readers, what poet on earth would choose to appear before the world with such a substitute for John Smith or Timothy Brown? No; let us leave Mr. Ernest Wheldrake the full distinction of his christian name and patronymic.

The present volume, we are bound to say, is a decided advance upon the author's *Eve.* Those who do not remember that remarkable poem, may require to be informed that it represented the expiring moments of our first mother. The opening scene was laid in Pandemonium, where a conclave of devils was assembled to debate on the means of getting spiritual possession of the deceased. The speech in which Lucifer introduced the subject to their notice was a masterly exposition of facts; towards the end, however, the honourable gentleman becomes slightly tedious, not to say maudlin. Discovering, however, that Mammon had dropped asleep (at least, so we construe the lines—

> Arouse thee, Mammon! is there room for sloth
> In this contracted parallax of time?)

81

Lucifer rebukes him as a "thunder-winged sluggard" and "a starry drone." He is then despatched to earth in a noticeably penitent condition: apparently to report proceedings, and ask leave to sit again.

We next find ourselves in the moon, which, we are informed is

> An extra-paradisal entity
> Swung by a cord athwart the howling night,
> Blackened with generations infinite,
> Whose dust lies thick as winter's leafy tears.

Here we are introduced to "Adam and Belial." These gentlemen discourse for about twenty pages in the style of the foregoing extract: on what subject, we are unable to discover: after which Belial becomes more lively, but decidedly blasphemous; not to mention his evident disposition to dwell upon such unbecoming topics as "wine-dishevelled tresses," "globed sapphires of liquescent eyes, warmed with prenatal influx of rich love," "luscious sweetnesses of vintage-tinctured raiment," etc., etc.[1] This behaviour Adam with great propriety rebukes, and puts to his companion the following query:

> Spirit! know'st thou not
> That the bad man is alien to the good
> As conch-like lustres to the rayless pearl?

Belial remarks that such language "doth blast his preconception," and announces a resolution to "depart for the inane"; whither he accordingly betakes himself.

We shall not follow him. We might indeed relate how Adam on his return to earth

> By starry passages
> Thrilled down the plummet of a cherub's plume,

is startled by the news

> That by the chill decrepitude of dawn
> Sharp cold has caught his Eve—

in other words, that the lady has taken cold—how the invalid has yet breath to lecture him for two hundred lines on his past life, and on the prospects of humanity—how the solicitous husband requests her to

> Dip her throat into this lunar bowl
> And drink a little, only for his sake,
> Lest med'cinable custom thwart itself,

how she positively refuses, and ultimately expires with the words,

> Eternity, unhand me! Is it there?
> Let me see—see—see; I feel very dead.

We at first, in common with other critics, took this *Mystery* as an irreverent parody of such poems as *Cain* and *Festus*. But we are now convinced that Mr. Wheldrake was in earnest; and so it seems are others. Certain periodicals, whose names we regret to say are new to us, have decided that *Eve* is "a happy overflow of young loveliness," "a green development" (this we entirely agree with), "a meridian imagining," and a "passionate revelation of purity"; also that it is "remarkable for nervous grace and [a] certain sinewy sweetness of expression." For one rash moment we did indeed believe that we had recognised here the fine Roman hand[2] of a well-known North British critic; but we have since been given to understand that this advertisement is a hoax played off by Mr. Wheldrake and his publisher. If this be the case, such an impudent attempt at imposition cannot be too severely reprehended: it shews, indeed, a degree of moral turpitude which far outweighs the sin of writing absurd poetry. These gentlemen may consider the occupation of literary forgery as remarkably humorous and amusing; but we can tell them that all honourable men will be revolted by such a flagrant instance of dishonesty. Our language may appear strong, but we must remember that the question at issue is one of far higher importance than any literary merit or demerit.

Mr. Wheldrake's present publication is, as we have said before, decidedly superior to his *coup d'essai*. It abounds, indeed, in such flowers of language as "a seraph's rainbow-cinctured pieties," "thunder-spurred immensities of space Sun-beamed with arrowy sable," "violet-poisoned subtleties of breath," "lotus-begotten happiness of scent," "blue raptures of predominating larks"; it is impossible to discover the construction of nine sentences out of ten: and the main poem is about as comprehensible as *Eve, A Mystery*. We defy any man to make sense of the following extracts:—

"Dismally they skipped me up and down
In bloody famine; rents of life were torn
From the red culmination of my heart,
Cored with unspeakable despondencies,
And pulsed with meditations of despair,
Thro' all the stagnant seasons?"

"Futurity
Is the dull owl[3] that croaks for any bone,
Ploughed over in the sepulchres of time."

"Love, crimson-hearted eagle, fed with stars,
Till he be potent (as my soul may be)
To brush the gold dust off the face of suns,
Assimilates all capability
In a mature parenthesis of thought.
Thought volatilatized by iris'd pain,
Thrice actuated by his own insolent sense,
Of muscular action, and destroyed disdain."

"By Heaven, had I the teeth of Caucasus
Red-hot from Promethean agonies,
And tusks more lucid than the lunar snows,
On those jagged lawns of Asia, cavernous
With many a dragon banquet-eyes like those
Minerva made of flint to shatter Jove—
I'd hurl their hate upon thee, and myself
Die in a red parabola of Fate!"[4]

This may be dramatically proper from the lips of a maniac, although we think a compassionate keeper would speedily put a gag in the poor creature's mouth: but a whole poem composed of such materials is surely too much. Let Mr. Wheldrake read *King Lear* with attention; he will see that the ravings of that monarch, in themselves meaningless and uninteresting, are duly subordinate to the progress of the plot, and the development of character.

The story of "The Monomaniac's Tragedy," as far as we can make it out, is briefly this: The hero is engaged in writing *Iscariot, a Tragedy;* and naturally feeling that, while yet innocent, he cannot enter into the feelings of thieves and murderers, he determines to acquire the requisite experience. With this rational object in view, he organises a burglarious attempt upon his brother's house, and wrings the neck of that gentleman's infant son: after which he reflects as follows—

> "Ay, I have seen the face of Theft,
> And tasted the red kiss of murder still—
> Large scope is yet for passion!
> > (*a very long pause*)
> > Oh! ah! oh!
> Ha! ha! it burns me. Have I found him there?
> Nay, thou dead pain, it shall not alter thee;
> Tho' I hurled heaven into the reeling spume
> Of thunder whitened ages, haled the moon
> At some red meteor's palpitating heels,
> A mangled residue of beams—what else?
> > (*a long pause*)

All this is a prelude to an attempt upon the life of his sister-in-law, whom he endeavours to poison in a Twelfth cake. He is, however, detected, and despatched to Bedlam

> With all the warmth of song
> Bubbled within him, tremulous with hope,
> Like a dead snow-drop.

Here he delivers himself of the interminable monologue which contains his life: and here we are happy to take leave of him.

The next poem is entitled "Keeping Cattle." One stanza we extract:—

> These meadows, cowslip tinctured,
> Fold-green dreams of May,
> The lowlands, pinespur-cinctured,
> Die into the day:
> The cow's breath pains me,[5]
> The vapour stains me,
> The sun disdains me;
> I know not what I say.
> Is it a bark far down? Hush! hark!

I heard him call the sweet old way
"Love, 'tis thy love overstrains me";
No! 'twas but the lark
And the red sunset hears the forest bray.

This idyl disposed of, we come to a Sonnet on the Emperor of the French, which we extract entire as a specimen of our author's saner mood.

Louis Napoleon.

He stands upon a rock that cleaves the sheath
Of blue sea like a sword of upward form;
Along the washing waste flows far beneath
A palpitation of senescent storm.
He, Lethean pilot of grim death,
Utters by fits a very potent breath.
He is the apex of the focussed ages,
The crown of all those labouring powers that warm
Earth's red hot core, when scoriac sorrow rages.
He is the breath Titanic—the supreme
Development of some presolar dream.
Owls, dogs, that bellow at him! is he not
More strong than ye? His intermittent love
The measure of your wretched hate keeps hot.
Ye are below him—for he is above.

We trust that Mr. Wheldrake's approbation will atone, in Imperial circles, for the publication of the "Châtiments." The English poet, indeed, seems determined to try for the post of Laureate at the Tuileries. In "A Dream of Ladies"—considerably altered from Tennyson—he is favoured with a glorified vision of

Her of the happy brows
Whom not in vain the Flemish sailor wooed;
First petal of our fair Imperial rose,
First dawn to France of good—

i.e. Madame de Saint-Leu![6] We trust the compliment will be as duly appreciated as it is happily chosen.

Of the other political poems in this volume we have not time to speak at length; but in passing we may recommend a lyric called

"Flowers from Naples," to the attention of M. Veuillot,[7] as a final refutation of the calumnies heaped by venal English and apostate Italian on his favorite monarch.

Next comes "Lines to ————." This person, it appears, died in Spring: and the result of her death to Mr. Wheldrake is described as follows:

> I put a smile about my face;
> Of tender doubts I cannot speak:
> I shudder in a sunny place;
> I tear a strip of tooth-shaped lace
> And press her skirt against my cheek.
> The luskish blossom near and far
> In shadowy pulses palpitates;
> The blooms that round her grave there are,
> Blot noon's extremest coping-star
> With black my lost heart emulates.
> A violet-vestured harmony
> Caps the composure of her grave;
> The voiced heaven's archæval sigh
> In plenilunar agony
> Dies round it like a broken wave.

We will go no farther. The above remarks were uttered with no intention of giving pain to Mr. Wheldrake: if they do so we are sincerely sorry. But if such books are published they must be criticised; and we only hope it is not too late for our author to profit by advice which has been offered in no unfriendly spirit.

Les Amours Étiques. Par Félicien Cossu

The advent of a new poet is notoriously matter of satisfaction to all wise men; especially we should imagine if the new poet give evidence of a quite original power, and be endowed with that clearness of eye, steadiness of hand, and vigour of touch without which no work of much worth can be well got through. How far these requisites are possessed by the author whose work we are to consider every student of the art must judge for himself. In several ways, as it seems to us, M. Félicien Cossu is a writer of a decidedly novel kind. His volume of verse, though as yet we believe unnoticed by English critics, has enjoyed a success not wholly unequivocal with at least a portion of the French public. A certain preparation as of men in training for some great work is perhaps necessary before we can relish the flavour of the fruit here set before us. And first of all we must warn the British reader that not one of the poems in question is fit to be read aloud in the hearing of Englishwomen. Many it is hardly possible to transcribe; some few it is hardly possible to allude to.

The book opens with a little poem entitled *Soupir,* of which we can only cite three stanzas—the first three—which may perhaps astonish some readers;

> À quinze ans je ne suis plus vierge,[1]
> O mes beaux jours épanouis
> Où le glas sonne, où luit la cierge
> De mille amours évanouis!
>
> Ton baiser m'a brûlé la bouche,
> Ton corps est chaud de mes sueurs,
> O fille indolente et farouche,
> Bel astre aux funèbres lueurs!

Mon âme au souvenir se baigne,
        Et mon corps en frissonne encore;
Mon cœur entamé vibre et saigne,
        O ma lune, ô mon soleil d'or!

To the writer of such lines envy herself will not refuse the praise
due to a strong imaginative power. We regret that want of space,
combined with other considerations, forbids our giving any further
extracts from this lyric, which is apparently addressed to five different ladies at once. In the next poem, M. Cossu thus addresses his
soul:

Aile brisée—empreinte d'un pied d'ange
Pris dans l'ordure et moulé dans la fange.[2]

From these briefer flights of the broken angel's-pinion we rise to a
wider sweep of wing and loftier scope of vision in the long poem
called *Une Nuit de Sodôme*. Singular as the choice of subject may
seem, there are glimpses of more power here than is frequent with
our poet. There is even some real elevation of fancy in the final description of an angel, clothed with fire and girt with a fiery sword,
pausing at sunset over the fearful city;

Et l'astre frémissant au front d'or noyé d'ombre
Semble une larme au fond du ciel azur et sombre.

The following passage is more in the author's usual fashion;

C'est la fin d'un été tout rempli de beaux soirs.[3]
On voit luire en passant par les carrefours noirs
Les jambes et les pieds des filles accourues.
La triste nudité ricane dans les rues.
On sent fuir et vibrer comme un souffle du jour
Les longs frémissements d'un effroyable amour.
Puis la nuit on croit voir, de sueurs arrosée,
Le corps trempé d'une âpre et fétide rosée,
Flêtrie et jaune comme une vieille putain,
10]   La lune aux yeux de nacre, au visage d'étain.
Tout est superbe, infâme, épouvantable et sale.
Voici venir la femme altière au teint d'opale
Montrant tout nu son sein qui brûle comme un four,
Son cou cicatrisé de morsures d'amour,

Son dos luxurieux fait de chair et de flamme[4]
Et son corps tout rongé des baisers d'une femme.
     À l'aspect de ce bel enfant, la flamme aux yeux,
Un vieillard pâle et flasque, horrible et radieux,
Murmure quelque chose abominable et tendre.
20]   L'homme s'accouple à l'homme et le néant s'engendre.[5]
Voici la nuit, voici la foule avec la nuit;
On entend haleter un vaste et vague bruit,
On entend passer comme un fourmillement d'ailes
Et chuchoter l'essaim hideux des filles grêles
Et crier la chair nue et rugir le baiser;
Et la volupté hurle et ne peut s'apaiser,
Et le soupir éclos de ces mille poitrines
C'est le cri de l'égout chanté par les latrines.
Lieu sinistre où le jour s'éveille en frémissant,
30]   Où le soir est mouillé de pleurs, taché de sang,
Où des membres sans sexe et sans sève se tordent,
Où les caresses sont des vipères qui mordent,
Où l'enfer tout entier éclate en floraison,
La luxure devient larve, et le pâmoison[6]
Se vautre, et l'amour sombre, obscène, morne, étrange,
Semble un démon moitié de feu, moitié de fange.

The monotony of rhymes and images here perceptible is a fault which frequently recurs. Metaphors drawn from sewerage and decomposition seem never to pall upon the taste of Mr. Cossu; neither does he ever tire of such epithets as swarm in the passage above cited. Certain of his erotic poems might have been written by a partially insane scavenger. We will cite four more lines from this poem and then dismiss it:

Et maintenant on voit dans ces plaines le soir,
Morne et visqueuse comme un grand suaire noir
Vide et taché, qui jette une odeur âcre et forte,
L'eau livide à grands plis ridés de la mer morte.

As a corrective to this mournful picture, the next poem opens thus cheerfully:

Pauvre fille! elle est ivre, et sa tête ployée
    Sur les grand pavés verse un long vomissement.
Dans la crapule et dans l'ordure elle est noyée;
    Son rire affreux et mou semble un hennissement.

That the desirable person whose attractions are thus invitingly set
forth in verse is the chosen mistress of our poet's affections, every
reader of intelligence and sensibility will at once have divined. All
doubt is happily removed by the following lines which occur in a
later poem—*Spasme d'Amour*—avowedly dedicated to the description of the lady of his heart.

        Sa voix glapissante a des sons doux et m'attire;
        Son rictus morne et flasque est un divin sourire;
        Sa crapule a l'odeur fraîche et chaste du lait;
        Et son vomissement quelque chose qui plaît.

So enamoured is M. Cossu of this adorable quality in the object of
his devotion that he recurs to it yet again: remarking with a profound sense of pleasure—

        Elle se vautre au sein du vice, et sans scrupule
        Son corps superbe et nu se plaît dans la crapule.
The following short poem we give entire, as being perfect in its way;

Rictus.[7]

Je vois grouiller les vers et croître les punaises.
Les hommes sont pourris comme de vieilles chaises;
La terre est faite avec des ossements humains.
Tout s'effeuille et s'éraille, et ce qui reste aux mains
C'est de la pourriture, hélas! ou de la honte.
Toujours le temps, marée intarissable, monte,
Et la luxure mord la chair des animaux,
Et Dieu ricane, et l'homme est mangé par les maux,
Et sur d'affreux débris mêlés d'or et de lave,
Ver gonflé de poisons, la femme rampe et bave.
Enfin, quand sonne l'heure auguste au glas fatal,
Tristes comme un mari qui se démène mal,
Ils s'en vont contempler Dieu, mâles et femelles,
Ayant toujours un peu de boue à leurs semelles.

By this time the reader is possibly qualified to appreciate the last poem from which we intend to make extracts of any length. It is entitled *Messaline*,[8] and is evidently the favourite work of its author. Unhappily, it is only from the opening part of the poem that we can select any specimen fit for citation; the rest being of a nature impossible, even after all we have now quoted, to so much as hint at. Thus it begins:

> Pourquoi ce son de fer et ces clameurs de bêtes?[9]
> Pourquoi ce sombre bruit qui plane sur les têtes
> Et se mêle en sifflant au cri tendre et mutin
> De l'amante aux abois près de l'amant lutin?
> Pourquoi ces yeux hagards remplis d'ombre et de flammes?
> Pourquoi ces hommes nus? pourquoi ces belles femmes
> Qui se tordent, montrant leurs gorges et leurs seins,
> Pour voir ces hommes nus et cambrés sur les reins?
> Pourquoi ces cous pliés, ces lèvres qui frissonnent,
> Ces trompes dont partout les vastes bouches sonnent,
> Et ces licteurs aux yeux d'acier, au corps de fer?
> On pressent vaguement quelque chose d'amer
> Rien qu'à voir chuchoter ces figures sanglantes
> Et frissonner la peau de ces femmes galantes
> Et luire ce regard lugubre de clarté
> Aux yeux ternes et froids de l'âcre volupté.
> Ah! c'est un monde abject que ce monde où nous sommes!
> C'est une triste chose, ô mon Dieu! que ces hommes,
> Ces femmes, cette foule ivre et morne qui rit,
> Cette chair qui ricane et foule aux pieds l'esprit!
> Pourquoi ce son rampant plein de choses lascives?
> Le grincement des dents, la bave des gencives,
> Le poison, la morsure et le glapissement,
> Et la bouche qui mange et la bouche qui ment,
> Et les membres tendus de la luxure nue,
> Et la sueur qui saigne avec le sang qui sue,
> Et le pourrissement de l'amour, et les pleurs
> De l'impuissance maigre aux débiles couleurs,
> Et ce que voit l'enfer et ce que vit Sodôme,
> File et remue au fond du grand cirque de Rome.

Au milieu de l'horreur des cris, des voluptés,
Des amours hideux pris au glu[10] des cruautés,
On reconnaît, en haut de l'arène infernale,
La femme au long cou blond, qui, stryge impériale,
Luxurieusement, d'un œil avide et doux,
Toute ployée, épie un gladiateur roux
Au ventre musculeux, à la cuisse abondante,
Et prend sur ses coussins la pose d'une amante
Dont la taille en sueur se crispe dans son lit;
L'impudeur enivrée et railleuse jaillit
De son œil fauve, et tord sa bouche sérieuse;
Elle sent s'échauffer sa chair luxurieuse
À contempler ce corps énorme au poil impur.
Pourquoi ce sang, ces cris, ce rire atroce et dur,
Hurlement de l'enfer aux monstrueuses bouches?
C'est que Messaline vient de faire ses couches.[11]

Chimère épouvantable et douce! ombre et clarté![12]
Chose impossible et folle! ô chaste impureté!
Ange hideux, meurtri de blessures infâmes!
Cynique Messaline, ô femme entre les femmes,
Démon pétri d'azur et mêlé de limon,
Fait de luxure et fait d'amour, ô cher démon,
Sombre reine aux seins durs, affreuse tentatrice,
Triste folle, superbe et forte impératrice,
Toi pour qui l'amour prit les muscles d'un géant,
Femme au corps famélique, épouse du néant,
Qui tordais l'infini sombre dans tes mains blanches,
Dont toujours une ardeur sans nom rongeait les hanches,
Enfant de Vénus ivre et de Mars éreinté,
C'est la douleur qui mord la pâle humanité,
C'est l'ennui que l'amour sous tes sourcils devine,
Et ta chair veloutée et ferme, ô Messaline,
Ta chair impériale où brûle un si fort sang,
Sous cette griffe saigne et va s'amollissant.
Les hommes après tout sont de mauvais ébauches,[13]
Rêves d'un dieu malsain assouvi de débauches,
Brouillons d'un poète ivre oubliés dans son lit.
Quand, le matin, le sang du grand soleil emplit

Tout un ciel rouge et morne, alors ce dieu qui boude
Sur un balcon cassé sinistrement s'accoude,
Se détire les bras, lâche un juron ou deux,
Chasse à grands coups de pied quelque ange hasardeux,
Bâille et tousse, et se trouve en humeur fort mauvaise,
Puis crache un monde affreux pour se mettre à son aise.

After this what can one do but admire the greatness of a creation which includes, among other things noticeable, a poet holding this opinion as to the manner of its origin? Another point we may remark, namely that here more than ever the faults of monotony, reproduction of unclean images, recurrence of the same phrases and the same rhymes, imitation of other men's words and ideas, abound almost to the ruin of any original power that may be in the man at bottom. In excess of beastliness indeed M. Cossu is perhaps original, and if so will, we trust, remain unparalleled; but in metrical cadence and turn of sentences he constantly recalls the verse of greater men, whose noble ideas, passed through the unclean filter of his fancy, reappear under some loathsome and devilish parody. The truth of this charge would be still more apparent than it is, could we venture to cite but a few lines more from the poem just considered; but it is impossible to tread a single step further than we have gone, under pain of being suffocated by the exhalations of this poetical sewer.

From the poem entitled *Christus* we dare not quote a single verse. It is upon the whole the most shamefully wicked production we have ever perused. Filth and blasphemy defile every line of it. Nevertheless it might perhaps be well to give some specimen of this foul thing as a warning sign of the unimaginable excess to which the corruption of French literature is now carried. But our pen refuses to trace the expressions of M. Cossu on a subject so awful and venerable. Let the reader conceive if he can the nature of this composition from the last two lines;

Alors du grand suaire une figure échappe,
Et je lui dis: Qui donc es-tu?—Je suis Priape.

Horrible as this is, it is only an instance of the persevering way in which M. Cossu insists on recognizing under all forms and in all religions the detestable likeness of the only god of his worship—

the foulest of all broken idols. In another poem, to which we dare
not refer by name, he justifies this leaning by arguments couched in
the misused and misunderstood verbiage stolen by men of his
school from the jargon of decayed oriental philosophies.

We will give but one or two more quotations, and those rather
laughable than horrible, before we thankfully wash our hands of
this hateful task. The following stanza is the first of a long poem
addressed *Au Peuple Anglais,* in which M. Cossu threatens us with
annihilation at the hands of indignant Europe in two years' time
at latest:

> Anglais, vous avez fait d'abominables choses.
> Vous avez effeuillé cyniquement nos roses
> Pour faire une guirlande à vos fronts rabougris;
> Vous volez nos lauriers pour en ceindre vos têtes.
> Ah! vous n'êtes qu'un tas méprisable de bêtes,
> Chenil que l'esclavage en ses griffes a pris.

Our next shall be a final specimen of M. Cossu's style of love-making:

> Cœur eunuque, âme étiolée,
> Femme morte et vivant souci,
> Nudité sinistre et voilée,
> Sais-tu bien que je t'aime ainsi?
>
> Quand je repasse dans mon âme
> Ta grâce et tes belles couleurs
> Dans mon cœur le désir se pâme
> Au souvenir de mes douleurs.
>
> Ah! réponds, cadavre implacable,
> Larve inutile de l'amour,
> Que de son poids le Temps accable,
> Nous reconnaîtrons-nous un jour?

We have but one word of comment to offer by way of conclusion.
Accusations are often put forward, at home and abroad, against
the restrictions imposed by a possibly exaggerated sense of decency
on the English literature of the present day. We have seen what are
the results of a wholly unfettered licence; base effeminacy of feeling, sordid degradation of intellect, loathsome impurity of expres-

sion, in a word every kind of filth and foolery which a shameless prurience can beget on a morbid imagination. Surely, whatever our shortcomings may be, we may at least congratulate ourselves that no English writer could for an instant dream of putting forth such a book as the poems of M. Félicien Cossu.

Les Abîmes. Par Ernest Clouët
Paris: Silvain, Libraire-Editeur, 1862.

In every age there is a certain quantity of moral force secretly at work, busied with whatever of skill and energy may be at hand to further it, in counteracting the tendencies of the time. Small bands of laborious believers gather in fierce heat and haste about some rallying-point of belief or disbelief, clutch hold of some weapon, blunt or sharp, anything to hit with—take to their fists even—use alike the flail and the rapier to hack or thrash withal at received opinions. Much chaff they do occasionally send flying from under the flails; occasionally too the flails recoil and thump the thrashers in the face. One quality these people have always in common; an infinite, indestructible belief in their own merit; a most supple, agile, vivacious, invincible confidence in themselves. They can wrestle, and they can wriggle; box, fence, leap, writhe, crawl to admiration. The muscles of their intellect are kept in excellent training by the sharp exigencies of their position. Apostles of the future, anatomists of the spiritual energy, regenerators of art or society—call them by what name one will—they must not rest on their oars. It is hard pulling against the stream. At times—for in every life of martyr or confessor there must be some soft rainy break of light, some breath from above or under of a sorrowful consolation—they get into the way of some groundswell or eddy setting against the main current which helps to keep them straight on their tack, perhaps even lends them a shove towards the haven where they would be. They are much given at such seasons of intervening good luck to raise with unanimous hoarse voices, throats roughened and rasped with sea-wind and salt of drifted spray, some shrill acclamation or outcry of thanksgiving easily distinguishable from the rowing songs and signal cries of ordinary weather. A coxswain in this service, one of a French squadron given overmuch to cruising in dangerous waters among sharp straits and shoals, lately took occasion to define the members of his crew as "témoins effarés de l'infini, portefaix flamboyants de l'idéal, chiffonniers étoilés ayant pour crochet la pensée, qui tiennent dans leur hotte l'avenir encore tout ruisselant des fanges du passé."

The duties, the day's work, and the day's wages of a starry rag-picker were then gone into at some length. One of their self-imposed tasks is, it appears, this: "ouvrir à coups de ciseau la matrice noire des siècles frémissants pour en dégager, fœtus radieux, la régénération humaine; éventrer le sphinx impitoyable, éviscérer Dieu." A labour in which we sincerely wish these male midwives of the infinite better success than we can in reason anticipate. A Caesarean operation performed upon the "Supreme Being" would be a feat worth chronicling in the annals of spiritual surgery.

It was not without some surprise that we came suddenly upon M. Ernest Clouët in his new character of a "radiant drayman of the ideal," fully equipped with the tools of his trade, and (we might say in his own florid symbolic style) employed mainly in shovelling stray rubbish into the rag-basket of journalism with the ragman's hook of bombast. We knew him merely as a writer of the musical articles in one paper, a collector of *faits-Paris* for another, a novelist in a very minor key for a third. A small and rickety book of his, touching on matters very common and rather unclean, called *Studies on England,* had also come once in our way. Three facts, notable and memorable, we gathered out of these *Etudes;* 1^0: that the lamented Prince Consort at one time enjoyed among the lower classes the nickname of *le prince prolétaire,* owing to his strong Chartist leanings; 2^0: that no laxity of prenuptial conduct is considered at all derogatory to the character of a jeune miss (a state of things which naturally ensures the fidelity and felicity of married people) but that a husband may dispose of his faithless wife to her lover for a sum of money not exceeding a thousand francs, or, on the lover's refusal to purchase, is free to blow out her brains on payment of a small fine to the Archbishop of Canterbury as national guardian of the sanctity of the marriage vow; 3^0: that the Lord Chancellor is annually elected by the "Central Committee of Aldermen" and that the grievances and abuses of the "Chancéri" are in the main attributable to the awful jobbing system prevalent in that powerful body, at whose meetings (one regrets to hear) there may be seen "le sourire de Torquemada, près du ricanement de Talleyrand; Laubardemont coudoyé par Metternich."

With a brain yet reeling from the shock of these revelations we turned to this present volume by the same hand; and having read it with some care, are bound to declare, as we now do, that it is a more wonderful, and a more disgraceful, piece of work than even the *Etudes Anglaises*. The chapter in M. Clouët's former book headed *Egout de Londres* was nauseous enough; but this book of *Les Abîmes* is simply—we know no English word for it—*inqualifiable*. Under the head of *Les Éclaireurs* our friend has thought fit to class some of the most unmentionable names in literary history. He anoints with a rancid oil of consecration the heads of men too infamous for open reference. A writer of monstrous books is with him "a force of nature—a spark blown by the wind of creation from the great palpitating source of generative fire hidden at the heart of the world." One of the "studies" here reprinted has for its subject a parallel elaborately worked out between Joan of Arc and Gille de Rays. Starting from the historical fact that these two served together in the war against the English, M. Clouët proceeds to draw upon a fertile and fetid imagination for details of their after intimacy. We have observed with some sense of relief that a critic of high standing and an unblemished reputation has condescended publicly to rebuke and chastise the author of this incredible outrage. "Eclabousser de cette fange sanglante la robe blanchie par les feux de la Pucelle," says M. Adolphe Vigniote with as much force as justice, "ce n'est pas seulement manquer à la France, c'est frapper par derrière toutes les croyances qui puissent fortifier ou soulager l'humanité." But this eminent journalist, it is too evident, is not one of that sublime crew out of which the scavengers of the Ideal and the rag-pickers of the Infinite are selected.

To justify the ways of Satan to man is one of the great aims of M. Clouët. Having as a first step demolished "le Dieu ganache des eunuques et des bourgeois" he rushes into a rapid analysis of crime such as probably was never before set down in human language. "La vertu selon les philistins," he affirms in a trenchant way, "c'est tout bonnement l'étiage de l'âme humaine." Crime, on the other hand, is the canal (*étier*) which serves to flood with strong tidal influx the stagnating marshes that lie dry at ebb-tide, along the coast of life, swarming as they are with a hateful brood of half-living animalcules—"the vermin of virtue—the sterile and sickly spawn of sexless moralities." The doctrine of moralists is to him a "croassement de grenouilles"; their daily life and practice a "croupissement de crapauds." Virtue indeed is as a red rag to this philosophic bull. "La crapule et le cynisme" he exclaims with a devout rapture "sont des travailleurs sublimes." One would take all this for dull and monstrous irony, but that the context in which these gems are set has evidently been wrought out with a serious purpose. "Le mal a pour moi quelque chose de mystérieux et de saint." He contemplates "avec un tressaillement d'entrailles farouche et voluptueux" the ugliest miracles of vice and the most inexplicable phases of crime. The odour of all these moral drains and sewers leaves, he says, in his nostrils the titillation of a pungent pleasure. Sin is his mental snuff. We recommend him to try the use of a milder sort, to accustom his "sensitive nose" by degrees to an adulterated kind. The pure essence is rather too high in flavour to be convenient for taking in public.

It is really a matter to think over as well as to wonder at, that such imbecile atrocities as these of M. Clouët can find an expression and an audience at the present day. Paradox has run mad in this miserable little book. Long since, in the full swing of romantic revolution, an ingenious poet, Pétrus Borel alias Champavert by his name, attempted to pass himself off as an actual live instance of lycanthropy; was indeed at the pains to write a book in evidence of the fact and call it *Contes Immoraux;* even to kill himself in print shortly after it appeared:[1] all in vain; an obdurate public bore up against both intimations with an admirable equanimity; did not seem very much to care whether or no a much-wronged poet, weary of long-suffering, took to devouring raw flesh as a stimulant (preferring, one would hope and suppose, the flesh of reviewers and publishers): and the result was that M. Pétrus, after a few more kicks, collapsed on a sudden; did not eat anybody; did not even choke, or cut his unfortunate wolfish throat, hairy on the inside as it was; but accepted an office under government (we think in Algeria), and died in the fulness of his time a peaceable Philistine. We sincerely wish M. Ernest Clouët as good an end as this. But such a book as *Les Abîmes* does look like the product of some disease—lycanthropy perhaps, or it might be hydrophobia: possibly, after all, it is but a determination of bad reading to the head, resulting in a case of moral sewerage or ditch-water on the brain.

Not that the whole book is made up of such stuff. There are passages here and there of real grace and power; at times too one gets glimpses of some vigour of invention. There is the making of a good critic in the man, if the mad and morbid spirit of paradox

were once well charmed out of him. The best paper in the book is
an essay on the *Fragoletta* of Henri de Latouche;[2] how it came there,
or why it was left there, the author of it only knows. At all events,
it is the best review we have seen of that singular, incoherent, admirable novel, so various and vigorous in manner of work; full of
southern heat, and coloured as with Italian air and light to the last
page of it. Another specimen of M. Clouët's saner and better mood
is the short chapter of description called "A Prose Idyl." This small
fragment of an essay is so delicate in touch, so soft and clear in
colour, so complete and pleasant in its slight way, that one remem-
bers it with a sort of gratitude. But a weary student never finds a
rest for the sole of his foot worth speaking of in such books as this.
Stepping off the good firm sward, he plunges ear-deep into some
unspeakable quagmire, to emerge therefrom defiled and stifled. The
longest section of *Les Abîmes,* that inscribed as "Prométhée," is a
deliberate attempt to explain and justify the work of a writer whom
most people would shrink from naming as they would from touching one of his books—the Arch-Unmentionable of literature. This
shamefully foolish article is dated 1800-1814; the new Prometheus
of M. Clouët had, it appears, during thirteen years, "Bicêtre for a
Caucasus and Napoleon for a vulture." Snuffing from afar off the
carrion of this congenial topic, M. Clouët warms by rapid gradations
into a style which recalls, in the dull shamelessness of its scientific
obscenity, the Abbé Domenech's famous preface to his invaluable
Red-Indian manuscript of last year. It is deplorable that the space
of a few months should have witnessed the appearance of two such
effusions on the same loathsome subject as Félicien Cossu's infamous
poem of *Charenton,* and this abominable notice in *Les Abîmes:* it
looks really as though there were now alive a small and unsavoury
crew of writers who cannot keep their fingers from poking and
paddling in this mire. We transcribe, as far as it is in any way pre-
sentable, the sentence in which our present author winds up his
article to a climax; for without some quotation no English reader
could be expected to take our word for the nature of it:

Au milieu de toute cette bruyante épopée impériale, on voit
passer en flamboyant cette tête foudroyée, cette vaste poitrine sillonnée d'éclairs, l'homme-phallus, profil auguste et cynique, grimace de
titan épouvantable et sublime; on sent circuler dans ces pages mau-
dites comme un frisson d'infini, vibrer sur ces lèvres brûlées comme

un souffle d'idéal orageux. Approchez, et vous entendrez palpiter dans cette charogne boueuse et sanglante des artères de l'âme universelle, des veines gonflées de sang divin. Ce cloaque est tout pêtri d'azur; il y a dans ces latrines quelque chose de Dieu. Fermez l'oreille au cliquetis des baïonnettes, au jappement des canons; détournez l'œil de cette marée montante de batailles perdues ou gagnées; alors vous verrez se détacher sur cette ombre un fantôme, immense, éclatant, inexprimable; vous verrez poindre au-dessus de toute une époque semée d'astres la figure énorme et sinistre du marquis de Sade.[3]

After this one feels bounden, as it were, to wash one's hands and rince out one's mouth in eastern fashion; however, like Jean Valjean in the great sewer, we are now well past this deepest slough of all, and it is at least some comfort to have done with the Arch-Unmentionable. No one will now be surprised to find the writer devoting a briefer article to the celebration of a still living notoriety—the pseudonymous authoress of *Rosine et Rosette, Confidences d'un Fauteuil,* and other books of as questionable a kind. We who have no inclination that way just now, will take leave of M. Clouët with a word of kindly counsel. We recommend him to give up all idea of making headway against the tide of modern morals, even with that Titan-phantom of the Arch-Unmentionable pulling stroke-oar in his boat. We do not believe he is really the sort of man to end in Bicêtre. We implore him to think of some honest trade—say of grocery—as an opening in life, feeling convinced that he would sleep warmly and well under protection of the proverbial *bonnet de coton;* and very heartily wish him speedy repentance, timely silence, and compassionate oblivion.

[La Soeur de la Reine]

Acte Second

(Scène première. Un salon superbe à Buckingham-House. Chaque meuble porte le chiffre et le blason de la reine. On voit par une fenêtre au fond les jardins de Kensington que surmonte le clocher de Saint-Paul. À gauche une petite porte qui donne dans la chambre à coucher de la reine. À droite une grande porte ouverte sur un corridor où l'on voit aller et venir des groupes de courtisans:
La Duchesse, *assise;* Sir Peel, *debout, tête nue.)*

La Duchesse.—Vous avez mal fait, milord, c'est moi qui vous le dis. Eh! mon Dieu, je ne vous cherche pas querelle; que vous aimiez d'amour madame la reine, il n'y a rien là qui ne soit assurément fort naturel; mais aller niaisement lui cracher votre amour à la figure comme cela! vraiment, il fallait être fou.

Sir Peel.—Que voulez-vous, duchesse! on n'est pas toujours maître de soi: il y a des moments où un amour comprimé déborde, éclate, jaillit des yeux, s'échappe aux lèvres. Voir cette adorable femme comme qui dirait aux bras d'un autre—tenez, à contempler ce beau couple enlacé qui valsait, qui valsait toujours, le bras de cet homme qui entourait sa taille frémissante, sa gorge qui palpitait, toute rose de chaleur, toute rougissante d'amour j'ai senti un vertige affreux de meurtre qui me montait à la tête—ma poitrine s'embrasait, mon cerveau était en délire—oh! j'ai bien souffert, allez! Et puis, ce n'était après tout qu'une indiscrétion bien mesquine, bien vénielle!

La Duchesse.—Une indiscrétion! ah! vous appelez cela une indiscrétion, vous! Savez-vous que j'ai vu pendre des hommes pour des indiscrétions comme celle-là!

Sir Peel.—Oh! je tuerai ce John Russell!

La Duchesse.—Plus bas donc, malheureux! *(Elle lui montre la porte de la chambre à coucher.)*

Sir Peel.—Il serait là? lui?

La Duchesse.—Vous ne m'écoutez pas, milord. Je vous disais

donc que du temps du feu roi il y avait un jeune homme beau comme les amours, svelte, gracieux, enfin quelque chose d'adorable.—Ne regardez donc pas cette porte pendant que je vous parle.

SIR PEEL.—Pardon, duchesse, je suis fou, la tête me bout.

LA DUCHESSE.—Ce pauvre jeune homme—il s'appelait lord Badger—s'avisa de tomber éperdûment amoureux de la reine Caroline, la plus revêche, la plus prude des femmes vertueuses, et un soir qu'ils valsaient ensemble—tenez, comme on valsait hier—il fit comme vous, il colla sa bouche fiévreuse sur les belles épaules de la reine. Il fut pendu le lendemain pour attentat à la personne de Sa Majesté. Vous, sir Peel, vous n'êtes pas même disgracié. Ah! c'était le bon temps que le temps de George IV. On avait alors de la morale. Cela me fait rougir pour ma pauvre fille.

SIR PEEL.—Oui—très bien—sans doute.

LA DUCHESSE.—Ah! milord, voilà qui est de la dernière inconvenance.

SIR PEEL.—Je crois qu'on a bougé là-dedans. J'en jurerais.

LA DUCHESSE.—En vérité, vous me faites pitié. Tenez, asseyez-vous là, j'ai quelque chose à vous dire.

SIR PEEL.—Oh! je souffre! Torturer comme cela un pauvre cœur d'homme, c'est épouvantable! Mais je tuerai ce beau muguet-là! oui, je le tuerai, prêtre, dans les bras de sa maîtresse. Je veux être damné s'il m'échappe, celui-là! Ah! elle devrait bien avoir pitié de moi! Cinq ans! voilà cinq ans que je baise le bout de son écharpe, le gant fané que j'achète à ses femmes à prix d'or ou bien à prix d'amour, la muraille que frôle sa robe, la poussière où s'est posé son pied! Et je souffre! et j'ai dans la poitrine un feu qui me ronge, un poison qui me mord les entrailles! O mon Dieu! je voudrais être mort! Ah! cet homme, cet homme maudit! il est jeune, il est beau, vigoureux, libertin—voilà comme elle les aime, elle! Faut-il être dépravée d'aimer un homme comme cela! Je l'aime tant, moi! Eh bien! je prendrai des maîtresses, j'aurai des filles à moi, je m'épuiserai, je me tuerai pour lui plaire! Mais je veux lui déchiqueter le ventre à coups de canif et faire manger par mes chiens sa chair et ses entrailles! Enfer! il lui parle amour, lui, et moi je lui parle politique! Ah! j'en mourrai. Ayez pitié de moi, madame! c'est votre fille, à vous! Allez donc lui dire de m'aimer un peu! enfin il faut avoir pitié d'un pauvre malheureux homme qui se damnerait pour baiser un ruban de soulier qu'elle aurait porté! Mais j'irai tuer ce John Russell! oui, Dieu me damne, je veux le tuer, moi vieux, moi chétif, moi impuissant!

La Duchesse.—Mais remettez-vous donc. Vous allez ameuter toute la cour.

Sir Peel.—C'est que cela doit lui faire grand plaisir de me broyer l'âme, de me tenailler le cœur avec un fer rouge! L'an passé c'était lord Palmerston, puis ce maudit quakre de Bright, puis Derby, puis—que sais-je, moi! quelque goujat ramassé dans les fanges, quelque artiste en haillons, quelque poète déguenillé, quelque homme de rien qui lui vend ses baisers à prix d'or! Cette femme mettrait dans son lit l'univers entier!

La Duchesse.—Milord, vous outragez la pudeur; vous manquez à toutes les convenances.

Sir Peel.—La pudeur! il s'agit pardieu bien de la pudeur! Tout le monde, hors moi! tout le monde, ô mon Dieu! Ce sont ses nuits d'amour qui m'ont fait venir des cheveux blancs. Je passe la vie sur un gril de fer ardent. Oh! c'est un véritable enfer que j'ai là;[1] cette femme me brûle à petit feu. Elle était toute enfant—oh! je me la rappelle bien, moi!—elle n'avait pas seize ans que son maître de musique—

La Duchesse.—Taisez-vous, malheureux!

Sir Peel.—Elle avait alors une petite robe brodée de fleurs, à quatre volants—elle avait une fraîcheur de pomme d'api, une bouche de framboise—maintenant, oh! maintenant, elle est mille fois plus belle de sa pâleur malsaine, de ses veillées amoureuses, de ses nuits de folle orgie! Et je l'aime, moi! Je l'aime, et je souffre plus qu'un damné.

La Duchesse.—Asseyez-vous là. Bien: je vois que la raison commence à vous revenir. À présent, écoutez-moi bien; je vous donnerai, si vous voulez, cet amour que vous souhaitez.

Sir Peel.—Vous, duchesse? vous?

La Duchesse.—Oh! ne vous effrayez pas, milord; je ne vous parle pas de moi, pauvre vieille à la figure ridée, à la bouche édentée; je vous parle de ma fille, de la reine Victoria, de vos amours, de mon enfant, qui est jeune, elle, qui est belle, qui a le cœur tendre et le visage radieux, qui a le corps fait d'amour et de lumière. Vous la posséderez, ma fille, si vous voulez. Vous trouvez que je tranche cyniquement le mot, n'est-ce pas? À quoi cela me servirait-il, de chercher de belles phrases pour envelopper, pour attifer, pour embaumer une chose malséante et cynique?

SIR PEEL.—Dieu! ma tête s'égare! c'est un rêve que je fais là, n'est-ce pas, mon Dieu!

LA DUCHESSE.—Je vous dis que vous la posséderez. Mais il faut faire quelque chose pour cela, milord. Si je vous livre la fille qui est à moi, vous me rendrez la fille que vous m'avez prise.

SIR PEEL.—Juste ciel!

LA DUCHESSE.—Ah! vous croyez qu'on oublie de ces choses-là? qu'on peut arracher des bras d'une femme épuisée, d'une malheureuse mère à l'agonie, son enfant, l'enfant de ses entrailles, son petit enfant, nouveau-né, pauvre ange qui lui sourit, qui pleure, et dont chaque larme et dont chaque sourire lui remue le ventre, lui fait vibrer jusqu'au fond du cœur, et que la mère n'en saura rien, et que tout se passera comme cela, et que rien ne lui remuera plus dans la poitrine, et qu'elle ne s'en souviendra plus, la mère! Ah! vous êtes un grand politique, un homme effrayant, et vous vivez d'une vie chaste et laborieuse, et voilà que soudain le feu vous prend au ventre, un amour vous embrase le corps et l'âme, et cela ne vous enseigne rien, et vous croyez toujours qu'il ne saurait être au monde d'autre amour que celui d'un homme pour une femme, que la fureur âpre d'une aveugle convoitise! Ah! ah! vous voulez tâter de la chair aux princes, milord? eh bien! moi, je veux tâter de la chair de mon enfant! Donnez-moi la cadette, je vous cède l'aînée. Il y a dix-huit ans que j'ai eu cette plaie au cœur. Osez maintenant venir me parler de vos souffrances d'amoureux! Cinq ans! je m'en fiche pas mal, de vos cinq ans de pleurs et de cris! Ah! je parle comme une poissarde, n'est-ce pas vrai? j'ai des phrases de canaille, hein? C'est que je ne suis plus ni duchesse ni régente, je suis mère, milord, et je veux revoir mon enfant, et vous voyez bien qu'il faut me la rendre, mon enfant!

SIR PEEL.—Nous rentrons en politique, madame. Ce que vous me demandez là c'est une chose impossible à faire. Vous n'avez qu'une seule fille, c'est la reine d'Angleterre.

LA DUCHESSE.—Vous mentez, milord!

SIR PEEL.—Madame!

LA DUCHESSE.—Je vous dis que vous mentez, et que c'est infâme, et que vous êtes le dernier des lâches, et que vous faites là un crime abominable et dont vous rendrez compte à Dieu! Elle vit, ma pauvre enfant, je sais bien qu'elle vit toujours, j'aurais eu là quelque tres- saillement horrible à l'heure de sa mort, si elle était morte—quelque déchirement de cœur qui m'eût dit—Ta fille n'est plus! Ah! vous mentez! C'est effroyable comme il ment, cet homme-là. Cœur de fange, bouche de couleuvre!

SIR PEEL.—Madame, je veux que Dieu me foudroie—

LA DUCHESSE.—Vous me soulevez le cœur! taisez-vous.

SIR PEEL.—Je vous jure sur la tête de ma mère que—

LA DUCHESSE.—Ah! tu n'auras jamais ma fille, toi! quand je dûsse la livrer aux chiffonniers de Londres! Moi qui m'étais toujours dit—que la reine ait des amants, qu'elle mène un train d'enfer, qu'elle traine par les ruisseaux sa couronne de vierge avec sa couronne de reine, qu'elle se laisse déshonorer, flétrir aux yeux de tout le monde, enfin, que m'importe! ce n'est pas ma fille à moi, c'est leur reine à tous ces gens-là; une reine, c'est chose publique, cela ressemble à une courtisane. Mais l'autre! la cadette! oh! celle-là, elle doit être bien véritablement mon enfant à moi, ma douce et chaste fille, ma colombe, mon ange aux yeux d'azur, au front de neige! Et tu me l'as prise, toi! et je me suis tu[e], j'ai eu peur, je n'ai rien dit, j'ai prié Dieu, j'ai pleuré, j'ai gémi, et je t'ai laissé faire! Et tu viens me demander l'autre, et te rouler en pleurant à mes genoux! Ah! ah! ah! c'est à mourir de rire! tu veux des reines, toi! On t'en donnera, des reines! Ah! tu te tords les mains, ta bouche se crispe, ta figure devient blême? Ah! tu souffres bien, toi, n'est-ce pas? Vieux farceur, va!

SIR PEEL.—Elle est folle!

(*On entend en dehors la voix de* LORD JOHN RUSSELL *qui chante.*)

> Ce qu'il faut chercher sur la terre,
> Nuit et jour,
> Ce n'est point la raison sévère,
> C'est l'amour!²

LA DUCHESSE.—Mon Dieu! j'avais oublié cet homme. Retirez- vous, mylord, j'ai à lui parler.

SIR PEEL.—Madame—

LA DUCHESSE.—Je croyais vous avoir ordonné de sortir.

SIR PEEL.—Malédiction! (*Il sort.*)

(*Entrent par la porte de la chambre à coucher la reine et*

LORD JOHN RUSSELL, *magnifiquement vêtu de costume de cour.*)

Scène II. LA REINE, LORD JOHN RUSSELL, LA DUCHESSE.

LA REINE.—Ah! c'est vous, ma mère! Il y avait quelqu'un ici?

LA DUCHESSE.—Apparemment que oui, puisque j'y étais, moi.

LA REINE.—J'ai cru entendre la voix d'un homme.

LA DUCHESSE.—C'était milord duc de Fuckingstone.

LA REINE.—Ah! j'aime beaucoup ce bon duc, quoiqu'il ait un nom des plus saugrenus.

LA DUCHESSE.—Ma chère, il faut vraiment que je vous le dise une bonne fois, vous ne devez pas vous compromettre ainsi que vous le faites.

LORD JOHN RUSSELL (*s'inclinant*).—Milady duchesse me flatte.

LA DUCHESSE.—Je ne vous parle pas, milord.

LA REINE.—Ma mère, il faut vraiment que je vous le dise une bonne foi, vous m'ennuyez. Je ne veux ni de vos sermons ni de vos avis. Faites de la politique tant qu'il vous plaira, mais laissez-moi faire l'amour. C'est ce que nous faisons de mieux toutes les deux. J'ai l'honneur de vous souhaiter le bonjour.

LA DUCHESSE (*furieuse*).—Adieu, miss. (*Elle sort en refermant derrière elle avec fracas la grande porte du corridor.*)

Scène III. LA REINE, LORD JOHN RUSSELL.

LA REINE.—Tu me boudes toujours, John.

LORD JOHN RUSSELL.—Moi! je me permettrais de bouder Votre Majesté?

LA REINE.[3]—Ah! tu n'as pas de cœur! tu n'es qu'un homme comme les autres. Moi qui le croyais un demi-dieu! Tenez, John, vous autres hommes vous ne comprenez rien à cela, mais c'est vrai cependant—mon Dieu! c'est bien affreusement vrai, qu'un regard boudeur, qu'une lèvre dédaigneusement pliée nous fait au cœur une bien profonde blessure. O mon bel amant! il y a dans mon âme quelque chose qui vibre, il y a dans mon sang quelque chose qui s'allume, au moindre de tes gestes hautains, au moindre de tes froncements de sourcils! Tu es fin, mon amour, tu es jeune, tu es beau, et tout cela me déchire parfois le cœur, je te voudrais laid, cynique, rabougri, rapetissé, vieilli, mais fidèle, mais amoureux. Mon baiser n'est pas séché sur ta lèvre, ta jolie chevelure brune et bouclée porte encore l'empreinte onduleuse de ma main caressante et je ne sais jamais si tu n'iras pas trainer jusque dans le lit d'une autre ces tristes gages d'un amour méprisé. Livrer ta bouche encore chaude des baisers de la mienne, ton corps encore fiévreux de mes étreintes passionnées, aux plaisirs fangeux de la débauche honteuse, et puis revenir m'apporter les restes de quelque misérable courtisane, ce serait un crime affreux, une trahison inqualifiable, et que je ne vous pardonnerais pas, milord—et qui me tuerais, John! O cher cœur! tu ne voudrais pas me tromper, dis, n'est-ce pas que tu aurais pitié de mon amour, que tu te dirais même au milieu d'un spasme amoureux—"Cette pauvre femme en mourrait"? et que cela te refroidirait les sens, et que cela me rappellerait ton noble cœur, mon amour?

LORD JOHN RUSSELL.—Jurez-moi du moins, Victoria, que c'était la seule fois—que ce misérable n'a jamais osé renouveler—Oh! j'en serais à renier Dieu!

LA REINE.—En vérité, monsieur, vous êtes un homme *shocking,* vous me dites là des choses—

LORD JOHN RUSSELL.—Ah! bon, nous aurons de la pudeur maintenant!

LA REINE.—J'espère, milord, que vous n'avez pas la prétention de me dicter des règles de convenance. Je vous préviens que je ne m'y soumettrai pas.

LORD JOHN RUSSELL.—Oh! Victoria! mais vous n'avez donc pas de cœur!

LA REINE.—Ah! c'est moi maintenant qui n'ai pas de cœur! Sur mon honneur, milord, vous êtes d'un ridicule achevé.

LORD JOHN RUSSELL.—Godam! je vais de ce pas livrer tous vos secrets au peuple! je dévoilerai les mystères immondes, j'éclaircirai les ténèbres sanglantes qui s'épaississent autour de votre lit! Tout le monde viendra vous cracher à la face la kyrielle des noms de vos amants!

LA REINE.—Vous feriez cela, milord?

LORD JOHN RUSSELL.—Oui, Dieu me damne! je ferais cela, sacrebleu!

LA REINE.—Avez-vous connu le vénérable docteur Ballok, président du collège d'Eton?

LORD JOHN RUSSELL.—Oui, nom d'une pipe! Le vieux cuistre m'a donné mille fois le fouet du temps que j'étais écolier. Après?

LA REINE.—J'ai appris qu'il enseignait à ses élèves l'histoire de Messaline. Je l'ai fait pendre. Du moins, je crois que cela doit être fait à présent, c'est midi passé!

LORD JOHN RUSSELL.—Mille godams! vous plaisantez, ma belle?

LA REINE.—Ah! je plaisante! Écoutez, milord, voici le mot de ma plaisanterie.

(*On entend tirer un canon au dehors.*)

LORD JOHN RUSSELL.—Sacré tonnerre! mille godams du bon Dieu!

LA REINE.—Milord, vous sacrez comme un alderman.

LORD JOHN RUSSELL.—Mille bouches! il y a de quoi!

LA REINE.—Jure-moi sur l'âme de ta mère que tu n'as jamais eu d'autre femme que moi—que, hors moi, tu n'as jamais aimé d'amour aucune femme et je te pardonnerai tes emportements. Sinon—

LORD JOHN RUSSELL.—Je le jure sur l'âme de ma mère, sur mon honneur de pair britannique! Que je sois damné si je mens!

LA REINE.—Eh bien! alors réconcilions-nous, mon beau seigneur. Je ne ferai jamais couper cette tête fière et douce, trancher ce cou souple et blanc. Il ne faut pas me garder rancune pour un moment d'humeur. Je te pardonne bien, moi. Oh! quelle femme ne te pardonnerait pas, mon amour! Que tu es beau, mon doux ami! que tu es noble et gracieux! Tiens, donne-moi un bon baiser, et nous oublierons tout cela, n'est-ce pas?

LORD JOHN RUSSELL.—Ah! femme séduisante! Tu as des colères de chatte qui te font mille fois plus adorable! Embrassons-nous.

LA REINE.—Mon amour! mon amour!

(*Entre* SIR ROBERTS PEEL. *Il est très pâle, mais sa figure rayonne. Il fixe sur les amants enlacés un regard plein de fiel et de triomphe haineux.*)

Scène IV. LA REINE, LORD JOHN RUSSELL, SIR PEEL.

SIR PEEL.—Pardon, madame, mais l'heure du grand lever a déjà sonné. Une foule de courtisans est là-bas dans les corridors.

LA REINE (*se dégageant des bras de Lord John Russell, et toisant Sir Peel avec une froideur dedaigneuse*).—Faites entrer, milord. J'avais oublié que c'était l'heure où les valets commandent. Tenez-vous près de la porte, afin de remplir dignement vos fonctions de concierge.

SIR PEEL (*saluant ironiquement*).—J'y veillerai, madame. (*Il se retourne vers la grande porte, qu'il ouvre à deux battants.*)

LORD JOHN RUSSELL (*bas à la reine*).—Cet homme vient de tramer contre nous quelque chose d'infernal. Sa figure de fouine me glace le sang.

LA REINE.—Voulez-vous que je le fasse arrêter?

LORD JOHN RUSSELL.—Gardez-vous-en bien! vous pourriez vous perdre. C'est un homme profond, et tout confit de trahisons.

(*Entre* LA DUCHESSE DE KENT. *Elle vient prendre place à gauche de la reine. Puis les évêques de Londres et de Canterbéry, les membres du concile particulier, les aldermen de la chambre haute, suivis de plusieurs lords et de quelques représentants du peuple. Chacun prend sa place dans l'alignement sans mot dire. Enfin plusieurs dames escortées de leurs pères ou de leurs maris, qui les présentent à la reine. Elle répond ordinairement à leurs révérences très profondes par un léger signe de tête, et ne leur adresse la parole que par intervalles.*)

L'HUISSIER (*à haute voix*).—Milady duchesse de Fuckingstone —mistress Rodger Cox Tandy—milady comtesse de Bitch—miss Sarah Butterbottom—milady Quim—milady marquise de Mausprick[4] —miss Polly Poke, presentée par milord duc de Shittinbags—milady Cunter, par milord marquis de Bumbelly.

LA REINE (*parlant alternativement à ceux qui l'entourent, et aux dames qu'on lui présente. Elle doit s'efforcer pendant toute la scène de prendre un air d'insouciance que dément son regard inquiet, toujours reporté sur* SIR PEEL.)—Bonjour, duchesse; vous êtes ravissante. Mistress Cox Tandy, charmée de vous revoir. —Mon cher M. Whitestick, dites donc à tous ces gens de me faire grâce de ces folies cérémonieuses; j'étouffe. On dirait un prêche le jour que vous êtes en chaire. —Miss Butterbottom, nous n'avons pas oublié notre vieille amie d'enfance. —Lady Bitch, vous avez vraiment une fraîcheur d'Hébé.

LORD JOHN RUSSELL (*à part*).—Je voudrais bien savoir le projet qu'il mâche avec sa moustache en souriant!

LE HUISSIER (*d'une voix éclatante*).—Miss Kitty,[5] presentée par Sa Seigneurie le lord Mayor!

(*Entre* LE LORD MAYOR *avec* Kitty, *habillée en princesse, qu'il amène en face de la reine.*)

La Reine.—Dieu! qu'est-ce que ceci?

La Duchesse (*avec un grand cri*).—Mon enfant! (*Elle s'éva-nouit.*)

Lord John Russell.—Malédiction! c'est elle! —Ah! démons!

Kitty.—John![6] (*Elle vient tomber à ses pieds qu'elle embrasse en sanglotant.*)

La Reine.—Mais, au nom de Dieu! qu'est-ce donc que cette femme?

Sir Peel (*faisant un pas en avant*).—C'est une fille publique!

La Duchesse (*se relevant*).—C'est la sœur de votre reine! Saluez, milords!

Sir Peel (*montrant du doigt* Lord John Russell *anéanti*).— C'est la maîtresse de cet homme!

Le Lord Mayor. (*Il relève* Kitty *et lui passe son bras autour de la taille.*)—C'est ma femme!

Fin du Second Acte

ACTE QUATRIÈME
(*Même décor qu'au second acte.*)

Scène première. LORD GOTOBED, LORD BUTTERS, SIR CHUMP.

LORD GOTOBED.—Tu l'as entendu, toi, Butters? Vous aussi, sir Chump, vous l'avez entendu?

LORD BUTTERS.—Elle a parlé d'un ton clair et net. Le mariage est cassé—oh! mais bien cassé!

LORD GOTOBED.—Mais—mais alors—on pourrait encore parvenir par ce moyen-là jusqu'à quelque chose—hein? quelque chose d'un peu joli? Ce digne Butters!

SIR CHUMP.—Vous vous trompez, milords. Personne au monde ne parviendra par ce moyen-là. Ce n'est pas un échalas politique que cette femme. C'est un cœur d'ange, une bouche de vierge; on n'achète pas de ces choses-là.

LORD BUTTERS.—Ah! ce pauvre lord mayor! comme il doit se ronger les mains!

LORD GOTOBED.—Voilà du moins un homme d'enfoncé. C'est toujours quelque chose.

LORD BUTTERS.—Qui sait? il pourra se relever un jour. On a vu de ces espèces-là.

LORD GOTOBED.—Allons donc! on en a vu, mais c'étaient des hommes. Il s'agit d'un—d'un lord mayor. Enfin, tu comprends, il y a des choses dont on ne se relève pas.

LORD BUTTERS.—Ce n'est qu'un mariage cassé.

LORD GOTOBED.—Cassé net—à cause d'impuissance.

LORD BUTTERS.—Diable! le malheureux! Femme adorable, du reste!

SIR CHUMP.—Adorable en effet. Oh! milords, si vous l'aviez vu, la figure voilée de ses mains—mains effilées, blanches, coupées du réseau frémissant de leurs veines azurées—les joues humides, moitié feu moitié larmes—la poitrine soulevée d'un chaste sanglot—le flanc palpitant d'un soupir virginal—prosternée aux pieds de la reine, le

113

corps étendu par terre, à peine un souffle douloureux à ses lèvres pâles—

LORD GOTOBED.—Tiens! sir Chump qui fait des phrases!

SIR CHUMP.—Riez tant qu'il vous plaira. Moi, j'ai versé des pleurs—et des pleurs bien doux, bien consolants, je vous l'affirme. Elle avait honte, la pauvre et sainte fille, elle rougissait, elle voulait se soustraire à cet affreux procès, à ces yeux lubriques. Pauvre ange!

LORD BUTTERS.—Simagrées que tout cela, mon bon Chump. Elle voulait se soustraire—à son bonhomme de mari.

LORD GOTOBED.—D'époux, tu veux dire. Mais, sérieusement, qu'en va-t-on faire?

LORD BUTTERS.—Ne sais-tu pas que ce vieux sournois de Peel a déterré une loi quelconque—loi de Sarmate, loi de Visigoth, enfin! —qui renverse d'un seul coup les prétentions de cette fille intéressante.

LORD GOTOBED.—Godam! ventre de pape!

SIR CHUMP.—Milord oublie qu'on a décrété contre les blasphémateurs la peine du tread's-mill, ou bien quinze pence d'amende par juron.

LORD GOTOBED.—Ah! nom d'un sacré godam! je m'en—

LORD BUTTERS.—Mais tais-toi donc! Il parait, comme je te le disais, qu'une fille—qu'une femme—enfin qu'une femme-là—

LORD GOTOBED.—C'est clair, ça, ventre d'un tonneau!

LORD BUTTERS.—Qu'une personne tarée enfin—

LORD GOTOBED.—Es-tu bégueule, mon pauvre Butters! es-tu bégueule! Dog's god!

LORD BUTTERS.—Aussi c'est un peu scabreux—qu'une telle personne ne saurait jamais s'asseoir sur le trône anglais.

SIR CHUMP.—Ah! ah! et la reine donc? j'espère qu'en voilà une qui n'est pas trop rosière!

LORD GOTOBED.—De quoi voulez-vous parler, sir Chump?

LORD BUTTERS.—Mais—j'aurais dû peut-être m'expliquer plus clairement. Mais c'est qu'il ne s'agit que des filles—que des femmes du sang royal, qui se seraient permis des—des écarts—avant de se faire reconnaître—comprenez-vous? La reine, elle était reine presque dans son enfance—on leur permet quelque chose, à ces reines-là.

SIR CHUMP.—Ah! mais c'est infâme, cela! mais c'est d'un cynisme odieux! Comment! on leur permet quelque chose, à ces femmes élevées au sein du bonheur, nourries du lait de la sagesse humaine, éclairées, échauffées au foyer de l'amour divin! à ces femmes qui ont des mères, des sœurs, des époux, des gardiens obséquieux et fidèles, on leur passe un peu d'amour par ci par là, on leur pardonne une petite dose de volupté prise au hasard dans quelque coin bien chaud, bien obscur, bien infâme! Pas de flétrissure pour elles! Cela rentre et se rassied parmi ses compagnes, sans s'essuyer la bouche, sans rajuster sa robe, sans rougeur au front, sans remords au cœur. Mais la pauvre femme faible qui pleure, qui rougit, qui se cache, qui va ramassant par les rues les morceaux brisés de sa triste vie, qui n'ose offrir qu'à Dieu les restes de sa pudeur mutilée—oh! à celle-là, honte et malédiction! à celle-là, tous les mépris du juste, tous les crachats de l'impur! Que voilà bien cette justice du monde! que voilà bien l'esprit de cette affreuse législature anglaise, le front souillé de boue, la main rouge de sang! En vérité, je vous le dis, milords, cela soulève le cœur.

LORD GOTOBED.—Vous êtes fou, sir Chump, ou bien vous êtes un homme déloyal et dangereux. Oseriez-vous par hasard prétendre—

SIR CHUMP.—Mais, sans doute, milord, j'ose affirmer que la reine a des amants, qu'elle mène une vie épouvantable, que nous vivons dans un temps inouï, que l'Angleterre, la tête couronnée de fleurs, les yeux rougis par l'ivresse, glisse du pied dans le sang répandu, rit, chante, et trébuche à chaque pas sur une tête coupée. J'ose ajouter, milord, que ce sont là des choses affreuses et dont nous rendrons compte un jour à l'humanité entière. A cet instant nous ferions horreur à tout le monde—mais heureusement nous sommes toujours la risée de l'Europe.

LORD GOTOBED.—Tas de godams! tête et ventre! sacré nom d'un chien!

LORD BUTTERS.—Calme-toi, cher Gotobed. Sir Chump, nous allons de ce pas vous dénoncer à la cour des aldermen. C'est un devoir pénible, et que nous ne remplirons que bien malgré nous, je vous le jure.

LORD GOTOBED.—Sacré godam! je vais le remplir de grand cœur, moi, diable d'enfer!

LORD BUTTERS.—Nous enverrons donc chez vous un homme de police, qui pourra vous y conduire. Adieu, sir Chump. Croyez à tous mes regrets.

SIR CHUMP.—J'ai l'honneur de vous saluer, milords. Vous êtes bien dignes tous les deux de remplir ce beau rôle de mouchards.

Scène II. La Reine, Sir Peel, Lord Butters, Lord Gotobed. (La reine *entre appuyée au bras de* sir Peel. *Elle est
très pâle, et parle d'un ton fiévreux et saccadé, avec des
gestes nerveux.*)

Lord Butters.—Quel homme abominable, mon pauvre Gotobed! quel discours atroce!

Lord Gotobed.—Chut! ce serait à perdre la tête. Voici la reine!

Lord Butters.—Ah! mon Dieu sauveur! Pardonnez, madame.
(*Il s'incline.*)

La Reine.—C'est bien, milord, c'est bien. Sortez, mais sortez
donc.

Lord Butters.—Ah! Majesté! que de regrets! que d'excuses!

La Reine.—Mais sortez, au nom de Dieu, monsieur. Vous me
feriez mourir.

(Lord Gotobed *et* Lord Butters *sortent.*)

Scène III. La Reine, Sir Peel.

La Reine.—Ah! je n'en puis plus. Ayez pitié de moi, mon Dieu!
mon Dieu! Je suis une pauvre femme bien malheureuse.

Sir Peel.—Mais, madame, de grâce, essayez de vous remettre
un peu. Vous ferez jaser les médisants.

La Reine.—Mon Dieu, milord, qu'est-ce que cela me fait à moi?
On ne dira jamais autant de mal sur mon compte que je n'en aie
encore mérité bien pis. Et puis, quand je serais innocente? Y-a-t-il
dans la parole humaine quelque baume qu'on puisse verser sur les
plaies du cœur et de l'esprit? Milord, regardez-moi bien en face,
voyez ces joues creusées de larmes, ce front pâli, cette bouche flêtrie;
considérez cette figure que ronge un désir inassouvi; dites, dites, re-
connait-on à tous ces signes une reine outragée ou bien une femme
qui a perdu son amant? Mais, s'il ne s'agissait que des médisants,
vous le savez, monsieur, j'ai mon bourreau. Souvenez-vous de ma
vieille devise. Ne touchez pas à la reine. Ce que j'ai dans la main,
répondez, milord, est-ce un sceptre? est-ce une hache? Est-il dans
toute cette infâme et misérable Angleterre une seule tête que je ne
puisse faire tomber d'un souffle? Ne suis-je pas l'église, moi? ne
suis-je pas la justice? Cette monarchie-constitutionnelle, comme vous
l'appelez—

(*Avec un mépris amer.*)

Etes-vous bien sûr que cela ne dépende pas de ma seule volonté? Le peuple avait un vieux ami parmi les rangs de la noblesse, un champion fidèle, un guerrier dévoué, un orateur vénérable et redoutable, sir Burdett;[7] mon grandpère l'avait jeté dans un cachot—il en sortit. Mon père l'avait envoyé au delà des mers; il en revint. Moi, je l'ai fusillé. Savez-vous, monsieur, comment est mort le doyen Smith? Il tramait des complots auprès de l'ambassadeur Américain: le parti démocrate l'appuyait de tout son intérêt. Il est venu souper à Windsor; milord Macaulay l'y a convié en mon nom. Dans trois jours, sa veuve éplorée est venue dénoncer au lord mayor un domestique soupçonné d'empoisonnement. On a pendu cet homme.

(*Avec un éclat de rire sauvage.*)

Ah! ah! monsieur, vous voulez me faire peur avec ces médisants-là? vous voulez que je songe à ce qu'on va dire de moi? Mais, mon pauvre et vieil ami, j'ai tenu tête à des géants, vous dis-je. Je suis bien jeune, et grâce aux bons conseils de mes bons amis, aux avis éclairés de ma mère, de cette âme forte, de cet esprit mâle et profond, j'ai déjà dompté les plus robustes lutteurs du parti populaire. Cinq fois on a tiré sur moi dans les places publiques. J'ai soulevé bien des haines; j'ai ensorcelé bien des cœurs. Bien des fois j'ai senti vaciller sous mes pieds le terrain hasardeux et perfide de la royauté; bien des fois, les yeux fermés, j'ai dû me raccrocher à quelque main amie sur laquelle j'ai senti la moîteur rouge et chaude du sang. Jamais je n'ai plié le genou; jamais je n'ai reculé d'un pas. Eh bien! maintenant je plie; maintenant je pleure, je frissonne, je chancelle.

(*Avec un sanglot déchirant.*)

J'ai honte, ô mon Dieu! je voudrais être morte!

SIR PEEL.—Mais c'est inouï! mais c'est insensé!

LA REINE.—Insensé, c'est le mot, milord. Je suis folle; je suis amoureuse.

SIR PEEL (*tombant sur un fauteuil*).—Amoureuse! Vous l'aimez toujours, cet homme maudit? Mon Dieu, Seigneur, donnez-moi des forces! elle me tuera.

LA REINE (*effrayante*).—Tu m'aimes, toi? tu m'aimes? Mais réponds donc!

(*Elle le secoue par le bras.*)

SIR PEEL.—Si je vous aime!

LA REINE (*avec un élan de joie funèbre et menaçante*).[8]—Il m'aime, lui! Voilà du moins un bras fort, une âme éprouvée. Merci, mon Dieu! —Tu m'aimes bien, n'est-ce pas?

SIR PEEL.—Oh! je rêve! je suis fou! C'est un délire affreux!

LA REINE.—Tu m'aimes—jusqu'au crime?

SIR PEEL.—Pour toi, je poignarderais mon père au pied de l'autel.

LA REINE.—Jusqu'à la mort? tu me donnerais ta vie, toi?

SIR PEEL.—Tu l'entends, ô mon Dieu! elle me demande cela!

LA REINE (*haletante*).—Eh bien! parle, veux-tu de moi?

SIR PEEL.—Ciel! je suffoque.

LA REINE.—Roberts! Roberts! à toi pour la vie! (*Elle se préci- pite dans ses bras.*)

SIR PEEL.—Allons! à présent, je suis bien véritablement fou.

(*Parait un huissier de cour.*)

L'HUISSIER.—Son Altesse Royale la princesse Catherine sollicite ardemment la grâce d'être admise auprès de Sa Majesté.

LA REINE.—Qu'elle attende. (*L'huissier s'incline et sort.*) Eh bien! Roberts? eh bien? Tu l'as entendu, cet homme?

SIR PEEL.—C'est un outrage infâme!

LA REINE.—Cette misérable fille qui m'a pris mon amant! Cette prostituée dont j'ai cassé le mariage! Faut-il être impudique! En vé- rité, je ne conçois point qu'il y ait des femmes comme cela. Mais, milord, cela ferait rougir un alderman.

SIR PEEL.—Voulez-vous qu'on la chasse de chez vous, cette ef- frontée?

LA REINE.—Non pas! Après tout—(*avec un sourire diabolique*) —après tout, monsieur—c'est ma sœur.

SIR PEEL.—Votre sœur! c'est absurde! c'est un conte pitoyable!

LA REINE.—Ah! les larmes d'une mère ne se démentent pas. Non, non, milord, la duchesse ne s'est point trompée. Et puis il y a des preuves—irrécusables. Je vous remercie de ce que vous avez fait contre elle, mais enfin c'est une chose constatée. Chose odieuse du reste, chose abominable, dégoûtante, effroyable; mais sûre, mais vé- ritable, mais apparente. Que voulez-vous! il faut s'y soumettre. C'est triste, cela: c'est même ignoble. Qu'en pensez-vous?

SIR PEEL (*soucieux*).—Je pense—que Votre Majesté a toujours raison.

LA REINE.—Pauvre mère! ç'a été pour elle un choc épouvan- table.

La Fille du Policeman
Étude historique

1. Quelques mots de politique.

Ce que nous écrivons, c'est quelque chose de plus et c'est quelque chose de moins qu'une brochure sur l'état social de l'Angleterre. C'est là une tâche austère que Dieu réserve sans doute à de plus puissantes mains. Nous ne voulons que constater quelques vérités tristes et navrantes sur les moyens qu'on a fait valoir en 1847 et en 1848 pour raffermir cet état, qui à cette époque chancelait sur ses bases. Et nous les consignons, ces faits douloureux, avec un profond sentiment de tristesse et d'amitié sincère pour le peuple anglais. Nous découvrons la poitrine de l'Angleterre non pas comme un assassin mais comme un chirurgien; c'est avec amour et compassion que nous en fouillons les plaies profondes. Ce peu que nous pouvons, nous l'offrons, non pas aux Anglais ennemis de la France, non pas aux Français ennemis de l'Angleterre, mais aux cœurs sains et aux âmes libres des deux nations. Nous n'écrivons ni pour les catholiques ni pour les protestants, mais pour l'humanité. Ce brin d'herbe que nous apportons sur son autel, il n'appartient du moins qu'à elle seule.

[*p.2* (A)] La société anglaise, envisagée d'en dehors, offre quelque chose d'informe; on pourrait l'appeler une chimère, dont les trois parties seraient la haute aristocratie, l'église, la presse. Cette dernière est (comme on sait) toute aux mains de la classe moyenne. Le duc de Wellington a fait sur le *Times* ce mot célèbre; Ça pue le Birmingham. Pour l'église, elle est souple, taciturne, sournoise; sa puissance est enracinée dans la haine du catholicisme et dans la peur d'une révolution. Entre ces deux rochers cette bâtarde de Calvin fait voguer sa galère chargée de mitres et de baïonnettes. L'armée lui est toute soumise: le soldat anglais, c'est un courage fait avec deux peurs; celle du fouet, celle du chapelain régimental. Quant à la monarchie, elle n'existe que par licence de l'aristocratie.

Donc, ces trois puissances s'affermissent et se replient l'une sur l'autre. Assez souvent elles font semblant de s'entrequereller, de se rallier au peuple; mais au fond elles sont amies et fidèles. Jamais il n'y aura pour le peuple anglais ni puissance véritable ni véritable liberté, tant que durera cette trinité sournoise et formidable; la tyrannie, l'hypocrisie, l'intérêt commercial et particulier.

Voilà l'Angleterre; voilà du moins l'Angleterre qui parle, qui crie, qui se remue, qui se pavane. Doit-on s'étonner qu'elle témoigne pour la France une [*p. 3* (A)] profonde haine et une méfiance profonde? Les gouvernements forts, libres, probes, sont tout naturellement en butte aux haines des sociétés débiles, fausses, tyrannisées par un despotisme masqué, menteur, cruel.

L'empire français, c'est la puissance, la lumière, le dévouement, la vraie liberté, la société saine et noble.

L'oligarchie et la théocratie anglaises n'ont rien de tout cela; elles n'en veulent pas.

Voilà le mot du problème.

Ce que veut le peuple anglais, personne à présent ne saurait le dire. Ce peuple pourrait être le frère cadet du peuple français; il n'est à présent qu'un séide frémissant.

Cela sera-t-il toujours ainsi? Dieu seul le sait.

En 1847, l'aristocratie avait une puissance extraordinaire. Elle avait rompu avec la royauté, elle s'était attachée à l'église. La mariage de la reine Victoria avec un étranger les avait mis en butte tous les deux à la jalousie et à l'insolence des aristocrates pur sang. Il suffit de faire les moindres recherches parmi les journaux de cette époque pour comprendre à quel point l'aristocratie poussait sa haine, comme elle maniait habilement les armes meurtrières de la calomnie.

[*p. 4* (A)] Du reste, le ménage royal offrait assez de prise à ces exagérations politiques. Nous renvoyons nos lecteurs à ces mêmes journaux pour les preuves de cette allégation.

Le prince Albert était mécontent de son impuissance sociale. La reine était mécontente de la méfiance populaire. Quelques esclandres de son époux contribuaient fort à la décider. Elle refusa nettement au prince quelques titres et quelques pouvoirs que sollicitait pour lui le parti allemand. Alors commença une lutte sourde entre ces deux intérêts.

Avant d'ajouter un seul détail, nous prions le lecteur de vouloir bien se rappeler l'époque dont il s'agit, de feuilleter les revues anglaises et les journaux contemporains, et surtout de croire que nous ne constatons aucun fait de moindre intérêt que nous ne tenons pas immédiatement d'une bouche ou d'une plume anglaise.

Ce livre n'est en effet qu'un roman: mais l'auteur a cru devoir à ses lecteurs et au sujet qu'il a entrepris de traiter une austère et sérieuse fidélité. Ce devoir a pour lui quelque chose de religieux.

On comprend qu'il a dû faire quelques changements, modifier quelques détails, assouplir quelques lignes trop prononcées; mais au fond de son roman il a mis une vérité historique pleine d'enseignements. Il a [p. 5 (A)] soigneusement étudié l'époque dont il va parler. Il a consciencieusement approfondi les problèmes qu'il se propose de soumettre à ceux qui voudront bien l'aider à les déchiffrer.

Pourquoi l'Angleterre eut-elle une révolution?

Pourquoi cette révolution fit-elle si peu de bruit?

Pourquoi enfin cette révolution échoua-t-elle?

II. Le tribun, le prêtre, l'aristocrate.[1]

Dites donc, Sir Jenkins, fit le policeman Hervey, est-ce que vous me prenez pour un baronet, moi? ou bien ma Nelli vous parait-elle fille à délaisser? Hein? Le père de la blanche Nelli se tenait accoudé sur le *wicket* d'un *chop-house*. Il portait un gros *overcoat* râpé, déteint, des manches duquel projetaient des mains singulièrement fines, arrondies, délicates. Sa figure puissante et douce était outragée de colère et de mépris; son œil sévère reluisait.

Le baronet Thompson Jenkins répondit par un mouvement d'épaules dédaigneux et stupide. C'était un gros petit homme ventru, louche, ayant des yeux jaunâtres à fleur de tête.

Williams Hervey prit un air menaçant. Sa main se reportait machinalement vers son fidèle blugdeon, terreur des coquins de Piccadilly.

—Sirs, au boxe! cria un *guardsman* étourdi qui [*p.* 6 (A)] sortait à cet instant d'un cabaret voisin, enivré à la fois du rhum et des baisers de son hôtesse, digne femme fort libérale des deux à l'endroit des beaux jeunes gens.

Williams fronça légèrement le sourcil; puis il sembla se remettre.

—Allons, sir Jenkins, dit-il d'un ton froid, je ne veux pas d'esclandre aux rues; ça ferait éclaboussure à l'honneur d'une jeune fille. Jurez-moi de ne remettre jamais le pied dans ma maison, et partez: vous êtes libre.

La figure bouffie et pesante du baronet s'injecta d'un vert bilieux. Il jeta sur Hervey un regard haineux et livide que celui-ci reçut en souriant, et partit en effet.

Au détour de la rue sir Jenkins rencontra un homme grand et maigre en costume de prêtre anglican. Cet homme lui prit le bras, et tous deux se mirent à arpenter le carré de Soho-square en se parlant à voix basse.

Nous citons quelques mots de leur entretien.

—Tiens, dit le prêtre, en se retournant, ça doit être ton policeman qui fume au devant de cette porte d'auberge les bras croisés? C'est pardieu un gaillard bien bâti.

A quoi sir Jenkins répondit avec une ferveur sentencieuse: —*God damn his eyes.*

—Amen! fit le ministre luthérien en ricanant. Et dire que cette espèce a de belles filles! Faut avouer que la beauté se loge mal. J'ai

connu, moi qui te parle, une comtesse [*p. 7* (A)] admirablement
laide qui ne sortait jamais qu'accompagnée d'une petite suivante qui
était bien la plus ravissante enfant du monde! Et d'une dépravation
—oh! Ça pourrait en remontrer à Messaline!

—Tu as le goût bien impur, toi, Whitestick. Moi j'aime l'enfance
innocente, la fleur mi-close.

—Choufleur! Du reste je ne te savais pas si poète; mais c'est une
idylle vivante que cette homme-là.

—Ris tant que tu voudras: je tiens à la Nelli, moi. C'est une eau
limpide et qui rafraîchie la bouche.

—Boisson fade, mon ami! Je voudrais bien pourvoir considérer
cet appétissant légume.

—Sais-tu, mon révérend, que tu m'embêtes avec tes filles perdues? C'est une si bruyante espèce! Aussi c'est indigne de songer
qu'un tel gaillard s'appelle évêque: mais, mon cher, tu dépasses
Dubois,[2] tu vas jusqu'à Borgia, Godam!

—Je vais jusqu'à Borgia, moi, Whitestick? Allons donc! C'était
un grand homme. Nous autres anglicans, nous sommes des nains pris
dans les bottes de sept lieues. Tu ne vois pas que la machine la plus
puissante qui soit au monde, c'est une église administrée par des
athées. Considère plutôt la renaissance. Vois comme Alexandre VI
fit marcher les choses. Eh bien! moi aussi, je suis athée, et cependant—

—Tu es athée, toi?

—Pardieu!

[*p. 8* (A)]—Alors, bonsoir. Je ne me frotte pas au diable.

—nom de Luther! serais-tu dévot, toi, par hasard?

—Mais sans doute. Un athée! cela sent l'enfer d'une lieue. Passe
encore pour les petits plaisirs défendus, mais renier son Dieu! c'est
affreux. Que diable! je suis bon chrétien, moi.

Whitestick éclata de rire.

—Combien en connais-tu de chrétiens qui soient coiffés de la
mitre? Tu es vraiment trop idyllique, je te l'ai dit et je le redis. Tu
vois que je ne crains pas de m'expliquer tout haut. Va me dénoncer à
Canterbéry, on te rira au nez. Le matérialisme fait rage parmi nous
autres pasteurs du peuple. Laissons cela. Je vais te prouver que la
robe vaut bien quelque chose. Dis-moi seulement où loge ta belle,
et tu verras.

—Eh bien, la voilà, regarde.

Le regard d'acier qui dardait des yeux de son interlocuteur sur la jeune fille insoucieuse, effaroucha le baronet. Il tira l'évêque par sa manche brodée.

—Elle est belle! articula Whitestick avec une profonde aspiration qu'on eût pu appeler un soupir de convoitise.

—Ah ça, ne va pas te mettre en tête de me l'enlever, à moi. Je te brûlerais la cervelle en plein prêche.

—Sois tranquille, cher ami. On est homme d'honneur ou on ne l'est pas.

Cependant Whitestick se répéta d'une voix basse et haletante.

—Elle est belle!

[*p. 9* (A)]—Elle est belle et même très belle, fit sir Jenkins d'un ton courroucé, et en fronçant légèrement sa narine épaisse: ce qui ne veut pas dire que tu y toucheras, bon ami.

—Moi, mon cher frère? fit le prélat avec un petit ricanement: à Dieu ne plaise! Aussi je n'aime plus ces filles du peuple, cela pue toujours son treadmill.

Expliquons cet affreux sarcasme. Du reste, nos lecteurs qui feuilletent quelquefois un journal anglais pourront bien le commenter sans notre aide.

Le treadmill, c'est le châtiment de la misère infligé aux misérables. C'est une machine à trois roues que font tourner trois malheureux attelés par le poignet, stimulés par le fouet, qu'on dépouille jusqu'au bas de la ceinture et qu'on attache à la roue pour la faire marcher en soulevant et en repoussant tout le poids de cette machine vraiment infernale. Enfin ce malheureux esclave succombe épuisé sous un tel fardeau. On le ranime à moyen d'une vigoureuse fustigation, ou bien en lui brûlant les chairs avec du plomb fondu. Cela s'est vu tout récemment. Puis c'est à recommencer. Et cela douze heures durant. (Voir sur les prisons anglaises le beau livre de M. Charles Reade où sont constatés des faits encore plus affreux.)[3] Et on s'étonne si les cachots anglais ne sont pas toujours remplis. Et on se croit le droit de mépriser, de conspuer les nations où le prisonnier survit [*p. 10* (A)] à son terme de cachot.

En Angleterre les pauvres meurent vite.

Cela débarrasse de ces importuns qu'on appelle la canaille, le marchand bouffi, le lord somnolent, le dandy radieux, la blanche et fière lady, le dévot à l'œil louche et lent, le *clergyman* boursouflé, l'évêque phariséen et débauché.

Cela est incroyable.

Cela est.

Nous le redisons encore, ce livre n'est pas seulement un roman: c'est de l'histoire taillée à vif dans les chairs de la vérité mise à nu et sanglante.

Chaque fait que nous constatons ici avec un frémissement douloureux, avec un sanglot indigné, c'est d'une bouche anglaise que nous le tenons. Nous pourrions citer plusieurs autorités devant lesquelles la dénégation baisserait la tête, muette, brisée, rougissante; nous n'en citerons qu'une seule; et que la presse anglaise y réponde.

C'est le révérend comte sir Shaftesbury.[4]

Le fait cité plus haut, nous l'avons extrait de son beau livre Les matinées anglaises (English mornings in the workhouse).

[*p. 11* (A)] Peu de temps après cette boutade épiscopale, ces deux amis se séparèrent. Sir Jenkins, l'homme charnel, le débauché vulgaire qui se tenait chaud dans sa boue et dans ses plaisirs fangeux, alla s'enivrer chez le lord mayor, son ami intime et le confident de ses débauches ordinaires. Et le prélat, l'homme sacré, l'appui des hommes profanes, la parole de Dieu habillée et qui marchait avec des pieds humains, que fit-il, lui?

C'est ce que nous allons voir.

III.   Un conciliabule de socialistes chrétiens.[5]

L'évêque de Londres se rendit chez le révérend Bobi Blubbs, chanoine de l'église du Temple, située comme on sait, entre le Holborn et les quais de la Thamise.

Le dit Bobi était un gros lourdaud de cinquante ans, très-ivrogne et très-égoïste: du reste, pas trop méchant, et d'une bêtise admirable.

Il salua profondément le grand évêque Whitestick, aumônier de la reine, primat du Sussex et des îles.

—C'est bon, fit celui-ci, assieds-toi. Nos frères sont-ils réunis?

—Ici même, Monseigneur.

La maison où se trouvaient nos interlocuteurs était sale, basse, et laide. Une moiteur graisseuse suintait par les murailles vertes. Le plafond échancré laissait passer par ses déchirures une lueur terne et lugubre. Les bruits d'une rue étroite et fangeuse venai[en]t frapper l'ouïe par les brèches du mur effondré. Les puanteurs insouffrables du fleuve emplissaient l'air épais et maladif, où se perdait l'haleine courte et pesante du bon gros chanoine. Les rumeurs assourdies, la lumière amortie venaient mourir sous ces tristes plafonds. Les parquets [*p. 12* (A)] humides, impurs, étaient empreints de boue et de fange: le pied glissait sur des ordures repoussantes mêlées à la paille fétide. On louait par semaine ce bouge affreux aux pauvres de l'environ.

Dans cette bâtisse qui appartenait au sieur Blubbs, attendaient trente hommes à peu près, tous à figure ecclésiastique, tous vêtus de soutane. On se leva pour saluer M. Whitestick, qui s'assit sur un dais élevé et promena sur ces têtes courbées sa prunelle d'aigle.

—Frère, dit un vieillard pâle et vigoureux, ayant bien le visage d'un des fils de Dominique[6] qui inondèrent de sang la Provence au temps de Philippe-Auguste, nous écoutons.

Whitestick prit la parole. Tous les yeux s'allumèrent.

—Mes frères, dit le puissant évêque avec sa grande voix tranchante, brève, accentuée, nous sommes ici réunis pour fait de politique. Ce que nous avons à chercher, vous le savez. C'est l'église anglicane perdue qu'il s'agit de retrouver, de ramasser, de ranimer. Le souffle seul du Tout-puissant donne la vie aux morts; aussi sans son aide ne ferons-nous pas un pas en avant. Mes frères, prions.

Aussitôt l'assemblée, comme un champ de blé que frappe et balaye une bourrasque subite, tomba la tête contre terre, les genoux pliés. L'évêque debout articula lentement ces paroles solennelles:

—Seigneur, nous sommes à tes pieds. Seigneur, nous croyons en toi, protège-nous. Tes brebis s'égarent, leur laine se déchire aux sentiers épineux de ce triste monde: leurs pieds boitent, leur flanc saigne. Verse sur eux les baumes de ta clémence céleste. Soutiens les pasteurs de ces ouailles; frappe les loups, chasse les tigres qui rodent, la gueule béante, l'œil rougi, autour de leur frêle demeure.

Tout le monde se releva et s'assit.

—Peters Prug, évêque de Lincoln, faites votre rapport.

Le vieillard pâle se leva, une liste à la main.

—Dans mon diocèse, dit-il, il se trouve à cette heure quarante-cinq fidèles, trois cents papistes, deux mille dissidents, quatre mille [*p. 13* (A)] incrédules, six cents républicains: le reste, prêtres et laïques, des indifféren[t]s. J'ai dit.

Un sourd murmure éclata. Aussitôt Whitestick le comprima d'un regard.

—Edwards Tonk, évêque du Lancashire.

Un petit jeune homme terne et cassé se leva.

—Moi, fit-il d'une voix aigre et glapissante, je compte deux cents fidèles, pas un papiste, vingt-trois républicains, douze cents incrédules, deux mille mondains. Il y avait des dissidents: mais chez nous cette engeance s'use vite. Du reste, on les chasse.

Les prêtres applaudissaient. Le sourcil froncé de Whitestick s'abaissa lourdement sur son œil courroucé.

—Votre police est mal faite, sir Tonk, dit-il. Vous êtes paresseux. Vous étiez comte; ruiné à la suite de vos débauches inqualifiables, vous vous êtes mis à l'église. Vous retournerez au monde: vous serez destitué. Pas un mot.

Un frisson circula dans l'auditoire.

—Rogers Fox, archidiacre de Somerset.

Celui-ci était un grand gaillard trapu, aux épaules fortes et larges, au ventre rebondi, aux poignets musculeux. Plusieurs bruits couraient dans le Somerset sur sa tyrannie louche, sur son inépuisable luxure. Ces qualités avaient valu à ce digne archidiacre les surnoms de Brisetout et de Mangefille (woman-eater). Il était lié fort intimement avec M. Whitestick.

—Vous avez la parole, sir Fox, fit ce dernier.

—Nos bons frères, dit le gros homme, pour savoir ce qu'il y a chez nous de papistes mâles il faudrait vous adresser [*p. 14* (A)] à mon sacristain, au digne Challs.[7] Pour moi, je vous assure que nous avons de petites papistes du beau sexe tout-à-fait propre à faire tourner la tête au saint Calvin de joyeuse mémoire. Il y a surtout une enfant fort sémillante qui donne des espérances on ne peut plus égrillardes. Tête et boyaux! c'est un morceau de pape. Au reste, assez bienveillante à l'égard de nos coréligionnaires et fort peu bégueule: aussi je ne crois pas, toute catholique qu'elle soit, qu'elle va jamais coiffer Ste Catherine.

Un énorme éclat de rire accueillit ces paroles évangéliques. Le seul Prug fit une moue de prude ou de dévot.

—Bien, bien, mon bon Rogers, dit Whitestick en souriant. Nous ne vous demandons pas de ces détails intimes. Seulement, croyez-vous que votre peuple soit bien soumis?

—Eh! nom de mille papistes! si je le crois! Mais nous les ferions rouer de coups, Godam! si ça s'avisait de grouiller. Par le diable! On est le maître ou on ne l'est pas.

—Assez, dit l'évêque de Londres. Maintenant, mes pères, il s'agit de nous organiser et de mettre en œuvre tous les moyens possibles pour combattre ce démon du socialisme qui nous envahit de tous côtés. Les flots bruyants d'une marée révolutionnaire menacent déjà d'engloutir tout ce qu'il y a de saint, de vénéré, de digne, dans ce malheureux pays. On dit déjà que l'église chancelle, que l'épiscopat vacille. Il faut que ces langues animées pas la haine, soldées par l'enfer, se taisent enfin et pour toujours.

[*p. 15* (A)]—Bien! bien! fit Prug en se frottant les mains; un éclair homicide incendiait de son reflet sombre la figure âpre du vieillard.

—Cependant, continua Whitestick, il faut surtout agir avec une lenteur sage et froide si nous voulons vraiment réussir. Laissons aux imbéciles le bûcher refroidi, le fer émoussé. Agissons par l'esprit sur l'esprit; étouffons le libre arbitre, non plus par la main brutale de la force, mais par la puissance profonde et calculée de l'âme. Frappons par la pensée ces penseurs, par la philosophie ces philosophes. Mettons sur la figure muette et patiente de l'église le masque voltairien; alors ces hommes maudits et aveugles accourront baiser cette bouche pleine de mots creux, d'amour, de liberté, de bienfaisance. Ce baiser leur sera mortel. Cette lèvre cachée leur mettra la fièvre au sang. Alors nous serons vraiment forts: alors nous écraserons du talon la tête monstrueuse de la liberté, de cette gueuse appelée par les coquins reine, par les sots déesse. Voilà.

Une admiration profonde, hébétée, s'était peinte sur les figures béantes de l'assemblée. Tonk essuyait la sueur qui coulait de son front à flots larges. Prug se mordait les lèvres; Fox palpitait, la bouche ouverte, l'œil fiévreux. Quant au gros Blubbs, il était anéanti.

—A Dieu ne plaise, mes chers frères, reprit le redoutable prélat, que je ferais douter de mon amitié profonde et sincère pour ces pauvres brebis égarés! Mon cœur, vous le savez du reste, mon cœur se gonfle et déborde de pitié en songeant à ces âmes que nous a confié Dieu même. Pour elles je répandrais mon sang: pour ramener à la foi ces âmes, Dieu [*p. 16* (A)] me pardonne si c'est un blasphème, je crois que je donnerais volontiers la mienne. Ils le savent, ces pauvres hommes; il me bénissent, tout indigne que je sois de leur bienveillance. Ces bouches républicaines croient me flatter en m'appelant prêtre selon l'évangile, socialiste chrétien. C'est par ce seul moyen que nous remettrons dans ces âmes flétries l'amour saint du christianisme, que nous ferons refleurir dans ces terres desséchées la fleur de la foi calme, éternelle, inébranlable.

On ne saurait décrire les nuances du sourire lent et mielleux qui glissait, doucereux et profond, sur les lèvres où vibraient encore ces paroles empreintes de charité et d'onction. Quelques ricanements sourds qui voltigeaient par l'auditoire prouvaient suffisamment que ses confrères savaient apprécier à sa valeur la foi évangélique, l'amour religieux, la fraternité candide et fervente du prélat Whitestick.

L'évêque Prug se leva. Cet homme, qui combinait dans son église protestante les sanglantes traditions de Laud et de Burnet, avait écouté avec un frémissement d'impatience féroce la parole onctueuse de son confrère de Londres.

—Fumée que tout cela! s'écria-t-il d'une voix vibrante. C'est en effet de l'indifférentisme tout pur. Moi, je me défie du libéralisme doucereux comme du libéralisme homicide. Je ne veux pas de la pensée! Je ne veux pas du libre arbitre. Notre frère de Londres est un homme fort savant; c'est un philosophe, c'est un idéologue: eh bien! qu'il mette le frein à cette cavale indomptée qu'on appelle la libre pensée; qu'il mette un mors à la liberté, un bâillon à l'humanité, avec ses beaux discours! [*p. 17* (A)] C'est puéril, c'est honteux que d'y songer. Tenez, moi, j'ai combattu le papisme, le libéralisme, enfants jumeaux de Belzébuth, quand vous autres vous vagissiez au maillot. C'est une chose pitoyable que d'entendre roucouler les jeunes gens d'aujourd'hui, les muguets religieux qui se repaissent de jolis mots, de phrases sonores. Nous, nous rugissions! Nous, nous mordions! La liberté saigne et frissonne encore des plaies que nous lui avons faites. La morsure de nos dents protestants entama profondément le flanc meurtri de l'Irlande papiste: et la verte Érin en gémit à cette heure. Vous voulez nous continuer? agissez comme nous. Que dis-je là! Vous, libertins cassés, efflanqués de débauches, mondains essouflés à la poursuite de la volupté aux lèvres humides, comment sauriez-vous continuer des hommes ridés à force de veiller, courbés à force d'étudier, desséchés à force de songer? Malheureux rapetissés! misérables ébauches de prêtres sans sève, sans puissance, sans virilité! Est-ce donc de votre chair usée aux plaisirs, de vos bouches enivrées par les baisers impurs d'un monde incrédule, que sortira la parole puissante et lumineuse qui éclairera, qui éblouira, qui brûlera, qui brisera? Enfantement sombre et douloureux! Croyez-vous par hasard que vos flancs sont de force à le porter? Accouplez-vous! engendrez! vous ne ferez jamais que des avortons, et c'est moi qui vous le dis: moi, vieux soldat de la religion, dont la lame a plus d'une fois entamé les chairs vives et saignantes de la liberté, dont l'ongle a plus d'une fois déchiré la blessure palpitante et envenimée du catholicisme! Après les géants, les hommes; après les hommes, les nains! Allez! agissez! je vous plains et je vous méprise.

[*p. 18* (A)] Après cette sortie foudroyante le vieux fanatique prit son chapeau à large bords, son bâton enduit d'argent, et voulut sortir pendant que l'éclair de ses yeux terrassait encore les diplomates et les quasi-libéraux parmi ses confrères. En effet, hors le seul Whitestick, tout le monde tremblait sous la puissance de cette parole sinistre, et de cet œil flamboyant. Mais lorsque Whitestick se leva pour répondre, tous ces regards se reportaient sur lui.

—Taisez-vous, sir Prug! fit-il d'une voix tonnante. Taisez-vous, et apprenez à respecter ceux qui remuent les ficelles par lesquels vous faites agir votre haine, votre énergie, votre autorité. Qui vous a donné l'évêché de Lincoln? serait-ce par hasard un de ces hommes dont vous nous parliez, de ces titans qui doivent nous faire honte et peur, à nous? Regardez et obéissez. En proférant ces paroles, Whitestick étendit vers le vieillard chancelant, ébloui, sa main blanche et robuste où scintillait un diamant superbe. Les joues de Prug blêmirent, son œil se voila, sa lèvre frémit . . . d'épouvante, non pas d'émotion.

—Apprenez, maître Prug, dit l'impitoyable Whitestick en appuyant sur chaque parole de tout le poids de sa voix sonore, que vous n'êtes pas la tête; vous n'êtes que la main. Frappez, ne pensez pas. Vous vous croyiez homme! mais ayez donc de la modestie! mais soyez donc raisonnable, mordieu! Vous n'êtes qu'une seule roue qui tourne dans la machine énorme, épouvantable, qui nous fait marcher tous. Vous manquez de pudeur, maître Prug: vous êtes indécent. Taisez-vous.

Le vieillard livide, haletant, épuisé, poussa un gémissement, s'inclina, prit la main de Whitestick et la baisa. Puis se retournant,

—Frères, dit-il, voici votre maître. Et il sortit, pâle, écrasé, ébloui, en vacillant sur ses pieds comme un homme ivre.

Alors, sans un mot de plus, Whitestick congédia l'assemblée d'un geste. Les prêtres sortaient en se chuchotant à l'oreille. [*p. 19 (A)*] Resté seul, Whitestick ôta son diamant, le regarda en ricanant, le mit dans sa poche, et sortit. Un reste de sourire crispait encore sa bouche, lorsqu'il se mit dans son *brogam* éblouissant.

—À Saint James! cria-t-il au cocher: et va vite!

Les chevaux firent jaillir les étincelles du pavé sombre et visqueux en partant au grand galop.

IV. La reine chez elle.

Une foule étincelante, bariolée, musquée, se pressait, surgissait, ondoyait sur les vastes escaliers de Buckingham-house! Au milieu de cette marée éblouissante qui montait toujours on vit surgir la tête pâle de John Russell, se dessiner la figure douce et sérieuse de Palmerston; on vit ressortir la bouche de vipère, la figure aplatie de lord Derby, rayonner l'œil puissant de l'Irlandais Mitchell, admis encore dans cette société radieuse et corrompue qui au premier mot de patriotisme devait le rejeter comme une lèpre; on vit se mêler, s'entrebaiser, s'entrechoquer en souriant, tous les intérêts, toutes les haines, toutes les intrigues: on entendit frémir et bruire les écharpes de soie chaude et parfumée qui voilaient à peine les seins adorables, les poitrines fécondes, les gorges haletantes des dames au regard velouté, chatoyant, doucement luxurieux, humide de voluptés in-décises: on sentit frissoner leur peau fine et neigeuse au contact subit de quelque main musculeuse, de quelque chair amie; on vit glisser sur les roses palpitantes de ces lèvres quelque vague parole d'amour furtif, de provocation voilée; on respirait les effluves de ces beaux corps, de ces épaules nacrées, de ces cheveux dorés: on s'enivrait à la vue de toutes ces blancheurs demi-vêtues, de toutes ces splendeurs demi-cachées. Une lady anglaise, c'est la pudeur lascive, la vierge courtisane.

[*p. 20*(A)] Cependant au milieu de ce monde bruyant, lumineux, se détachait comme sur un fonds de lumière la tête belle et sombre, le front fier et pâli, de la reine Victoria. La douce et noble créature que Dieu fit asseoir sur un trône chancelant sentit déjà percer les épines de sa couronne de martyre. Elle pliait déjà sous ce fardeau surhumain d'un énorme empire malade. Son beau teint blond s'altérait sous ce poids de tant de milliers d'homme qui pesaient sur elle.

Une douleur sourde effaçait les méplats flêtris de sa figure vir-ginale, estompait les nuances nacrées de sa peau lisse et délicate.

Elle pleurait sans doute l'idéal doré, les illusions riantes qui voltigeaient autrefois autour de son cœur de jeune fille, pour s'enfuir hélas! à tire d'ailes.

Près d'elle, sévère et beau, veillait d'un œil soupçonneux celui qu'on nomme aujourd'hui le prince consort, qu'on nommait alors le prince prolétaire. (Voir le *Times* et le *Morning News*.) Derrière l'époux royal s'était amassée une petite bande de ses fidèles, parmi lesquels on distinguait la figure soucieuse et sournoise du célèbre Bright, alors jeune homme plein d'entrain et de fougue, qui débutait aux *meetings* de ses confrères avec grand éclat.

Le chef du parti quakre avait alors ses entrées chez la reine à toute heure. On les lui retira en 1854, à propos de son fameux discours sur les sucres bruts, dans lequel il soutenait le droit reconnue aux nobles par la loi anglaise de prélever un impôt sur la bière, le tabac, le thé, la poivre rouge, destinés à la nourriture du peuple des champs.

C'est que le gouvernement de cette année frisait le libéralisme.

Aussi depuis ce temps le grand orateur s'est-il fait réformiste.

Tout ce monde se remuait, vibrait, refluait dans les corridors, éclatait aux miroirs, foulait incessamment les tapis somptueux du grand salon.

Et à trois pas de là la misère populaire grouillait dans sa fange.

Et personne ne venait cracher à la figure de cette reine, de ces hommes dorés, de ces femmes musquées, le nom de l'Irlande crucifiée.

[*p. 21* (A)] Cependant un frémissement d'intérêt, de plaisir, d'admiration, se fit sentir parmi les plus prochains de la grande porte. Un homme de haute taille, portant sur son habit noir le seul ordre de la Jarretière, s'avançait dans la foule.

Le huissier ému annonça d'une voix retentissante;

—Sa Grandeur, milord évêque John Whitestick de Londres!

En effet, Whitestick, l'œil souriant, le front serein, la bouche placide, se dégageait de l'étreinte de tout un monde d'amis et de courtisans qui se pressaient pour le saluer.

Le prince vint à lui et lui prit la main. Whitestick l'écarta doucement, et s'avançant vers la reine il mit un genou à terre et lui baisa le bout des doigts.

—Soyez le bienvenu, mon cher lord, dit la reine.

Whitestick salua.

—Il y a longtemps que vous ne nous ayez fait ce plaisir, milord. J'espère toutefois que vous n'avez pas à vous plaindre de nos procédés. Le prélat passa une main caressante dans la belle chevelure bouclée d'un adorable enfant de quatre ans, fils aîné de la reine, qui jouait avec les anneaux de sa mère. Alors, tout en glissant dans la main du petit un papier de dragées, il répondit avec un flegme aussi parfait que s'il eût parlé aux sieurs Prug ou Blubbs:

—Madame, le moindre de vos serviteurs n'a jamais osé penser que sa présence pût être en quelque sorte agréable à son aimable souveraine. Autrement il se serait chaque matin empressé de se mettre à ses pieds.

—Eh bien! mylord, et la mission Irlandaise?

—Nous avons deux cents catholiques de convertis, madame.

—Ah! c'est bien, dit la reine. Puis elle se remit à babiller avec son enfant.

—Bonjour, mon ami Bright, fit Whitestick en se retournant. Ah ça, il parait donc décidément que nous nous réconcilions avec l'église de nos pères.

—Je suis anglais loyal, sir Whitestick, répondit l'orateur d'un ton sec.

—J'en suis ravi, sir Bright. La loyauté, c'est comme l'écusson d'un négociant.

—Monsieur, dit Bright fièrement, je suis gentilhomme de vieille roche.[8]

—Ah!

—Les Bright combattaient sous Macheath la tyrannie de Henri huit.

[*p. 22* (A)]—Ce qui n'empêche pas que leur fils ne vende de coton à très-bon marché.

—Mylord, je vends aussi le fer.

—Tiens! tiens! fit le prélat d'un ton passablement impertinent.

—Monsieur, mes ancêtres combattaient sous Clarendon et Strafford pour la cause de Dieu et du peuple-roi. Rien en moi que je sache n'a taché ce nom respectable.

Hé! mon cher, qui vous dit que le commerce soit une tache? Vous lavez du linge blanc. C'est perdre votre savon.

—Monsieur! fit Bright écumant. Ce sarcasme ne mordait que sur lui seul attendu que sa mère avait été blanchisseuse.

—Mais, mon cher M. Bright, ne vous échauffez pas, je suis prêtre.

—Et damn! quand vous seriez pape!

—Messieurs, messieurs! fit le prince Albert.

—Mylords, dit la reine, en se retournant pour la première fois, si cette conduite inqualifiable ne tire pas à sa fin, vous coucherez tous deux à la tour de Londres.

—Veuillez agréer mes excuses, sir Bright, dit Whitestick.

—Monsieur l'évêque! fit le grand quakre d'un ton ému . . . .

—Et un handshake assez cordial termina cette scène un peu inconvenante. Alors le prince prenant M. Whitestick par le bras le tira à l'écart et entama à voix basse la conversation suivante.

—Eh bien! mon cher, et les socialistes chrétiens?

—Ils sont à nous, sire.

—Très bien! Et les pusséites?

—Sire, j'ai sur moi les signatures des chefs de ce parti. Seulement, vous donnerez au comte Ashley le titre de duc, vous ferez une gratification de 20,000 livres sterling au maire d'Oxford, vous ferez baronet et paire d'Angleterre notre révérend père M. de Canterbéry.

—Diable! diable! fit le prince en se mordant la moustache.

—Mais, sire, il faut payer pour avoir ces gens-là. Ce ne sont pas des niais. Enfin, que voulez-vous! il faut avoir avec nous tout le monde.

—On payera, M. l'évêque.

—Sire, on m'écrit des provinces du midi que le chartisme a [*p. 23 (A)*] gagné les soldats de garnison posés dans les petites villes. On brode des bannières ayant pour devise ces trois mots, 'la liberté, le prince, la charte.' L'Irlande, vous le savez, sire, nous assure son appui.

—Hum! hum! fit le prince Albert.

—D'un mot, sire, nous faisons tomber la tête d'O'Connell.[9] Il est maintenant tout à nous; en se dégageant du parti solidaire, il se perd.

—Vous êtes un homme impayable, M. Whitestick.

—Sire, Votre Majesté me flatte.

—Allons donc!

—Et les aldermen, sire?

—Oh! les aldermen! regardez dans ma poche. Cela donnerait son âme pour un penny de plus ou de moins. Cette espèce me rebute, vraiment.

—Sire, défiez-vous de la bourgeoisie.

—Eh mon Dieu! je les attends: qu'ils s'avisent après de grouiller! On leur remettra les menottes.

—Bien, sire! À propos, après le coup fait, je vous demanderai la permission de faire destituer le vieux Prug. C'est usé.

—Comme vous voudrez, mon ami: mais pour Dieu! assez de politique comme ça. Parlons un peu plaisir.

—C'est à dire que Sa Majesté me congédie?

—Mais non, mais non. Restez, godam!

—Sire, le temps presse. Veuillez remettre à la reine mes excuses sincères. Les deux complices échangèrent un sourire plein de sombres réticences, de nuances perfides, et se séparèrent. Le prince prit la belle main de lady Cobden[10] et l'entraina dans le tourbillon de la valse. Le prélat se glissa par les antichambres en saluant seulement de la tête ses chiens empressés, sans accorder même l'aumône d'un sourire aux regards provocateurs des jolies comtesses, et parvint au bas de l'escalier. Là veillait un petit jockey à l'œil vif, ficelé dans un étroit habit galonné, à la livrée Whitestick.

[*p. 24* (A)]—Viens ici, Spanks, dit le prélat, arrivé sur le perron. Puis se penchant vers l'enfant il lui souffla ces mots à l'oreille. —Tu n'as pas perdu de vue notre policeman chartiste?

—Non, mylord.

—Bien. Tu retourneras chez lui dans quelques jours. En attendant, va chez sir Jenkins, à Pimlico: fais-lui remettre en mon nom ce petit flacon. C'est de l'opium: aussi tu n'y toucheras point. Tu ne comprends rien, soit; il comprendra, lui. Alors tu te tiendras à l'écart, pour le veiller soigneusement; quand il sortira, tu le suivras. Il ira sans doute vers le Soho; tu auras soin de ne jamais le perdre de vue. Quand il rentrera chez lui, viens m'avertir. Après, si j'eusse à quitter Londres, tu sais ce qu'il faut faire. À la garde de Dieu, mon petit!

V. Le peuple chez lui.

Assez longtemps nous avons pataugé à travers les fanges amoncelées du grand monde. Reposons-nous un peu en contemplant l'asile chaste et frémissant, azuré par un coup d'œil de Dieu, irisé par un reflet du paradis, où s'abrite en souriant la pauvreté vierge et dévouée, ayant à sa droite l'amour de la patrie universelle, à sa gauche l'amour du foyer paternel—Williams Hervey, figure que nous avons vu flamboyer un instant sur le seuil de cette histoire pareil à l'archange en colère sur le seuil d'Éden, et que depuis nous avons perdu de vue—Williams Hervey, génie lumineux et sévère, enfant du peuple qu'il aimait, qu'il instruisait, qu'il soutenait de toutes ses forces—Williams Hervey, policeman et orateur populaire, jouissait en paix d'une petite propriété dans Suothwark, quand la voix de ses frères affamés, quand le son de la trompette ressaisie par l'Irlande meurtrie, était venu l'arracher à ce doux repos de corps et d'âme. Cet homme qui aurait pu vivre toujours dans une oisiveté humble et tranquille sentit alors bouillir dans sa poitrine les flots de la colère, monter à son cerveau les ardeurs de la pensée. Il se fit policeman [*p. 25* (A)] afin de pouvoir à tout instant venir à l'aide du peuple qu'on opprimait, enseigner ce peuple qu'il vénérait. Par son moyen le culte libéral s'était propagé en mille endroits où sans lui n'aurait jamais pénétré la lumière de l'idée puissante et douce. Tout en réprimant les turbulences populaires, il avait soin de faire toujours peser le coup de son autorité, le poids de son blugdeon officiel, sur les têtes des gentlemen qui s'y mêlaient en raillant ce bon peuple stupide. Aussi les jeunes aristocrates tapageurs, les eccentrics de Paddington et de Blackfriars, connaissaient-ils bien ce poignet ferme, cette arme redoutable, et s'empressaient-ils de fuir à son aspect. La fille de ce lion, c'était naturellement une colombe. La blanche Nelli était l'idole d'un faubourg entier. Plusieurs lords avai[en]t essayé de la séduire; Hervey leur avait cravaché la figure et les avait jetés dehors. Nelli avait à cette époque dix-huit ans. Pâle, svelte, gracieuse comme un lis, elle faisait néanmoins en marchant ondoyer la souplesse de ses hanches arrondies avec la volupté la plus virginale du monde. Dans sa prunelle d'azur doré l'amour se noyait dans la rêverie. Son cou délicat avait une cambrure de reine; sa jambe parfaite avait une grâce de paysanne. Un teint rose et douteux[11] éclatait à peine sur sa belle joue charmante.

Ce soir elle brodait assise aux pieds de son père qui prenait le thé, son blugdeon sur les genoux. Une larme bien douce brillait au bord de son cil noir. Elle venait de s'entretenir avec le seul être qu'elle aimait au monde, du seul être qu'elle connaissait au paradis. La défunte mistriss Hervey avait été une femme sainte, chaste comme épouse, noble comme mère, éclairée comme esprit.

—Mais où donc s'est-il égaré, ce gamin de Joë? dit après un instant Hervey, tout en posant la tasse dont il venait d'effleurer le bord de sa lèvre.

[*p. 26* (A)]—Pauvre petit! soupira la douce Nelli.

—Croit-il qu'on s'amuse à ramasser comme ça les orphelins du hasard pour l'amour de leurs cheveux couleur carotte? Ma fille, ouvrier ou noble, tout homme doit travailler. Celui qui essaie de se soustraire à cette loi, c'est un voleur, c'est un lâche. J'ai recueilli par amour du prochain ce moutard qui grelottait dans les ruisseaux de cette Babylone fangeuse, mais je n'ai pas voulu l'élever dans l'oisiveté. Etre sorti deux jours de la maison, c'est un dérèglement. Tout le poids de notre modeste ménage vient de retomber à l'improviste sur les épaules fatiguées de cette pauvre vieille Deb. C'est mal. Je n'aurais pas cru cela de ce petit fainéant à poils roux.

—Songe donc que c'est un enfant, mon père, et un enfant des rues. Meurtri depuis le berceau par le talon des grands, repoussé, conspué, au nom de l'ordre social, il ne peut pas encore s'arracher aux tristes habitudes d'une vie vagabonde. Il faut bien commencer par lui pardonner ces quelques écarts. Après, il se formera à l'ordre, aux douceurs d'une vie d'aisance honnête. Tu verras à son retour comme je le morigénerai. Pauvre enfant! Il nous aime tant!

Le policeman baisa le front sans tache de sa pudique enfant, et lui répondit d'un ton grave et doux.

—C'est beau ce que tu dis là, et cela peut être vrai. Mais j'ai du reste mes soupçons à cet endroit. On m'assure qu'un enfant du même âge, d'une figure toute pareille, est allé dernièrement roder à l'entour d'une maison que tout honnête homme sorti du peuple doit éviter comme une peste, comme une lèpre—d'une maison infecte, maudite, impure, damnée, repaire où se chauffe le vice, tanière où s'abrite le crime—de Lambeth-Palace, enfin!

[*p. 27* (A)]—Oh mon Dieu! fit la jeune fille en frémissant. Une vive rougeur colora aussitôt ses joues de nacre.

—Tu vois, ma fille, que c'est grave. Le bon Irlandais O'Swocks, que tu connais, affirme aussi avoir reconnu dans un petit laquais galonné qui montait derrière la voiture de Sa Grandeur M. Whitestick les traits de notre prétendu orphelin.

Or, s'allier en quelque sorte aux puissants de ce monde, c'est à mon avis une honte; se souiller les doigts du contact de leur or, c'est une trahison; mais qu'un fils du peuple se fasse laquais, qu'il endosse la livrée d'un riche,—et de quel riche, mon Dieu! d'un prêtre fourbe, d'un scélérat doucereux, d'un Judas souriant, d'un démocrate à bas de soie et à manches de dentelle, d'un assassin mielleux qui caresse et qui poignarde, de M. Whitestick, enfin!— c'est un opprobre si affreux, c'est une lâcheté si inqualifiable, c'est une infamie si effrayante, que le sang me bout rien que d'y songer. Oh! ma fille chérie, Dieu garde tout bon citoyen de toucher à la main de cette homme! c'est un poison qui marche, c'est une contagion qui parle. Il embrasse, il étouffe dans les replis de sa pensée tortueuse, dans les anneaux de sa politique de vipère, les imbéciles qui se laissent prendre à ses belles couleurs, à sa parole chatoyante et dorée. Passe encore pour l'ennemi brutal, pour l'insolent insoucieux, pour un faquin de vieille souche comme ce misérable Jenkins: mais un prêtre! c'est plus et c'est moins qu'un roi, c'est pis et c'est mieux qu'un homme.

Le policeman essuya du revers de sa forte main la sueur qui coulait de son front. Puis il reprit, en attirant sur ses genoux Nelli toute palpitante.

—Ecoute, mon enfant, je vais te raconter une chose qui s'est passé—oh! il y a de cela bien des années. Tu n'étais pas née alors. Ta mère avait une sœur, belle comme le matin, chaste comme la rosée. On l'appelait la belle Bab. Elle gagnait à broder [*p. 28* (A)] de quoi s'assurer une aisance humble et pure. Un jour un passant la vit sortir: il la suivit. C'était sir Whitestick. Ce Judas n'était alors qu'un pauvre curé aux habits râpés, aux bottes éculées, à la soutane tachée, au linge graisseux. Cependant toute la puissance du génie, toutes les ardeurs de la débauche, fermentaient déjà dans ce cerveau profond, dans ce cœur sans pitié. Il voulut la séduire; elle le repoussa, en le menaçant de le faire citer devant la cour des aldermen. Cet homme s'inclina et sortit de sa mansarde où il s'était glissé sous l'habit d'un facteur qui lui apporterait des lettres. Deux jours après, tout le faubourg tressaillait de douleur, la belle Bab avait disparu.

—Ciel! dit Nelli avec un sentiment d'effroi profond.

—C'est hideux, n'est-ce pas, ma pauvre enfant? Et bien! nous eûmes bientôt de ces nouvelles et quinze jours de cela, on retira son cadavre presque méconnaissable des eaux de la Tamise.

—Oh! mon Dieu! mon Dieu!

—On fit des recherches. Un homme soldé par Whitestick déclara la reconnaître pour une drôlesse ivre qu'il avait vue dans le Strand suspendue aux bras d'un coupeur de bourses. Un chiffonnier jura qu'il l'avait vu courir comme une forcenée vers le pont de Londres, prenant les rues Tottenham et Audley. Personne ne doute plus qu'elle ne se fût suicidé. Eh bien! un chirurgien fit ouvrir son corps: il reconnut dans l'estomac les traces d'une drogue puissante, d'un philtre amoureux qui corrompt le sang, qui entraîne la fièvre, la folie, la mort.

—Grâce, mon père! grâce! fit Nelli qui étouffait.

—Cet homme avait mêlé un philtre à sa boisson; il l'avait enlevé toute engourdie du sommeil pesant que le philtre avait versé sur ses paupières: il avait lâchement, honteusement mis à profit l'accablement de la chaste victime. [*p. 29* (A)] Il l'avait violé: puis sans nul doute à son réveil il l'avait chassé de chez lui à coups de pieds. Alors, mourante, désespérée, souillée, assassinée, elle s'est trainée vers la rivière, elle s'est précipitée dans son abîme fangeux, pour s'abriter contre le mépris affreux des hommes ou contre leur amour plus affreux. Violà l'histoire de la belle Babby Prawns.

—Et cet homme vit encore! On ne l'a pas envoyé pourrir sur les pontons!

—Que pouvions-nous faire? pas de preuves, pas d'intérêts, pas d'argent. Tu vois maintenant que si en effet quelqu'un que j'appelais mon ami se serait fait laquais de M. Whitestick—oh! je ne peux dire ce que je lui ferais, à cet homme. Mais je suis fou! le souvenir de ce prêtre m'a monté la tête.

Il déposa un dernier baiser sur les blonds cheveux de sa fille et se leva.

—Où donc vas-tu, bon père?

Il y a réunion pour ce soir des amis du peuple. O'Swocks, le représentant de l'Irlande, y doit apporter les noms des irlandais fidèles. Moi, je parlerai pour Londres: j'expliquerai la position actuelle; je remuerai les âmes, je sonderai les poitrines, je fouillerai dans les idées. Ce sera une belle et magnifique chose que de voir se réunir toutes les douleurs, toutes les aspirations, tous les patriotismes. Ah! mon enfant, c'est pourtant une lourde responsabilité que la mienne! je dois prendre en main tous ces hommes, enseigner toutes ces souffrances, mener à bien toutes ces passions! —Il s'arrêta et poussa un soupir: puis relevant le front, il sortit sombre, silencieux, auguste.

La jeune fille restée seule se laissa aller à un rêve d'amour qui teignait de rose sa figure moite que mouillait de pleurs son œil baissé. Quelle souffrance altérait ce doux visage? quel regret mordait ce cœur virginal? [*p. 30* (A)] Etait-ce un désir? Etait-ce un remords qui éclatait dans ce sanglot brisé?

Un bruit subit la fit frissonner. Elle leva les yeux et vit entrer une figure bien connue—la figure du patricien insolent et stupide qui depuis longtemps la poursuivait tout doucement de son amour hypocrite et sournois—de sir Thompson Jenkins esquire.

VI. Le verre d'eau de M. Whitestick.[12]

Les mains du baronet tremblaient et son œil fiévreux rayonnait d'un éclair douteux mais effrayant.

Nelli se détourna avec un frisson de dégoût comprimé, car cet homme suait l'ivresse et la luxure: elle appela la vieille Deb.

—Oh! miss, dit sir Jenkins, ne vous égosillez pas à crier, on ne répondra point. Savez-vous que c'est un trésor que Deb—oui godam, un vrai trésor, une ménagère modèle? Aussi vous l'ai-je soufflé ce trésor—cette chère Deb est maintenant établie chez moi; elle dirige l'économie internelle de Jenkins-House.

—Monsieur!

—Que Dieu me foudroie si je mens! je viens de l'y installer.

—Mon Dieu!

—Vous voilà seule avec moi. N'ayez pas peur, je suis bon diable. Mais ne vous mettez pas à crier, à faire du vacarme. Votre père est à une bonne lieue d'ici, il harangue sur la morale humaine et l'évangile social deux cents coquins pris de gin: occupation apostolique qui me procure le plaisir de vous dire que vous êtes véritablement la plus jolie et la plus effrontée petite coquine que je connaisse. Là, là, ma colombe, là, ma fille, ne nous effarouchons pas.

—Sortez, monsieur!

—Que Dieu me damne si je bouge!

[*p. 31* (A)]—Vous êtes un misérable! Laissez-moi!

—Oh! la farouche! oh! la mijaurée. Allons, baise-moi, méchante.

—Lâchez-moi, malheureux!

Sir Jenkins lui prit la taille en riant à gorge déployée.

—Là, viens sur mon cœur, pauvre chérie, dit-il en l'attirant dans ses bras. N'aie pas peur, personne n'entrera. Conviens qu'on ne saurait être mieux que cela. Damn! le gentil pied! devil! la jolie jambe! Cela doit avoir un genou rond, joli, satiné—Tiens! décidément tu as le diable au corps! veux-tu bien te tenir tranquille?

—Oh! misérable! à l'aide!

—Godam, quelle vertu! Feu Lucrèce n'était qu'une éhontée auprès de toi. Pourtant, faut bien être raisonnable, ma pouponne. On ne gagne rien à se tordre les bras. Oh! que c'est mal de meurtrir à coups de pieds les jambes du plus tendre des amants. Aussi n'est-on pas plus respectueux et dévoué que ce pauvre Jenkins. Mais tu veux donc me faire enrager? Ah! je ferais des choses affreuses!

Tout en proférant ces gracieusetés, le digne baronet couvrait de baisers les épaules pantelantes de Nelli en pleurs, qui se débattait dans l'étau de fer de ses mains crispées, et dont la voix étranglée ne devint bientôt qu'un râle.

—Allons, allons, cela marche, dit le Céladon ventru. Heureusement que le jour baisse. Cette petite folle qui ne veut pas se laisser faire! Damn my two eyes! —l'adorable sein et la gorge laiteuse que voilà! Dire que l'on trouverait de ces choses-là chez le peuple! c'est vraiment mirifique, et cela convertirait des athées—s'il n'en faisait pas.

L'héroïque baronet poursuivait ses recherches philosophiques en anatomie vivante lorsque Nelli, écrasée, étouffée, s'évanouit tout à fait. Alors sir Jenkins prit un verre, le remplit d'eau pure, [*p. 32* (A)] y versa le contenu du petit flacon que lui avait remis une main fidèle, et le fit boire à la jeune fille accablée.

Alors une moiteur plus humide, une pâleur plus mortelle, se répandit sur ses traits, un ton bleuâtre voila les fraîcheurs de sa peau, elle s'affaissa lourdement, les yeux chargés de sommeil, la paupière cerclée de bistre.

Sir Jenkins la prit dans ses bras en ricanant, l'enveloppa d'un manteau, la porta sur l'escalier de la maison déserte. Ce petit bâtiment étroit, humble, obscur, n'était habité que du policeman et de sa fille.

À la porte stationnait une grande voiture armoriée.

Sir Jenkins se demanda s'il fallait conduire chez lui sa victime, ou la transporter dans un cottage qu'il louait à Billingsgate, endroit propre aux amours cachés.

Il ne voulut pas que quelqu'un pût y voir stationner une voiture qui porterait le blason des Jenkins.

Il se décida donc pour le premier parti.

Personne ne passait dans la petite rue, triste et silencieuse.

D'un pas rapide il transporta sur les coussins moelleux du carrosse son fardeau soigneusement empaqueté et cria au cocher d'une voix de maître;

—Chez nous!

La voiture se mit en motion. Alors un enfant de douze ans,

couvert à peine d'une méchante souquenille immonde et trouée, se leva d'une borne où il était assis et se mit à la suivre en courant.

Cet enfant, Hervey l'appelait Joe, Whitestick l'appelait Spanks.

Tous les deux avaient raison, il se nommait effectivement Joe Spanks.

[Ce qui peut se passer dans un cab-safety][13]

[*p. 33* (B)] Une vieille femme affreusement maigrie, désséchée par la faim, rongée par le besoin et les veilles, fendit la foule et se précipita aux genoux de l'évêque. Ce cri sortait rauquement de sa poitrine haletante;

—O notre John! soyez béni! Puis elle alla rouler aux pieds des assistants. On la releva. La pauvre femme était morte. Cette suprême bénédiction s'était envolée de ses lèvres au même instant que l'âme qui avait vibré dans ce dernier souffle d'un séraphique amour, d'une sublime reconnaissance, était parti pour la rejoindre devant Dieu et y mêler sa chaste haleine.

L'évêque sut aussitôt profiter de cette sainte et consolante mort. La voix brisée et soupirante, il put néanmoins articuler ce peu de mots;

—Mes frères, vous nous accorderez à ma sœur et à moi quelque charrette, n'est-ce pas, pour nous conduire chez nous? Vous voyez si l'émotion la gagne.

En effet, Nelli, presque étouffée de honte et d'horreur, l'élan triste et sympathique qu'elle ressentait à cette vue, se pâmait dans les bras du démon qui en faisait pour ainsi dire sa complice dans cet effroyable et infernal forfait.

—Un cab-safety à M. l'évêque!

—Un cab-safety à John!

[*p. 34* (B)] Frémissante, elle hésita. Cette hésitation décida de son sort et du sort de son père. A cet instant un prolétaire s'approchant presque amoureusement de M. Whitestick lui dit;

—Mylord, veuillez vous remettre dans votre voiture. On se ferait hacher en morceaux plutôt que d'y laisser toucher.

—Non, non, mon cher frère, dit le prélat d'une voix étouffée par une émotion sourde. Le soleil de la fraternité ne s'est-il levé pour nous tous? Loin de moi ces galons de fripier que j'ai déjà maudit mille fois en songeant aux citoyens qui s'en allaient pieds nus par la boue glaciale! Au feu cet écusson que m'ont légué des hommes ennemis du peuple! A l'oubli ce nom que m'ont legué des tyrans! Jamais je ne me nommerai plus que John tout court. N'est-ce pas le nom du peuple?

—Vive John! s'écria la foule extasiée, éblouie en face de cette suprême vertu plus que civile!

Le prélat serra la main endurcie par l'honorable travail de l'ouvrier qui fondait en larmes. Les pleurs ruisselaient sur sa figure basanée. Whitestick lui même commençait à larmoyer. Alors ce ne furent plus des applaudissements, ce furent des cris, entrecoupés de spasmes, des sanglots, des hurlements d'enthousiasme.

[14]Le Prince Prolétaire.

Maintenant, récapitulons un peu l'histoire de ces jours terribles sur lesquels l'histoire contemporaine n'a pas encore dit son dernier mot. Ce fut à cette époque que le prince Albert, génie sombre et profond, cœur sec et sévère, conçut l'affreux projet de détourner à son profit l'élan républicain du peuple anglais si longtemps tristement comprimé.

Jusqu'alors, cet homme n'était que la chose de la reine, qu'une machine à lui faire faire des enfants. Or, cet homme voulut devenir le roi d'Angleterre. Pour se conquérir ce titre il s'appuya sur le peuple, peuple méconnu, peuple meurtri, peuple brisé.

La vieille aristocratie, inepte, chancelante, ridée, se mit à hurler et à glapir après lui de sa vieille voix cassée et stridente.

La bourgeoisie commerciale, la triste noblesse de Manchester, aiguisa pour le déchirer ses dents d'airain.

L'église anglicane vomit contre lui les plus sales injures. On fit pendre un curé;* l'église se tut.

Cependant le prince s'avançait, porté sur les épaules du peuple. Pensif, il se penchait sur l'avenir sanglant; [*p. 36* (C)] sa narine crispée humait déjà l'odeur de la guerre civile.

Il fut surnommé le prince prolétaire; titre magnifique et trompeur, qu'il a depuis effacé avec du sang.

Le 24 Avril 1847, cet homme envoya chercher le lord mayor. Le lord mayor s'appelait Tom Boggs. C'était un homme d'environ une cinquantaine d'années, maigre, voûté, l'œil louche, la voix mielleuse, le front plissé. Il se rendit à Buckingham house. On lui fit dire que le prince se trouvait dans un pavillon à lui, petit bâtiment obscur, placé à l'endroit où le Haymarket, écorné par la Tamise, débouche dans Charingcross vis-à-vis de la tour de Londres. Sir Clunk, valet particulier du prince, l'y introduisit. Alors, entre ces deux hommes il se passa une chose affreuse.

—Sir Boggs, dit le prince qui affectait déjà des façons de parler royales, nous vous connaissons pour un fidèle.

Le lord mayor baisa le pied du prince. C'est là un homage que l'Anglais refuse au pape, qui ne représente que Dieu, qu'il accord au roi constitutionnel, qui le représente, lui.

*Le révérend Swigs, pasteur de Bolbreth-sur-Wear.

—Je me charge de vous faire entrer au concile particulier. Fiez-vous-y. [*p. 37* (C)] Tu dois penser, mon cher, que je ne fais rien pour rien. Si, comme je l'espère, je peux te compter parmi mes amis—

—Oh! Altesse! fit le pauvre homme en chancelant.

—Va, nous nous connaissons tous deux. Tiens, Boggs, veux-tu que je te parle avec franchise? Nous sommes de vieux camarades, *my dear*. Eh bien! franchement, Boggs, est-ce que tu me trouves un homme bien heureux, bien puissant?

—Franchement, non, Altesse.

—Ni moi non plus. Je sens toujours renaître sur ma figure le soufflet de cette aristocratie orgueilleuse et brute, le crachat de cette église éhontée et rampante. Cela me fatigue. Tiens, vraiment, le sang me monte aux joues, me siffle dans les tempes, quand je songe que moi, prince de naissance, moi, mari de la reine d'Angleterre, je suis condamné à subir chaque jour quelque nouvel outrage sourd et haineux de ces hommes de clinquant, taillés, dans des bâtons de parade: cette petite noblesse découpée dans le tronc moisi d'une société qui déjà s'effeuille et dépérit mordue au cœur par la vétusté, brisée dans ses ramages par les premiers souffles de l'orage révolutionnaire. Non, décidément, Boggs, cela ne sera pas.

—Altesse, balbutia le lord mayor effrayé.

—Je t'ai pris pour un homme fort, mon pauvre Boggs. Ne me force pas à démentir cette idée que j'avais conçue sur toi.

[*p. 38* (C)]—Son Altesse viserait-elle par hasard à la régence? Ce serait d'un grand génie—il faudrait pour cela une hardiesse, une souplesse d'intrigue.

—Allons, dit le prince, je me serai trompé. Bonjour, M. Boggs. Vous êtes un honnête homme, gardez-vous de faire de la politique.

—Mais, Altesse, il n'existe pas d'homme plus dévoué, plus soumis.

—Monsieur, dit Albert, je veux des complices, non des esclaves.

—Altesse—en vérité—

—Ayez la bonté, sir Boggs, de m'envoyer M. Clunk; vous le rencontrerez en sortant d'ici. C'est un homme précieux que celui-là.

—Altesse, donnez-moi des ordres à remplir, montrez-moi quelque chose à faire! Mon Dieu! Mon Dieu! suis-je malheureux! Un serviteur si fidèle et si obséquieux! Le lord mayor suait à grosses gouttes et se tordait les mains.

—Ecoutez, sir Boggs. Je ne vise point à la régence. Ce serait pour moi un sentier trop épineux.

La figure du lord mayor s'épanouit comme une pivoine qui éclaterait en boutons. Il ouvrait une bouche vaste, pareille à celle d'une vache haletante de soif, et se pencha vers le prince en frémissant de tous ses membres.

—Je vise au trône.

Boggs faillit s'évanouir, il se maintint en s'accrochant des deux mains à la table où siégeait l'époux royal.

—Et vous me céderez les clefs de la tour de Londres, ajouta celui-ci en fixant sur Boggs accablé son regard chargé de sombres éclairs. Le lord mayor, magnétisé par ce regard puissant, lumineux,[15] sentit vibrer sous son effrayante lumière ses nerfs électrisés. Il tira les clefs de sa poche, et les déposa aux pieds du maître avec un gémissement.

—Bien, dit le prince. Maintenant, je vais vous mettre au courant de mes plans. Ecoutez bien, car ceci est sérieux. Premièrement, je soulève le peuple.

—Miséricorde! articula le lord mayor épouvanté.[16]

[*p. 39* (C)]—Majesté! fit Boggs ébranlé.

—Le ballot y pourviendra, dit Albert en souriant.

—Ah! je comprends.

—Pas encore. Je livre au peuple les vastes magasins de gin, de rum, de porter.

—C'est sublime!

—J'enivre cette canaille de liqueurs fortes, je fais mouvoir cette masse aveugle qui fourmille et se replie dans les bas-fonds de Lambeth, qui croupit dans les repaires de Grosvenor, qui croasse dans les marais de Bayswater.

—Godam! fit le lord mayor en pâlissant.

—Ce n'est rien. Tous ces marauds, toute cette horde débraillée, ivre, affamée, vêtue de haillons, rongée de vermine, que crois-tu que j'en fasse? Eh bien, Sir Boggs, j'en soufflette la royauté de l'Angleterre.

—Devil take it! fit Sir Boggs.

—J'en écrase l'aristocratie.

—Very good sir!

—Je m'en sers pour abîmer la bourgeoisie.

—Heah!

—Pour enfoncer l'église protestante.

—Bless you!

[*p. 40* (C)]¹⁷—Je fais tout cela, ou sinon—

—Sinon?

—Ou sinon, on me proclame roi à l'instant; ce que du reste je ne crois pas qu'on fasse.

—Altesse, vous êtes un grand homme!

—Je veux l'être.

—Ne se pourrait-il pas que cela se fît sans le sang répandre?

—Je ne sais pas. Mais, avec ou sans, je trônerai.

—Vous êtes un grand homme!

—Et vous, Boggs, vous siégerez dans mon concile particulier.

—Majesté, vous êtes un grand roi!

[18]Les écoliers britanniques.

Une belle matinée se levait sur les fraîches collines qui bordent la plaine jaunissante de Warminster. Les blés naissants ondulaient sous un vent humide, qui balayait doucement les nuages lents et vacillants éparpillés comme une troupe d'oiseaux farouches sur le bleu verdâtre d'un ciel printanier. Les boutons blanchissants, les fleurs teintes d'un rouge timide, des pommiers et des cérisiers, se balançaient à ce souffle plein de rosée et de parfums fugitifs. A peine un reste de vapeur jaunie souillait-il les bords du fleuve, masquait-il les contours des belles groupes d'osier, de saule, de bouleau, qui en frangeaient les rives sereines.

Toute cette douce nature apaisée riait sous un ciel dont l'azur, de plus en plus foncé, se colorait de nuances d'un pourpre chaud. Les feux du soleil brûlaient les touffes de bois embaumées et dorées où l'avril voltigeait d'une aile insouciante parmi les herbes, les feuilles, les fleurs des champs.

Une bande riante de jeunes garçons âgés de dix à seize ans se dirigeait vers le bord du fleuve. C'étaient les élèves du célèbre et révérend docteur Swutchin[19] ministre anglican. [*p. 42* (B)] Des vingt garçons qui en ce moment se dirigent vers les bords de la rivière, douze ont été fouettés hier. Ils en montraient bien les marques visibles sur leur peau. Les cicatrices, les sillons leur vergetaient de rouge les chairs du bas des reins jusqu'aux cuisses.

—Tiens, Frédéric, fit le premier d'entre eux, tu l'as eu serré. (Notez que ces enfants s'étaient dépouillés pour prendre un bain froid au fleuve.)

—Pour Dieu! n'y frappe donc pas; ça cuit encore.

—Ça cuit? Ohé! le beau coup!

—Ce damné cuistre de Swutchin!

—Hein? prends garde; ce serait à recommencer.

—Figure-toi qu'il m'a fait monter sur les épaules du gros Pierre, qu'il m'a ajusté de ses propres mains.

—Et puis Zou! Zah! flip! flap!

—A-t-il de culotte rouge ce Frédéric!

—Et de culotte rayée donc!

—Regarde, Arthur, ne vois-tu pas quelque chose là-bas, entre les saules et les bouleaux, de ce côté?

—Cela me vient encore parler de bouleaux!

—Pourquoi pas?

—Parle donc des verges tout de suite, petit nigaud!

[*p. 43* (B)]—Je comprends que cela te fasse frissoner.

—Tiens, tu dis que je frissonne?

—Comment donc!

—Sais-tu que je te ferai goûter de mes poings?

—Mon pauvre Arthur, on nous ferait goûter du fouet tous les deux.

—Goûte-moi donc de cela en attendant! fit le jeune flagellé en lui assenant un vigoureux coup de poing sur le nez.

Ce spectacle intéressant de deux grands garçons nus comme la main qui s'apprêtaient à se mouler la figure de coups fut malencontreusement interrompu: autrement en peu de temps les deux enfants auraient été tout noirs au devant, tout rouges au derrière ce qui aurait été un assemblage on ne peut plus joli de couleurs artificielles sur la chair humaine. C'est qu'un carrosse armorié venait de rouler sur le grand chemin. Par un élan de chasteté louable, les écoliers s'étaient blottis à l'eau. On voit que l'enfance anglaise est à la fois modeste et guerrière. Lycurgue l'aurait approuvé. Cependant la voiture s'était arrêté; une tête passait par la portière. Cette tête criait:

—Holà, mes enfants! holà!

[*p. 44* (B)] Quelques-uns des plus hardis et des moins prudes s'élancèrent hors du fleuve. On voyait reluire au soleil leurs beaux membres blancs et ruisselants, leurs corps sveltes et gracieux qui éclataient dans leur nudité de marbre antique. Deux enfants de treize ans, encore tout mouillés, n'ayant pour tout vêtement que le pantalon et la chemise ouverte sur la gorge ronde et ferme, se présentèrent. Ils reconnurent l'illustre évêque Whitestick, l'ami de leur maître, et surtout l'ami de mistress Swutchin. Il avait à son côté une femme demi-vêtue, à demi éveillée. C'était la fille de Williams Hervey.

—Mon garçon, dit l'évêque de sa voix tendre, veux-tu aller dire à ton maître que je l'attends ici?

—Yes, sir, fit l'enfant qu'on appelait Frédéric.

—Il serait pourtant bien que je t'accompagnasse, fit M. Whitestick d'un ton encore plus doux. Oui, c'est mieux.

Il descendit. Le cocher, espèce de quadrupède sur deux pattes, idiot abruti par le rum, qui conduisait machinalement la voiture de l'évêque, ne bougea pas. Il se serait maintenu tout roide sur son séant quand la terre se fût ouverte pour l'engloutir à deux pouces de ses chevaux.

[*p. 45* (B)]—Toi, dit l'évêque à l'autre enfant, qui n'était autre que le héros imberbe du pugilat ébauché, veille bien sur cette dame: sinon, mon jeune ami, je te traduis devant le docteur Swutchin, et ta peau lui en répondra.

M. Whitestick et Frédéric s'éloignèrent. Arthur restait sur la place, tout boudeur, presque furieux. Ce prêtre l'avait menacé: et ce prêtre n'était pas son maître à lui. Quand Swutchin le faisait châtier, Swutchin était dans son droit; Swutchin pouvait le fouetter jusqu'au sang en pleine salle de collège: du reste, cela lui arrivait assez souvent, à cet enfant mutiné, mais que cet homme, qu'un étranger le menaçât—L'écolier indocile en était là de ses méditations quand il sentit une main humide et frissonante, une main de femme, se cramponner au bras qu'il appuyait sur la portière. Il se retourna. La malheureuse Nelli, hagarde, l'œil égaré, les cheveux dénoués, eut à peine la force de lui crier:

—Sauvez-moi! faites-moi évader, pour l'amour de Dieu.

Arthur, la bouche entr'ouverte, la regardait avec de grands yeux bleus plein d'admiration et d'épouvante.

—Oh! tenez, tenez, fit Nelli en frémissant, ne voyez- [*p. 46* (B)] vous pas qu'il va revenir, cet homme maudit? ne voyez-vous pas que je suis perdue, et que je suis une pauvre créature qui ne fait du mal à personne? Pourquoi m'en ferait-on? Mon bon jeune monsieur, vous avez une mère, des sœurs, vous devez bien avoir pitié de moi! Oh! mais cet enfant ne me comprendrait pas! C'est affreux, mon Dieu! Il me laisserait assassiner, il verrait sur moi les mains abominables de cet homme d'enfer, qu'il n'y comprendrait rien! Mon père, mon père, sauvez-moi! Tenez, monsieur, je ne sais ce que je dis, mais, pour Dieu, ayez donc pitié de moi! Vous comprenez n'est-ce pas, qu'on me fait du mal? vous êtes jeune, beau, cela ne vous ferait pas plaisir, dites, que l'on me fît du mal? mais vous ne laisseriez pas maltraiter votre sœur, qui doit être belle comme vous êtes beau? Oh! mon Dieu, c'est que l'homme va revenir, secourez-moi donc! Oh! oh!

Elle gémissait, sanglotait, se tordait, pleurait, étreignait le bras d'Arthur; il n'avait jamais rien vu de si affreux et de si beau que le désespoir de cette femme.

—Madame, fit-il tout ébranlé, je ferai tout ce qui pourra vous plaire; mais ne pleurez donc pas! allons, je ne vous dénoncerai donc pas!

[*p. 47* (B)] Il la descendit du carrosse armorié et voulut la poser sur le gazon: mais elle se releva, se pencha sur lui, déposa un chaste baiser sur ses cheveux blonds et humides, et s'enfuit. Quand l'enfant, qui haletait et rougissait du plaisir de ce baiser qui lui électrisait la tête, regarda après elle, la blanche suppliante avait disparu. Quant au cocher, ce digne anglais n'avait pas sourcillé.

—Tiens, mon pauvre Arthur, lui dit une voix à l'oreille, tu seras joliment étrillé!

—Hé bien! fit Arthur en soupirant; l'on m'écorchera, qu'importe!

—Hein? il t'émouchera rudement le derrière!

—Si, dit Arthur tout rêveur.

Alors, apercevant Whitestick et Swutchin qui venaient vers eux d'un pas rapide, l'enfant marcha droit aux deux hommes et leur dit;

—Vous pouvez vous épargner la peine de courir, messieurs, la dame n'est plus ici.

—Où donc? fit Whitestick haletant.

—Elle est en sûreté, M. l'évêque.

—Veux-tu bien parler, méchant garnement! qu'en as-tu fait?

—Je l'ai aidé à s'évader.

[*p. 48* (B)] Comme nous allons voir, si le peuple bougeait, M. Whitestick pouvait aider à le faire massacrer. Comme nous allons aussi voir, si un écolier bougeait, M. Swutchin ne pouvait que le faire fouetter. C'est vrai qu'il fouettait bien. Mais qu'est-ce que c'est, à côté du gibet et de la corde, qu'une misérable cinquantaine de coups de verges vertement appliquées sur la chair nue d'un seul garçon? Qu'est-ce donc que de faire saigner la peau quand on pourrait faire tomber les têtes? Donc, chaque fois par jour que M. Swutchin fustigeait les parties charnues de quelque malheureux élève, il les fustigeait d'autant plus serré qu'il se sentait impuissant de lui faire couper le cou. Tous les pères, tous les oncles, tous les tuteurs de jeunes garçons un peu vifs, un peu mutins, disaient donc de M. le docteur Swutchin: C'est un homme impayable. Nous l'avons dit, le père ou le tuteur anglais aime à voir tout rayé, tout rouge de coups de fouet, le derrière de son fils ou de son pupille. C'est un caprice charmant de cette aimable nation. M. Swutchin fouettait donc en plein soleil de prospérité.

[20]L'époux de la reine.

Revenons maintenant au policeman, que nous avons laissé à la tête d'une foule rugissante qui se ruait vers Buckingham-Palace en débouchant de tous côtés. De Holborn, de Chelsea, du Haymarket, d'Oxford-street, ces vastes masses se dégorgeaient en face du vieux palais gothique. Il semblait que les figures des rois d'Angleterre sculptées sur la façade grisâtre avec cet art merveilleux, ce goût admirable du moyen âge, tremblaient et fléchissaient vis-à-vis de ce grand torrent populaire.

C'était affreux et c'était superbe.

Cependant les cours s'emplissaient d'hommes armés, l'air s'emplissait de hurlements, les cœurs des courtisans s'emplissaient d'épouvante.

Le ministère de lord Derby avait alors le dessus. Ce lord s'est toujours vanté de son influence auprès du peuple. Il a depuis réclamé sa part de l'honneur sanglant que se sont acquis ses collègues.

Eh bien, à ce premier jour d'alarme, on le cherchait pour qu'il pût parler à la foule, l'enivrer, la courber de son souffle puissant.

Ce lord s'était réfugié, dit-on, auprès de la reine. [*p. 50* (C)] C'est ce qu'ont affirmé les journaux anglais. Personne, même parmi ses ennemis les plus acharnés, même parmi les quakres, même parmi les tories, n'a jusqu'ici osé faire publier la vérité. Cette vérité, on l'a chuchoté, on l'a soufflé tout doucement à l'oreille, on l'a rapetissé, on l'a châtré, on l'a fait avorter, on l'a étouffé entre une huée et deux rires. Cette vérité, nous la publions aujourd'hui.

Ce lord s'était réfugié dans les cloaques. Là, tapi dans l'égout, là, blotti dans la vase, il attendait en frémissant les suites de cette émeute.

Revenons encore une fois au peuple. La foule commençait à appeler la reine à haute voix. On ne disait plus la reine; on disait Mistress Cobourg. La pauvre femme pleurait dans son cabinet. Douce et frêle créature, papillon éclos à la chaleur d'un soleil d'or, elle ne put comprendre que ce lion démuselé qu'on appelait le peuple lui en voulût à elle. Elle demandait aux courtisans effarés son mari, son soutien, son élu. Les ladies blanches et frissonnantes s'agitaient autour d'elle comme des flocons d'écume au vent. [*p. 51* (C)] Les lords s'arrachaient les favoris et juraient. Un pas rapide retentit dans les corridors. La reine poussa un cri. Trois ladies se jetèrent devant elle et lui firent un frêle rempart de leurs beaux corps.

Le prince Albert entra. Il portait l'habit complet d'un ouvrier journalier. Gros souliers, redingote longue et râpée, cravate blanche, ceinture de cuir brodé en pincebêche[21] que fermait un boucle d'airain. Il était grave et triomphant. Un sourire sévère voltigeait sur ses lèvres, crispait sa moustache menaçante. Il avait à la main un énorme bludgeon. Ce détail baroque avait pour lors une signification tragique. Aussi personne n'en rit.

—Madame, dit le prince d'une voix lente et hautaine, cela vous étonne de me voir ainsi habillé?

La reine, étouffée d'angoisse, muette et furieuse de sa peur, fit signe que oui.

—Madame, c'est vous qui m'avez mis cet habit sur le dos. Vous me traitez en laquais, je me fais prolétaire. Il me semble que c'est bien là un pas en avant. Qu'avez-vous à redire à cela? Oui, mylady Victoria, c'est vous, ce sont vos lords, ce sont vos paires, ce sont vos ladies, qui m'ont flétri de leur mépris, qui m'ont frappé [*p. 52* (C)] de leur sarcasme, qui m'ont voulu ravaler au niveau de leur froideur et de leur morgue. Je ne suis pour eux qu'un gentillâtre allemand, qu'un pleutre demi-couronné, qu'une souche de grande maison, qu'une rature faite par hasard dans le livre d'or de la noblesse anglaise? Eh bien, j'accepte ma position. Pardieu! Mylady, vous me mettez des armes à la main et vous vous flattez que je ne saurai point m'en servir? Perdez cet espoir. Je croupissais, fourmi, sous votre talon? eh bien! oiseau de proie, je plane sur votre tête.

—Mais enfin, mylord, fit la reine en sanglotant, que me voulez-vous donc? Mon Dieu! vous ne voudriez pas ma mort? Au nom de nos enfants dont vous ébranlez le berceau plein de gémissements, ayez pitié de leur mère.

—Votre mort, madame? mais vous êtes folle—oh! plus folle encore que vous ne l'étiez lorsque vos dédains vinrent me frapper au front. Votre mort, non; votre couronne, oui.

—Alors, monsieur, dit la reine en se levant avec une majesté qu'on ne lui avait jamais vu, prenez les deux ensemble.

—Hurrah! fit un lord qui pendant tout le discours du prince s'était mordu les poings de rage.

[*p. 53* (C)]—Madame, imposez donc silence à votre valetaille. Je le redis, je veux l'une de ces deux choses, je ne veux point l'autre.

—Accomodez-vous de cela. Seulement, hâtez-vous. Je représente ici le peuple anglais; la populace, la canaille, la crapule, les débris de la société. Cette canaille, madame, a le bras fort et peu de patience. Elle n'est point habituée à guetter une réponse qu'elle a mendié avec toutes les façons de la diplomatie britannique. En dix minutes je vais leur porter votre réponse. Songez-y.

—Albert! Albert! vous ne feriez pas cela!

—Je le ferai aussi vrai qu'il y a un Dieu au ciel. Arrangez-vous, madame, il faut y pourvoir.

—Saisissez cet homme, mylords! fit la reine en étendant le bras, avec un rugissement de colère.

—Arrière, laquais! dit l'Allemand en tirant de sa poitrine un pistolet tout chargé.

Les lords se reculèrent, gelés d'épouvante.

—C'est là votre réponse définitive, madame? Soit! j'en rendrai compte au peuple.

Il se retourna sur le seuil de l'appartement.

—Songez-y bien! lui cria-t-il: c'est la guerre!

Puis il sortit, faisant craquer le plancher sous ses pas puissants. La reine s'était évanouie.

[22]Un irlandais.

La lueur grise du matin baignait les brumes noircissantes des quais de la Tamise. C'était une aube terne et triste: Whitestick arrivait avec sa victime près de la maison des Swutchin: Hervey après une nuit de fatigues surhumaines ralliait sur la grande place du Wauxhall le peuple éparpillé en escadres par les rues, jeté pêle-mêle sur les squares. Il avait à sa droite un homme de taille élevée, dont l'œil plein de puissance et de dévouement ressemblait à celui d'un chien fidèle: il s'attachait au pas de son ami avec un respect, une dévotion admirables à voir.

Cet homme, c'était Patrick O'Swocks, le représentant de l'Irlande républicaine. Résumons en quelques mots l'histoire d'un cœur vaillant, d'un esprit religieux. Agé de douze ans, O'Swocks avait vu gémir sa mère catholique dans les bras d'un landlord protestant qui prélevait sur les belles femmes la moitié des rentes qu'il extorquait à la sueur de sang de leurs maris; il avait compté les râles sourds de son père agonisant sous les yeux du pasteur britannique qui lui refusait et le baume triste et consolant que verse sur le front pâli du moribond la main du prêtre compatissant, et les maigres patates cultivées à la sueur de son front; il avait écouté pendant deux ans entiers les pleurs de ce paysan privé et du pain du corps et du pain de l'âme; il avait senti tirailler ses entrailles par les doigts crochus de la faim aux joues bleues; il avait senti mordre son cœur par les dents aigües de la honte, s'épuiser son sang sous la pression du besoin abrutissant. Déchiré à coups de fouet par les gentlemen, meurtri à coups de poings par leurs fils, le malheureux avait grandi en sentant sur sa joue le soufflet perpétuel du pouvoir, dans son cerveau la fièvre constante d'une colère âpre et folle. Vigoureux garçon de seize ans, il avait su plaire à une grande dame anglaise, femme du bon propriétaire qui usait si largement de ses droits de seigneur, par la fraîcheur et l'éclat de ses belles joues rebondies, de sa bonne santé de paysan; leste, vermeil, découplé, il apparaissait comme un ange aux yeux de cette pauvre femme habituée à ne voir autour d'elle que les figures hâves et blanchies des jeunes anglais débauchés au corps grêle, à la voix sifflotante. Elle voulut acheter à prix d'or ce beau corps amoureux du jeune irlandais. Mais le pauvre Paddy aimait d'un amour fidèle; il avait pour maîtresse la plus belle fille de son canton, la blanche Norah, fille du vieux Fitz-Brown: l'amour brutal de lady

Chops effaroucha cette âme vierge et fière. Repoussée par [*p. 55* (A)] cet enfant, par une des choses de son mari, lady Chops livra le malheureux aux fureurs de ce fidèle époux. Elle l'accusa de vol et de tentatives par voies de fait sur une vieille suivante ridée, boiteuse, chauve et borgne, autrefois nourrice de milady. Ce mensonge échoua devant des preuves irrécusables. Alors lady Chops fit fouetter publiquement Paddy par ses domestiques; elle-même contempla de sa fenêtre ce spectacle obscène, si hideusement saugrenu, de son amant rétif livré au châtiment d'un écolier paresseux. Toute la maison Chops vint rire de ce misérable, qui, nu, dépouillé, rugissant, se débattait aux mains d'un groom herculéen, tandis que deux autres gaillards énormes labouraient de coups de verges sa chair sillonnée et rougissante. Deux jours après cet outrage inqualifiable Paddy cassa la tête au groom d'un coup de pistolet. Amené devant lord Chops, il avoua son fait, et demanda la mort à grands cris: la vie lui paraissait une flétrissure de plus. Seulement il voulut qu'on lui permît de prendre congé de Norah. Lord Chops éclata de rire, et fit entrer Norah magnifiquement vêtue à l'anglaise. Maîtresse du lord, cette fille n'avait plus un regard de pitié pour son amant outragé. Paddy tomba la face contre terre. Lord Chops le fit relever, et ayant fait sortir tout le monde il apprit en ricanant au jeune homme accablé qu'il était son fils à lui Chops, et que par conséquent il aurait la vie sauve pour l'amour de sa mère. Du reste, ajouta l'anglais, tu m'as pris la femme, mon bon, je te prends la maîtresse; épouse pour épouse, c'est assez raisonable, hein? J'ai toujours quelque chose à te pardonner, car lady Chops a été pour moi d'une humeur massacrante pendant trois jours. Tu me l'as gâtée, va! Voyez-vous, ce petit libertin! Tu tiens cela de bon papa, mon ami. Aussi je te pardonne pour l'amour des beaux souvenirs que tu me rappelles. Sais-tu que je pourrais toutefois te faire pendre comme incestueux? Mais j'ai pitié de toi, car je sais ce que c'est que le sang jeune. Ici lord Chops poussa un soupir gonflé de regrets: Va, mon gaillard, tu auras toujours la bénédiction paternelle. Quant à cette fille, si tu veux, je te la rendrai dans un mois. Autrefois j'aurais dit—dans un an, mais que veux-tu! on vieillit toujours un jour, mon pauvre O'Swocks. Va donc, petit, et surtout tâche de ne plus avoir rien à démêler avec lady Chops; c'est une femme forte que milady. Va-t-elle me faire des scènes à propos de toi! Adieu; songe à te ranger.

[*p. 56* (A)] Ce discours cynique glaça de dégoût le sang du jeune homme. Il put à peine se tenir sur ses pieds: il sortit en comprimant dans sa poitrine bouillante les rugissements de haine et de honte. Le lendemain, il agonisait dans l'étreinte d'une fièvre mortelle; grelottant sur la paille, il se battit corps à corps avec la mort pendant deux mois. Aussitôt relevé du fumier infect qui avait vu tordre ses membres dans l'étau de la douleur, il sortit à jamais de la chaumière de sa mère souillée. Lady Chops se consola près du ministre anglican.

Arrivé à Londres, le malheureux enfant de la douce Erin fut recueilli par la charité sainte et profonde de ses pareils. Williams Hervey prit pitié du misérable trainé par tous les ruisseaux de la Babylone anglaise. Il le reçut chez lui, l'éleva, le consola, lui enseigna les vastes devoirs de l'homme, le destin radieux de l'humanité. Pour la première fois ce grand mot chaleureux de fraternité vibrait aux entrailles du bâtard rejeté par ses frères, du triste avorton de l'ordre social. À partir de ce jour Paddy O'Swocks devint homme politique; il sentit sa valeur; il vit poindre à ses yeux l'aube de la liberté; il comprit tout ce qu'il avait à faire. Il étudia profondément les besoins de son époque; il pesa tous les partis, il sonda toutes les politiques; il se lia avec les chefs irlandais, avec ces grands hommes qui faisaient à cette époque frémir l'Angleterre jusque dans la moelle de ses os: il dépensa au profit de sa patrie toute la sève, tout la puissance de sa belle et noble jeunesse. Hélas! les amères déceptions qui l'atteignirent à ses premiers pas dans la vie avaient fermé à jamais son cœur aux tendres émotions, desséché dans sa poitrine fiévreuse les doux élans de l'amour. Pour lui, la femme du peuple, c'était toujours Norah Fitz-Brown, la femme noble, c'était Miss Peggy, baronne de Chops.

Cependant et à de rares moments cet homme de flamme et d'airain devenait homme de chair et de muscles: une rosée rafraîchissante désaltérait ses paupières humectées, une douce pensée déridait son front sombre, dépliait sa figure soucieuse. Ces pauvres bonheurs passagers, [*p. 57* (A)] il les devait à la belle fille du policeman, à la radieuse Nelli. On doit comprendre que dans ce jour de deuil l'aiguillon de deux haines, l'éperon de deux devoirs, lui mordait le cœur, lui déchirait le flanc. Jamais, même sous l'œil agaçant de lady Chops, même sous le fouet de son cynique époux, il n'avait senti bondir ses veines avec un si fiévreux élan.

Trahison.

En sortant du cabinet de sa femme évanouie, le prince Albèrt s'était remis à la tête du peuple qui l'attendait; il avait excité par un discours plein de feu, rapide, concis, énergique, un vrai speech de prolétaire, l'âme orageuse et facile à remuer de cette masse vacillante. Il leur avait promis à chacun son part de pain, son part de gouvernement; lui, le premier citoyen, il voulait, dit-il, rallier autour de lui tous les citoyens, pourvoir à tous les besoins d'âme, de corps, d'esprit. Enfin, il parla chaleureusement pendant une heure entière, il se posa en demi-dieu, il enivra les âmes, et puis—

Et puis?

Et puis, il enivra les corps. Il ne voulut point, le bon allemand, faire une révolution au profit de l'idée démocratique. Il n'oublia point, le digne père du peuple, ce que c'est que les appétits de la chair.

Il ordonna qu'on livrât au peuple les immenses magasins Alsopp-Barclay. Le peuple ébloui jeta les armes, fondit comme un essaim ivre sur les barils de bière.

Le prince Albert, tête forte, âme profondément cynique, avait calculé que cela donnerait le temps aux conseillers de la reine de peser ses offres, de songer aux moyens de salut. Ils accepteraient peut-être ces offres, il voudrait peut-être de ces moyens. Alors il se raillierait à eux; il serait régent, il tiendrait dans ses mains tout hors le seul titre de roi. Ce titre, il se le ferait accorder plus tard par le suffrage parlementaire. Alors aussi il supprimerait à l'instant même toute cette émeute qui sans lui allait devenir révolution. Il ferait tomber la tête à ses chefs, il ferait écrouer au bagne les plus forts parmi leurs sectateurs; il ferait pleuvoir sur ses fidèles l'or, le pouvoir, les dignités.

[*p. 58* (A)] Si le parti aristocrate qui masquait à cette époque la reine impuissante, écrasée, s'obstinait toujours à repousser la main qu'il leur étendait, alors seulement il lacherait contre eux toute la puissance du parti démocrate.

Alors les hommes tels que Hervey, tels que Paddy O'Swocks, pourraient se frotter à cette aristocratie qui les avait brisés sous son talon. Le profit de cette guerre de titans reviendrait toujours à lui: il tiendrait toujours dans le creux de sa main la palme sanglante de ces énormes combats.

On le voit, il y avait loin de cela aux projets paisibles de 1851.

En 1851, ce tigre était devenu mouton, il broutait paisiblement parmi les hautes herbes du Hyde's-Park.

En 1847, quelques mois avant l'énorme écroulement de trônes qui remua l'Europe entière, lui portait déjà dans sa tête courbée le vaste fourmillement des idées politiques qui devaient changer la face de l'Angleterre.

Un seul homme avait sondé ce cœur corrompu, avait jugé cette âme ténébreuse, cet homme, c'était John Whitestick. L'intelligence froide, avide, inexorable du grand évêque lui suffit pour mesurer de toute sa largeur, de toute sa hauteur, celle du prince sombre et patient. Aussi Whitestick avait-il usé au profit de son maître de toutes les ressources de son immense volonté, de sa puissance d'intrigue. Il va sans dire qu'il se réservait au besoin la liberté de comploter à son tour contre le prince Albert, au cas où celui-ci deviendrait par trop révolutionnaire. Whitestick, nous croyons l'avoir dit, ne voulait point que l'on entamât les droits de l'église, les propriétés de ses chefs. Aussi se préparait-il maintenant à les raffermir.

A douze heures du matin, Whitestick se mit en route pour Londres accompagné de la malheureuse qui lui avait un instant échappé. À deux heures, il entrait chez soi, il retirait du cab-safety le corps meurtri de la jeune fille échevelée. À trois heures, il avait rejoint devant la grande porte du palais le prince Albert, qui, rongé d'un souci vague, contemplait l'œil dédaigneux, la lèvre recourbée, les ébats de la foule enivrée qui venait de le saluer roi.

Le prince et l'évêque échangèrent quelques mots. Whitestick s'avança vers les sentinelles du palais, et leur donna le mot d'ordre. On le fit entrer chez [*p. 59* (A)] la reine accompagné de M. Brigth, de lord Palmerston et de quelques autres des amis du prince.

Cependant O'Swocks et Hervey après vingt-quatre heures d'un affreux travail, étaient parvenus à ranger en ligne droite le bataillon rassemblé des quatre coins de Londres. Deux fois repoussée, deux fois victorieuse, cette armée de citoyens emplissait les rues du Wauxhall jusqu'au Haymarket. À peine une goutte de sang avait-elle taché la robe blanche, souillé la cause sainte du peuple. C'eût été une belle chose que cette révolution toute paisible, toute morale, écrasant des hauteurs de sa pensée la calomnie acérée comme elle écrasait du revers de son talon la force brutale. Tout était si bien combiné pour cela!

Hélas! on avait compté sans deux choses: la trahison et le hasard.

Hervey s'était effectivement toujours défié et du prince et du lord mayor; mais la plupart de ses concitoyens se trouvait ébloui par ces mots sonores. Des princes, des lords maires qui prêchaient, qui pratiquaient les règles de l'égalité humaine! La belle chose que cela!

La moitié du bataillon républicain était composée d'irlandais. Il va sans dire que ceux-là avaient su résister et à l'éclat du parti du prince et aux tentations funestes des magasins de bière. Ceux-là, c'étaient des hommes forts, des cœurs sains, dignes de comprendre la liberté. Il y a toujours quelque chose du stoïcien antique chez le fils de la verte Erin. Des siècles d'esclavage, qui n'ont point amorti en lui l'amour de la patrie, ont donné à son tempérament bouillant le caractère du fer éprouvé.

Ah! quand viendra le jour si longtemps attendu de son émancipation, cette belle Irlande aura un noble rôle à remplir devant les peuples!

Et ce jour arrivera, l'Angleterre expiera tout le sang versé, toutes les vies épuisées au profit de son despotisme. Ah! ne doutons pas de Dieu; ce jour arrivera.

Williams, nous l'avons dit, était entouré de ces irlandais fidèles, bras vaillants, esprits éclairés, cœurs sobres et fermes. La douleur, en ce moment d'attente, venait de retomber sur son front nuageux. Tout à coup, un cri jaillit de ses lèvres, sa figure devint livide. Il venait d'apercevoir une jeune fille aux vêtements déchirés, à l'œil hagard, qui se trainait lentement vers lui. La foule compatissante, et qui pressentait quelque chose de sombre, faisait place à cette malheureuse. Enfin, folle, égarée, elle vint tomber aux pieds du policeman.[23]

[*p. 60* (A)] Hervey traina par les poignets sa fille dans une chambre de l'auberge la plus prochaine. Là s'asseyant sur une chaise de paille à moitiée rompue, il lui prit les mains et dit: J'écoute.

—Mon bon père! fit la malheureuse d'une voix brisée, rauque, étouffée de pleurs. Mon pauvre père, si bon, si doux!

Les larmes lui serraient la gorge; sa paupière rouge et flétrie battait sur une prunelle terne et décolorée par la souffrance. Elle était affreuse à voir.

—Ce qu'on t'a fait, pauvre enfant, je le sais, dit Williams. Maintenant il me reste à apprendre le nom de l'infâme.

Nelli se tordit de douleur. Une convulsion affreuse semblait prête à briser les articulations de ses membres. Williams échauffa de baisers ses mains amaigries, ses lèvres blanchies. —C'est pour l'amour de moi que je te le demande, mon ange adoré, dit-il, les larmes aux yeux.

—Non! non! c'est trop affreux! c'est effroyable à dire!

—Mon Dieu! mon Dieu! sanglota le policeman.

—Je ne pourrai jamais proférer ce nom! Tenez, tuez-moi plutôt, mon père bien-aimé. Un baiser, et la mort.

—Il est donc de ces douleurs! fit Hervey d'un air égaré.

—Eh bien! c'est—

—Mais parle donc! Songe que tu me déchires le cœur! que chacune de tes paroles c'est comme la morsure brûlante du fer dans la plaie! Mon Dieu! faites-la parler.

—C'est John Whitestick, évêque de Londres!

Un blasphème effroyable ébranla les poutres du taudis où s'était assis le malheureux policeman. La rage de sa douleur venait d'arracher Dieu de ce cœur profondément chrétien.

—Mais c'est impossible! Elle est folle! Il nous manquait cela! Oh! j'en maudirais le ciel!

[*p. 61* (A)]—Hélas, Dieu a vu cela, il l'a souffert!

—Donc, Dieu n'est pas! hurla le policeman.

—O mon père! l'enfer s'est mêlé de tout ceci. Cet homme m'a enivré d'opium, il m'a accablé de coups, il m'a tué—

—Damnation sur lui! vociféra Williams Hervey. Oh! si je pouvais enfoncer ma main dans sa poitrine, en tirer son damné cœur, le broyer entre mes dents!

—Le peuple m'aurait sauvé, il leur a dit qu'il était leur ami, leur père à tous—il a fait profession de foi républicaine.

—Enfer! grinça le policeman. Il était épouvantable et beau de colère: le sang lui emplissait la figure.

—Il a dit—mon Dieu! il a juré que j'étais . . . sa sœur!

—Malédiction! Et tu l'as laissé dire?

—Mon père, c'est un Satan que ce prêtre. J'étais écrasée, abrutie de peur. Je l'aurais démenti que l'on ne m'eût pas même écouté. De plus il a menacé de vous perdre, vous! Plaignez-moi, mon père! J'étais maudite. Voyez-vous cela devait être ainsi. Et puis il y a toujours la mort. Oh! mon Dieu! ai-je assez souffert! Tenez, mon cœur se brise, je crois que je vais mourir.

—Quel homme! quel homme!

—C'est un démon. Il y avait aussi une femme, une femme affreuse.

—Dire qu'on est taillé comme cela! Tu as raison, il faut que l'enfer s'en mêle. Dieu ne fait pas de tels hommes.

—Oh! j'ai peur! fit la pauvre petite en frémissant.

—Remets-toi, ma fille chérie. Vierge devant Dieu, relève la tête devant les hommes! A lui la honte! à lui la mort! Tu vivras honorée, sainte, respectable!

—Ah! tu me fais du bien! Comme c'est étrange de se sentir [*p. 62* (A)] au cœur un peu de cette bonne chaleur! Cher père! va, je vivrai pour te soigner. Mais tu me vengeras?

—Par le Dieu qui m'entend! fit le policeman en levant vers le ciel son poing droit fermé.

—Non! non! pas de sang! pas du talion! Pardonne-lui! C'est la loi, c'est la règle. Dis que tu lui pardonnes! Dieu te sourira de son paradis. Faites cela, mon père!

—Tu es folle, malheureuse! Puisse la foudre m'écraser si je pardonne à ce misérable! Comment! il t'a ravi ton chaste voile de jeune fille, il t'a jeté dans sa fange, il t'a meurtri de ses coups et de ses baisers, il t'a trainé par les ruisseaux, toi, ma fille, ma blanche et chaste enfant, toi dont le front présentait l'auréole à demi éclose, dont les ailes semblaient déjà pousser pour te remporter dans l'azur —en un mot, il t'a violé! Et tu veux que je lui pardonne!

La voix du policeman prit une nuance encore plus effrayante; d'un ton cassant il proféra cette lugubre parole;

—Tu l'aimes donc?

Nelli poussa un cri effrayant.

—Je l'aime, moi! Mon Dieu! Est-ce que les damnés ont de l'amour pour celui qui les a perdu? est-ce que la victime va s'amouracher du bourreau? Moi, j'aimerais ce Whitestick, ce monstre, cet évêque, ce démon fait de fange et de sang! Hélas! on me demande cela! A lui, mon amour! à lui, mes rêves de jeune fille! il a pris de force mon corps, et moi j'irais lui donner mon âme! Oh! tu le sais, mon Dieu! si c'est lui que j'aime!

—Tu as donc de l'amour pour quelqu'un? Hélas!

—Oh! oui, fit la jeune fille avec un admirable élan du cœur, j'aime, oui, j'ai toujours aimé!

[*p. 63* (A)]—Et qui donc? au nom de Dieu!

—Oh! ne le demandez jamais! je mourrais d'une honte nouvelle qui viendrait s'ajouter à l'ancienne!

—Mon Dieu!

—Écoute, mon père, j'étais folle. Supposons que j'ai aimé quelqu'un de plus haut que moi, qu'une pauvre enfant du peuple, et n'en parlons plus.

—Sache, mon enfant, qu'à l'heure qu'il est, une fille du peuple, chaste de cœur et d'esprit, vaut mieux, même aux yeux de la raison sociale, qu'une lady corrompue de cœur, vierge d'habits, tachée, souillée par le contact des mille impuretés qui fourmillent sous les dehors étincelants du grand monde. Parle donc librement.

—Il est marié!

—On brisera ces liens. L'amour, c'est désormais la seule loi.

—Eh bien! mon père, écoutez. Il y a deux ans de cela. Je brodais à la fenêtre de notre doux logis du Southwark. Une procession passa. Je vis briller parmi toutes ces têtes radieuses une figure mâle, et forte, avec de grandes moustaches, des lèvres serrées, des yeux noirs, profonds, lumineux. À son aspect je sentis se dilater [*p. 64* (A)] mon pauvre cœur de seize ans; une volupté humide assombrissait mes yeux penchés, baignait mes cils tremblants. Lorsque tout le monde eut passé, je demandai son nom. On me dit que c'était le prince Albert.

—Fatalité! murmura le policeman.

—Je tombai à la renverse. C'est alors, vous vous le rappelez, mon père, que je fus prise d'une maladie de langueur. Vous me soignâtes —mon Dieu! avec quelle adorable bonté! Je me souviens encore du goût des tisanes que vous me fîtes boire mêlées de votre propre main dans les intervalles de vos rudes travaux.

Une larme jaillit de l'œil sombre du policeman et vint rouler sur la joue pâle de Nelli.

—Mon père, tout cela, c'est l'histoire de ma pauvre vie. Une autre fois je le vis de plus près. Il marchait dans les rues par une soirée d'automne. Il courtisait des filles que je ne connaissais pas. Il leur disait de si douces paroles! Ces femmes riaient. Je ne pus m'empêcher de pleurer. Il avait avec lui quelqu'un de très grand—je crois que c'était le lord mayor. Lui cajolait une harengère. Tout à coup le prince leva ses yeux sur moi. Il me dit; Bonsoir, la belle. Et toutes ces femmes de chanter; Bonsoir, la belle! bonsoir! Oh! j'avais honte. Je me suis enfui. Tu le sais [*p. 65* (A)] je ne t'en avais jamais parlé. Je crois que le lord mayor lui a dit quelque chose sur moi. Cet homme me fit peur.

—Pauvre enfant chérie! dit Williams en soupirant.

—Tu me pardonnes, mon père, n'est-ce pas?

—Enfant au front candide! ange aux chastes rêves! je ne te pardonne pas, je te bénis! Ange consolateur de ma vie, sois bénie dans ton triste amour, dans ton songe virginal. Ma fille, prie Dieu pour moi.

À cet instant, pendant que Nelli éclata en de doux sanglots, la porte violemment heurtée céda à l'impulsion, un prolétaire hagard, pâle, souillé de sang et de poussière se précipita vers Hervey.

—Nous sommes trahis! s'écria-t-il. Le prince s'est rallié au parti Victoria. Il a entraîné avec lui le lord mayor, les aldermen chevau-légers, les mousquetaires du duc de Wellington. Les Irlandais sont massacrés dans Holborn. On nous fusille dans les rues. Tout est perdu.

En proférant ces mots, un flot de sang jaillit de sa bouche, ses yeux se voilèrent, ses jambes plièrent, il tomba mort aux pieds de Nelli.

Celle-ci jeta un cri.

—Je te quitte mon enfant. Je vais mourir sur une barricade, dit Hervey. La république en ce jour de [*p. 66 (A)*] deuil doit m'être plus chère que ma fille même. On l'outrage comme l'on t'a outragée. Adieu.

Nelli tira en souriant une petite fiole de sa poitrine.

—J'ai pris ceci, dit-elle, dans la maison maudite. Quand je suis revenue de mon mortel évanouissement, j'étais toute seule, je l'ai trouvée sur une console auprès du lit souillé où l'on m'avait déposé. C'est de l'arsenic.

Hervey frissona. L'homme d'acier sentit se détendre les ressorts de ses nerfs puissants.

—Adieu! dit-il.

Il se précipita dans la rue. Nelli le suivait lentement.

Au détour de la place grondait une vaste foule, qui se reculait devant les chevau-légers (queen's own aldermen). L'épée d'un de ces hommes tournoyant comme un éclair vint s'abattre sur la tête du vaillant et dévoué [O']Swocks.

Williams Hervey se jeta dans cette bagarre en rugissant;—Oh! malédiction! malédiction!

[24]Révolution manquée.

En voyant entrer chez elle les ambassadeurs de son mari, la reine avait senti courir un frisson dans ses veines. Ces hommes venaient-ils lui demander compte au nom du peuple entier de ce qu'elle avait laissé faire contre lui? L'échafaud se dressait-il derrière ces pâles figures de démocrates?

La vue de M. Bright lui rendit un peu de courage. Elle savait que cet homme n'était pas de la taille des régicides: elle crut aussi pouvoir compter sur les restes d'un amour que lui avait autrefois témoigné le chef quakre, amour depuis longtemps étouffé dans les réseaux de la politique, mais auquel, s'il en faut croire aux bruits répandus par la cour, la belle jeune femme n'était pas toujours demeurée insensible.

—Sauvez-nous, sir Bright! lui dit-elle d'une voix faible.

Elle s'était levée; sa belle tête défaillante glissait sur la poitrine du grand orateur. Cette poitrine sentit-elle un battement plus rapide au contact de ce sein charmant, de cette gorge superbe?

Nous n'oserions l'affirmer. Toutefois M. Bright sut-il comprimer cet élan, si toujours cet élan existait. Il aida la pauvre femme rougissante à se remettre, et lui baisa dévotement la main.

Il fallait voir les lords se ronger les lèvres, se mordre les poings à cette vue si écrasante pour leur orgueil, d'un quakre qui soutenait dans ses bras la reine d'Angleterre, la *tête suprême* de l'église protestante!

Cependant M. Bright s'effaça presque aussitôt pour démasquer le véritable maître du jour, le puissant et audacieux escamoteur qui faisait à son gré sauter les cartes, danser les marionnettes de la révolution.

Sans doute à ce moment suprême il se glissa au fond du cœur ténébreux de Whitestick une joie sombre, immense, dédaigneuse. Cette reine, ce peuple, ce prince, ces puissants esprits, ces cœurs dévoués, tout cela lui tenait dans la main. Sa vaste volonté froide et compassée allait réduire en cendres tous ces beaux rêves que lui-même il avait aidé à rallumer dans les poitrines profondes des fils du peuple abattus, abrutis. Tout cela passerait comme un éclair.

Lui Whitestick resterait seul, et plus fort que devant.

[*p.* 68 (A)] Oui, plus fort de toutes ces têtes tombées, de toutes ces espérances brisées. Comme démocrate, Whitestick aurait renversé le trône anglais pour asseoir sur ses débris une poupèe dont il tiendrait les ficelles: homme d'église, Whitestick vit bien qu'il fallait arrêter à mi-chemin la révolution, éteindre cette flamme populaire qui venait mordre aux pignons de son palais épiscopal. Albert serait devenu roi, qu'eut[-il] fait de l'homme qui l'aurait mis sur le trône, son premier ministre; Albert restait prince, Whitestick, le sauveur de la monarchie, se rattachait d'un lien bien autrement fort à la royauté qui lui devait la vie. Tout ce hideux calcul dut sourdre longtemps aux coins obscurs de ce cerveau puissant; à présent il tenait bien solidement, bien véritablement les rênes du pouvoir dans sa forte main.

—Madame, dit-il à la reine d'un ton grave, compatissant, où frémissait pourtant un accent étranglé de menace, nous vous apportons les dernières volontés—il s'appuya sur cette phrase—le dernier mot de votre auguste époux. Pesez bien ce que vous allez répondre. Ce n'est plus au peuple orageux et stupide, c'est au prince lui seul que vous avez affaire. Ne lui accorderez-vous rien à cet époux, à ce prince?

—Tout, dit la reine en pleurant, j'accorderai tout, hormis le seul titre de roi. Ce titre, je ne puis l'accorder: un serment religieux me le défend—un serment exigé par mon père mourant, par mon père adoré! Elle éclata en sanglots. —Il me fit jurer, moi enfant, sur sa vénérable tête grise, sur ses cheveux blanchis que je baisais en les arrosant de larmes! Oh! oh, mon Dieu, soutenez-moi!

Une larme aussitôt comprimée glissa sur la paupière agitée de M. Bright et vint briller au bord de son cil épais. Mais son regard vaguement obscurci tomba sur le fils de la reine, qui, muet et blême de peur, se tenait blotti dans un coin, et cette larme se sécha. Cependant la reine l'aperçut.

—Ah! monsieur, dit-elle avec un douloureux gémissement, ah, monsieur, plaignez-moi!

M. Bright dévora un sanglot qui lui serrait la gorge.

—Assez, dit durement Whitestick. Madame, on vous demande par ma voix [p. 69 (A)] si vous consentez à céder au prince Albert la régence de l'Angleterre? Veuillez lui remettre une réponse définitive.

—Et si je ne veux pas, monseigneur? dit la reine irritée par ce ton sec.

—Alors, madame, à lui la couronne, à vous—l'exil.

—La couronne, à lui? à ce prince allemand? Allez, monsieur, votre esprit si ferme me parait tomber en faiblesse, vous divaguez.

—Madame, je n'ai jamais eu l'esprit plus sain. Demandez plutôt à M. Bright, qui représente ici la moitié des anglais, un corps commercial et religieux énormément puissant. Vous oubliez, madame, qu'il ne s'agit pas ici d'un royaume où prévaut le dogme monarchique. Vous tenez la couronne, vous, non par droit divin, mais bien comme l'élue du peuple, comme l'ont tenue vos pères. S'il plaît à ce peuple de vous l'ôter, il vous l'ôtera. S'il lui plaît de vous chasser, il vous chassera. Rappelez-vous les Stuart. Demandez-en des nouvelles à mylord Palmerston, qui s'en souvient, lui. Eh bien! madame, vous chassée, pardonnez le mot, ce n'est pas moi qui ferai la chose—pourquoi le peuple n'irait-il point élir pour la deuxième fois un prince allemand, allié de l'Angleterre, ami de ce peuple? Allons, madame, il est toujours temps d'empêcher tout cela. Le voulez-vous?

—Oui, dit la reine d'une voix étouffée. Mais il me garantira des colères du peuple? N'est-ce pas qu'il ne me laissera pas faire du mal? Je l'ai tant aimé!

La figure de M. Bright devint livide, sa poitrine haletait, sa bouche convulsive laissait voir des dents qui grinçaient.

—C'est dit, madame. Le peuple ne bougera point. Vous accordez la régence?

—Non pas! non pas! le nom de régent me serait trop odieux, il me rappellerait mon père.

Les sanglots de la pauvre martyre débordaient encore une fois.

—Finissons, dit Whitestick. Voulez-vous du titre de prince consort?

La reine fit signe que oui. Son dernier souffle semblait prêt à lui échapper des lèvres.

—Ouvrez la fenêtre, sir Bright, dit l'impérieux prélat.

Le ministre, les dents serrées, les lèvres blanches, mit la main sur l'espagnolette, et se retourna pour contempler la reine.

[*p.* 70 (A)] Elle gisait étendue dans une chaise longue, lourde, inerte comme un corps mort. Bright soupira, il parut un moment près de s'élancer à la gorge du prélat qui torturait cette femme; mais il se retint.

La fenêtre ouverte laissait voir la place remplie d'hommes armés.

Un vieux levain de religion fit pâlir le quakre qui fit place à son complice plus hardi, et surtout plus incrédule. Pour Whitestick, un forfait ne devenait pas plus noir parce que l'évangile le défendait, et qu'il fallait l'exécuter à main armée. Il se mit à la fenêtre et cria d'une voix ferme;

—Vive la reine et le prince consort!

C'était pour les soldats de la reine un signal convenu.

Pour le peuple soulevé, c'était un arrêt de mort.*

Mille voix répétèrent ce cri de loyauté.

Bientôt on entendit tirer les premiers coups d'une fusillade lointaine.

La reine frissonnait de tous ses membres.

Bright s'était rapproché du prélat, et lui disait à l'oreille:

—Mais le prince, que fera-t-il?

—Mon cher, dit Whitestick, il fera des exhibitions d'industrie.

---

*Voir le dernier discours de M. Bright (1860) dans lequel il qualifie tout haut de 'massacre' cette violence des troupes royales qui étouffa de vive force le chartisme en Angleterre. En 1848, lui comme tout le monde il l'appelait 'justice faite.' Il était pourtant constaté, alors comme aujourd'hui, que plusieurs citoyens y eussent péris. Mais que voulez-vous! il y avait un danger, le chartisme était devenu un danger, il fallait bien le suprimer.

Double mort.

Le feu ne dura pas cinq minutes.

Hervey, nous l'avons dit, s'était précipité au milieu du tumulte, il avait vu abattre devant ses yeux la noble tête de son ami—Paddy O'Swocks râlait à ses pieds. En mourant, il venait de reconnaître la figure du vieux militaire qui l'avait frappé. Cet homme commandait la troupe royale. Il portait l'uniforme chamarré d'un colonel de brigade irlandais. C'était son père, c'était lord Chops.

Le malheureux ne poussa qu'un gémissement et expira sur-le-champ.

Le seul nom de Nelli avait vibré sur ses lèvres mourantes.

À son coté était couché un autre irlandais, la tête fendue.

—Erin! Erin! criait ce moribond. À toi mon sang! à toi mes adieux! Et il mourut. Un divin sourire resta sur sa bouche inerte, comme un oiseau céleste qui se serait posé sur un cadavre.

Williams avait enjambé les corps de ces deux martyrs pour se ruer sur lord Chops, qui, le sabre à la main, regardait son fils tué. Il riait:

—Tiens, c'est drôle, dit-il à son voisin, c'était là mon gaillard à moi. Et du plat de son sabre il souffleta la joue morte de Paddy. —Allons, dit-il. Toi, Jenkins, prends à droite; on se bat à gauche.

Et il riait toujours, lord Chops, en considérant la figure ébahie de son lieutenant, de l'héroique sir Thompson Jenkins, qu'il avait déterré, au fond de quelque bouge de Kensington où l'avait enseveli Whitestick, et qu'il avait forcé de prendre place à son côté en tête du régiment. La couardise éhontée du baronet le faisait tant rire, de son bon rire franc, le cher homme! Ce digne lord Chops avait quelque machine à rire au fond de sa poitrine qui lui tenait lieu de cœur, à cet excellent vieillard. Du reste, il ne craignait pas grand'-chose, lui; Dieu pas du tout, un peu la reine, un peu plus les hommes d'église, beaucoup lady Chops. C'est qu'il s'y connaissait.

[*p. 72* (A)] L'étrangeté de l'aspect de ce vieillard rieur glaça de stupéfaction le cœur bouillant de Williams, et l'arrêta en plein élan. Il regarda autour de lui. Partout des ennemis, nulle part des amis. On tuait bien un peu, mais la résistance était si faible, la proie si mesquine! on laissait fuir et on riait.

Williams, frappé à l'âme, blêmit et chancela. Le peuple éperdu fuyait honteusement vers le Wauxhall. Là il s'était réuni le matin, là il se réfugiait le soir. Williams rallia autour de lui une demi-douzaine d'hommes dévoués, et essaya de tenir tête à la cavalerie qui s'amusait mollement à déchiqueter les derniers fuyards. Il leur tint tête en effet pendant cinq minutes. Ce peu de résistance anima les soldats, toute la troupe vint fondre sur les six ou sept chartistes.

—Feu! criait lord Chops, qui étouffait de son gros rire: feu!

—Feu! lui répliqua une autre voix.

Hervey se retourna et vit sur le seuil du Wauxhall Whitestick debout, l'œil allumé, le sourire aux lèvres, et près de lui Nelli qui se débattait, renversée dans les bras du lieutenant de lord Chops. Sir Jenkins à l'aspect de la pâle jeune fille entraînée parmi les fuyards, s'était détaché de son régiment, et s'était jeté en bas de son cheval pour courir vers elle et l'enlacer de ses bras. La rage de sa luxure deux fois trompée éteignait sa peur. Il haletait et mordait comme une bête sauvage.

Toute cette vague d'hommes était venue se briser, lame orageuse et sonore, aux portes de Wauxhall: ceux qui combattaient, ceux qui mouraient, ceux qui fuyaient. Au milieu de ce bruit et de cette fumée d'enfer, les regards de Whitestick et de lord Chops se croisèrent comme deux épées. Ces deux hommes se comprirent. Le prêtre étendit le bras; le rire de Chops devint un rugissement. Il signa aux soldats de se jeter sur le policeman, qui hurlait de colère comme un lion blessé, et dont la figure était toujours foudroyante de puissance et de lumière sous le sang qui l'inondait.

L'apôtre était devenu gladiateur, le père était devenu tigre.

[*p. 73* (A)]—Mort! mort! hurlait-il toujours; mort à toi! mort et malédiction! Whitestick souriait. Une haie épaisse d'hommes armés l'entourait et le garantissait de toute atteinte.

Enfin Hervey parvint à rompre le cercle de fer qui le comprimait de tous côtés. Il enjamba le cadavre cette fois de son dernier ami, et se précipita en rugissant vers le ravisseur de sa fille.

Mais Whitestick ne venait pas de remuer des trônes pour mourir d'une si banale et si petite mort. Whitestick ne s'était pas donné ce plaisir de venir contempler la révolution qui agonisait, brisée sous son pied puissant, sans se munir contre toutes les chances d'une émeute qui expire noyée dans le sang. Williams le frappa en pleine poitrine; son arme glissa sur la cotte de mailles fine et cachée que portait sous son habit épiscopal le prévoyant homme d'église. Alors, frappé de mille bras, il disparut parmi les satellites de Whitestick.

En tombant, il entendit lord Chops qui riait.

Il sentit l'œil fixe de Whitestick qui le perçait de son éclair ironique. Le flot de fer passa sur sa tête mutilée. Quand ce flot s'écarta, les rayons rouges du soir éclairèrent une chose lugubre à voir. Hervey, renversé sur les dalles ensanglantées du Wauxhall, agonisait aux pieds de l'évêque. Le malheureux était percé de quatre bludgeons. Des flots de sang jaillirent de ses blessures et inondèrent le pavé sombre. Un souffle douloureux flottait encore sur ses lèvres immobiles. A cet instant Nelli, se dérobant à l'étreinte redoutable de sir Jenkins, vint tomber sur ce corps avec un cri navrant. Sa tête rebondit sur le pavé; elle était morte.

Williams, d'un effort surhumain, parvint à se dresser sur son séant, et de la main droite éparpillant sur la robe noire du prélat quelques gouttes de son sang répandu, la main gauche menaçante et fermée, il proféra ces suprêmes paroles: —Vieux cuistre de Whitestick, va!

Puis il retomba roide mort.

Lord Chops vint à Whitestick et lui serra silencieusement la main.

Sir Jenkins, assis près du cadavre blanc et chaste de Nelli, pleurnichait comme un homme ivre.

[*p*. 74 (A)] Le lendemain on entendit retentir ces paroles sous le dôme flûté de Westminster, où l'on offrait à Dieu des remerciements solennels pour sa miséricorde envers l'Angleterre en garantissant la famille royale des violences révolutionnaires.

—Nous, John Whitestick, évêque, de par[t] la reine et le prince consort, faisons prohibition à toute âme chrétienne d'ensevelir ou d'enterrer en terre sainte le nommé Williams Hervey, policeman, convaincu d'athéisme et de haute trahison, témoins le très noble lord Chops et l'honorable sir Thompson Jenkins.

—Et de plus confisquons au profit des pauvres de l'église tous les immeubles, terres et autres propriétés du dit Williams.

—Que Dieu conserve la reine!

EDITOR'S
Commentary and Notes

DURIESDYKE

Next to Swinburne himself, who wrote but did not publish it, this poem owes most to Anne Henry (Ehrenpreis), who, though *all* the verses appeared in print four or five times after Swinburne's death, was the first person to perceive that the seventy-six lines entitled (by Swinburne) "Duriesdyke" were the opening two-thirds of the same work of which the thirty-two lines mistitled "Lady Maisie's Bairn" were the concluding third. The opening portion first appeared in a pamphlet *Border Ballads,* privately printed by T. J. Wise in 1909, and was included in Gosse and Wise's edition of Swinburne's *Posthumous Poems* (1917) and in the Bonchurch Edition of his complete works. The concluding third first appeared in *Lady Maisie's Bairn and Other Poems,* privately printed by Wise in 1915 and, like the truncated "Duriesdyke," was collected in *Posthumous Poems* and in the Bonchurch Edition. Mrs. Ehrenpreis's astute detective work, joining together what had been put asunder, set forth in her article "A Reconstructed Swinburne Ballad," *Harvard Library Bulletin,* XII (autumn, 1958), 354-62, should be consulted for details, of which I give only an abstract here.

The manuscript of lines 1-76 is in the Harvard College Library, of lines 77-108 in the British Museum. Both pieces are written on blue foolscap watermarked E TOWGOOD/1859, and, according to Mrs. Ehrenpreis, "the handwriting is identical, [and] there is even a similar smear of ink at the top of the recto of each leaf in both portions." As long ago as 1922, Constance Rummons, in an article "The Ballad Imitations of Swinburne" in *Poet Lore,* suggested that the so-called "Lady Maisie's Bairn" had been intended as the conclusion of "Duriesdyke," but she supposed that it was a later try and that some of the intermediate portions had never been written. It remained for Mrs. Ehrenpreis to demonstrate that the poem was complete once the two portions were joined. She was able to prove it by examining the manuscripts, for only such an inspection could expose the crucial error that had no doubt kept Constance Rummons herself from perceiving the truth. "Maisie" of Gosse and Wise's "Lady Maisie's Bairn" never existed: she was simply a misreading of "Maisry" in line 102 and therefore bore the same name as the heroine of "Duriesdyke." "Neither the appearance of the manuscript nor the continuity," Mrs. Ehrenpreis observes, "supports the theory of a lost intermediate portion of the ballad."

My text is, of course, that established by Mrs. Ehrenpreis, and I reproduce it here, with her kind permission, from the *Harvard Library Bulletin.* C. K. Hyder's "Swinburne and the Popular Ballad," *PMLA,* XLIX (March, 1934), 295-309, discusses that subject generally, and Mrs. Ehrenpreis's recent study, "Swinburne's Edition of Popular Ballads," *PMLA,* LXXVIII (Dec. 1963), 559-71, is the final word—long overdue—on Swinburne's projected anthology of ballads.

CHARENTON EN 1810

For once it is possible to assign a precise date to an early work by Swinburne—in this case, October 27, 1861. There are two manuscripts of the poem. The earlier one, formerly in the collection of the Marchioness of Crewe and now in the library of Trinity College, Cambridge, consists of four blue foolscap leaves, of which the first and fourth are watermarked 1861, and is dated at the end "Dimanche, 27 octobre, 1861." The other, written on two blue foolscap leaves watermarked 1863 and now in the Library of Congress, is the basis of my text. The earlier version was printed by James Pope-Hennessy in *Monckton Milnes, The Flight of Youth, 1851-1885* (1951), pp. 257-59. Apart from the advantage of having this poem in the same volume with its siblings in "Félicien Cossu," it seemed to me worth while in this single instance, for the sake of the many variant readings, to disregard my rule against reprinting works already published elsewhere in hard covers.

The poem was an apocalypse, and in several senses—initially, if not principally, because it was written nearly ten months before Swinburne had read the works of the Marquis de Sade, of whom these verses are a sinister prevision. Writing on October 15, 1861, to his new friend, patron, sponsor, admirer, and Young Man's Guide, Richard Monckton Milnes (later Lord Houghton), who six months earlier had added the youthful poet to his collection of *objets d'art et de curiosité,* Swinburne mentioned his promise to send to Milnes a comedy by Henri de Latouche. "Reserving always your corresponding promise, which I do not forget," he went on (*Letters,* I, 46), "that I am yet to live and look upon the mystic pages of the martyred marquis de Sade; ever since which, the vision of that illustrious and ill-requited benefactor of humanity has hovered by night before my eyes. . . ." He which testified these things came quickly indeed and, before a fortnight had gone by, the pillar of fire by night had guided Swinburne if not to the Promised Land or even to the top of Pisgah at least to the lower slopes of Parnassus.

This poem, which should be read in conjunction with those in "Félicien Cossu," below, is, like practically all of Swinburne's French verse, Hugolian to the last degree. It would be fanciful to draw a comparison between Hugo's Booz, another "vieillard," who fell asleep and in a vision saw an oak tree growing out of his belly up to the blue sky, while Ruth the Moabite, "le sein nu," reposed at his feet, but there are in Hugo other confrontations and other visions that cannot easily be passed by—primarily the great "vision d'où est sorti ce livre" that opens *La Légende des siècles,* the extraordinary description of Shakespeare and *his* vision in "Le Poète" (*Les Contemplations,* XXVIII), Napoleon's confrontation with the personified vision of his past in "L'Expiation" (*Les Châtiments,* XIII), and, deliciously enough, the satyr's arraignment before Jupiter and Jupiter's revery ("Le Satyre," *La Légende des siècles,* XXII), in which Swinburne surely saw himself in a kind of double exposure, the schoolboy in the bill at Eton showing through beneath the later image of the fledgling poet reading *Justine,* drawn so tremulously yet irresistibly to its creator.

1. Charenton is the asylum in which the Marquis de Sade (1740-1814) was confined from 1803 till his death. I do not know the significance of "1810."

2. A Hugolian beginning in both letter,

"En ces temps-là, c'était une ville tombée . . ."

("Toulon," *Les Châtiments,* I.ii)

and spirit,

"Un soir, dans le chemin, je vis passer un homme
Vêtu d'un grand manteau comme un consul de Rome,
Et qui me semblait noir sur la clarté des cieux.
Ce passant s'arrêta, fixant sur moi ses yeux
Brilliants, et si profonds qu'ils en étaient sauvages. . . ."

("Ecrit sur un exemplaire de la 'Divina Commedia,' " *Les Contemplations,* III.i)

3. "Caprée est sous tes yeux" (Henri de Latouche, *Fragoletta,* p. 4)
"Il contemple la foule avec son regard fixe. . . .
Le monde tout entier passe à travers son crible;
Il tient toute la vie en son poignet terrible. . . ."

("Le Poète," ll.4, 11-12,
Les Contemplations, III.xxviii)

The allusion to Capri is explained in the section of Suetonius's "Tiberius," cited below.

4. See Suetonius, "Nero," 28-29, *The Lives of the Caesars.*

5. See Suetonius, "Tiberius," 43-44.

6. Sappho (based on Fragment 31.9-10).

7. Pasiphaë.

8. Aphaca, according to Lempriere, was "a town in Palestine, where Venus was worshipped, and where she had a temple and an oracle."

9. Cf. l. 98. Nothing could be more Hugolian, as can be seen in these instances from *Les Châtiments* alone:

"Toutes les voluptés avec tous les oublis" (I.xiv.8)
"Et que tout ce qui rampe et tout ce qui se traine" (II.vi.31)
"Toute une nation avec toute sa gloire" (III.iv.94)
"Tout ce peuple conquis, tout ce peuple stupide" (III.ix.5)
"Toutes les voluptés et toutes les ivresses" (VI.xiii.212)
"Et Rome tout entière avec tout son passé" (VII.iv.74)

10. Ovid, *Metamorphoses*, X.298 ff. (esp. 462 ff.). In the fragment "Herbert Winwood, Uses of Prosody" Mrs. Winwood reads a passage from an "infamous" French novel beginning: "La tête renversée dans les seins de Cécile, qui haletait comme une moribonde" (see *The Novels of A. C. Swinburne*, with an introduction by Edmund Wilson, New York, 1962, p. 373).

11. Cf. Spenser, *The Faerie Queene*, III.vi.7, and Shelley, "The Witch of Atlas," 57-64.

12. Swinburne canceled "gros ventre ouvert" for this reading.

13. Two occasions on which Sade was as Sadique in life as in literature. For details, see Gilbert Lely, *Vie du Marquis de Sade* (Paris, 1952), I, 163-253, 310-55.

14. "Puis plus grand que Titan, puis plus grand que l'Athos" ("Le Satyre," l.686, in *La Légende des siècles*, XXII).

15. Cf. Gautier's "Son épaule de nacre et son dos de satin" ("À un Jeune Tribun," l.106).

16. Cf. Gautier, "Dis, que fais-tu donc là, vieillard . . . ?" ("La Mort dans la vie," vi.103).

Or Hugo: "Qui donc es-tu?—Je suis ton crime, dit la voix" ("L'Expiation," l.380, *Les Châtiments*, V.xiii).

17. "Maintenant, je suis homme, et je m'appelle Dante" ("Ecrit sur un exemplaire de la 'Divina Commedia,' " l.14, in *Les Contemplations*, III.i). Swinburne put quotation marks only here and in line 79.

AMARI ALIQUID

The only version known to me of this little poem is the manuscript in the Library of Congress—a blue foolscap leaf, watermarked 1863, which contains, also, "Caprice" and the poem "Rictus," from "Félicien Cossu." The manuscript is a fair copy, and the date of composition may well be earlier than 1863.

The title, which has been rendered as "something bitter" or "a bitter taste" or "a drop of bitterness," comes from *De rerum natura,* IV.1134:

> nequiquam, quoniam medio de fonte leporum
> surgit amari aliquit quod in ipsis floribus angat . . .

"but all is vanity, since from the very fountain of enchantment rises a drop of bitterness to torment even in the flowers . . ." (trans. W. H. D. Rouse in the Loeb Classical Library).

The poem may also owe something to Gautier's *Mademoiselle de Maupin,* especially chapter five:

> Colosses du monde antique, bat sur mes faibles côtes un cœur aussi grand que le vôtre, et, à votre place, ce que vous avez fait je l'aurais fait et peut-être davantage. Que de Babels j'ai entassées les unes sur les autres pour atteindre le ciel, souffleter les étoiles et cracher de là sur la création! Pourquoi donc ne suis-je pas Dieu,—puisque je ne puis être homme?
>
> Oh! je crois qu'il faudra cent mille siècles de néant pour me reposer de la fatigue de ces vingt années de vie.

CAPRICE

The sole text of this poem is, as far as I know, the manuscript in the Library of Congress. It is written on the same leaf (watermarked 1863) as "Rictus" (which appears also in "Félicien Cossu") and "Amari Aliquid," the title and first four lines on the same side, the remainder on the back, and, like them, is a fair copy. In "forêts pleins" (line 11) Swinburne evidently preferred metrical to grammatical correctness.

Here, as in "Amari Aliquid," Swinburne is still Hugolian, though now it is neither the furious titan, exiled in Guernsey, of *Les Châtiments* or the deep-browed visionary of *La Légende des siècles* that guides his hand, but the Hugo of *Les Contemplations,* "les Mémoires d'une âme," as the author described them in the brief preface: "toutes les impressions, tous les souvenirs, toutes les réalités, tous les fantômes vagues, riants ou funèbres, que peut contenir une conscience, revenus et rappelés, rayon à rayon, soupir à soupir, et mêlés dans la même nuée sombre."

A few passages from *Les Contemplations* may be helpful in showing the similarity of mood:

(a) Je m'en vais courbé, las, sombre comme un aïeul;
Il semble que sur moi, secouant son linceul,
Se soit soudain penché le noir vieillard Décembre;
Comme un loup dans son trou, je rentre dans ma chambre;
Le chagrin—âge et deuil, hélas! ont le même air—
Assombrit chaque trait de mon visage amer,
Et m'y creuse une ride avec sa main pesante.
Joyeux, j'ai vingt-cinq ans; triste, j'en ai soixante.

(II.viii.29-36)

(b) Je ne vis qu'elle était belle
Qu'en sortant des grands bois sourds.
—Soit; n'y pensons plus! dit-elle.
Depuis, j'y pense toujours.

("Vieille Chanson du jeune temps," ll.33-36,
in *Les Contemplations*, I.xix)

(c)   Vere Novo
Comme le matin rit sur les roses en pleurs!
Oh! les charmants petits amoureux qu'ont les fleurs!
Ce n'est dans les jasmins, ce n'est dans les pervenches
Qu'un éblouissement de folles ailes blanches
Qui vont, viennent, s'en vont, reviennent, se fermant,
Se rouvrant, dans un vaste et doux frémissement.
O printemps! quand on songe à toutes les missives
Qui des amants rêveurs vont aux belles pensives,
A ces coêurs confiés au papier, à ce tas
De lettres que le feutre écrit au taffetas,
Aux messages d'amour, d'ivresse et de délire
Qu'on reçoit en avril et qu'en mai l'on déchire,
On croit voir s'envoler, au gré du vent joyeux,
Dans les prés, dans les bois, sur les eaux, dans les cieux,
Et rôder en tous lieux, cherchant partout une âme,
Et courir à la fleur en sortant de la femme,
Les petits morceaux blancs, chassés en tourbillons,
De tous les billets doux, devenus papillons.

(*Les Contemplations*, I.xii)

The Ballad of Villon and Fat Madge

The manuscript, in the British Museum, consists of two leaves of white foolscap paper, watermarked 1861. Because of this watermark and the handwriting, which seems to belong to the early sixties, as well as Swinburne's references to the poem in 1876 (*Letters*, III, 132, 136), which pretty certainly include this poem among his "old versions," I take the date of translation to be 1861-63.

In *Poems and Ballads*, Second Series (1878), Swinburne published ten of his translations from Villon along with his own poem "A Ballad of François Villon" (Bonchurch, III, 125-46), but from this collection he excluded the two translations printed here, both now published for the first time in book form. In 1878 it was considered necessary to suppress six lines of "The Complaint of the Fair Armouress," two of which were restored in the six-volume collected *Poems* (1904); and all were printed, finally, in T. J. Wise's *Bibliography* (Bonchurch, XX, 162). Swinburne refrained from printing any of his "Ballad of Villon and Fat Madge"—Villon's "Ballade de la Grosse Margot"—because, as he put it (*Letters*, III, 270-71), "it has not six decent lines (nor a single bad or weak one) in it from beginning to end."

The translation was privately printed by T. J. Wise in 1910. Gosse's statement, in the introduction, that the poem "was written in 1877" must be read with the same lightheartedness that one reads his opening sentence (quoted in Bonchurch, XX, 336): "It is with reluctance, and in order to make this series of Swinburne's posthumous writings complete, that we add to it the translation of the *Ballade de Villon et de la Grosse Margot.*"

As Swinburne pointed out (*Letters*, III, 136) to his friend Watts, he made no attempt "to reproduce the exact metre by adherence to the limited number of rhymes," and it will be observed that the Envoy is shorter by one verse than in the original. The verses that he subjoined with an asterisk are the final stanza of Villon's "Ballade des femmes de Paris." I add here a variant version, put together from interlinear second thoughts (not canceled) in the manuscript, of the last dozen lines (a slightly different version of the Envoy is printed in *Letters*, III, 271):

> Then her womb's lust awakes: I must be ridden;
> To save her seed she gets me well bestridden
>   Wheezing and whining, flat as planks are laid:
> And thus she spoils my taste o' the fruit forbidden
>   Inside this brothel where we drive our trade.
>
> Blow, hail or freeze, I've bread here baked rent free!
> Whoring's my trade, and whoring pleases me;

Like cat, like rat; we're just the same if weighed.
We that love filth, filth cleaves to us, you see;
Honour flies from us, as from honour we flee
Inside this brothel where we drive our trade.

It is convenient to include here the fragment of an essay on Villon, of which the manuscript is in the British Museum: four blue leaves folded once each to make sixteen foolscap pages, with half of another leaf used as page three. The writing occupies pages 1, 3, 5, 7, and 9. Pages 10 to 18 are blank except that the last half-dozen lines, heavily corrected, of the fourth chorus of *Atalanta in Calydon* are scribbled on page 18. None of the paper is water-marked, but from Swinburne's explicit statement (*Letters,* III, 272) we know the date of composition to be 1863.

FRANÇOIS VILLON

Of gallows-birds there are various kinds and classes, not undeserv-ing scientific study; but as yet never properly mapped and marked out by the moral ornithologist. It has been found not impossible to train these interesting fellow-creatures into some musical proficiency; grace of wing and suppleness of throat have not been by any means univer-sally denied to this fugitive and predatory tribe of varied feather and vigorous claw. The Montfaucons and Tyburns have turned out, rather often than not, samples of the hangdog poet; fiddlers of varying value have played springs and danced rounds beneath the gibbet; the Heli-con of Newgate has before now echoed to the notes of many a gallows-bit or gallows-finch; but once only within the memory of retrospective science has the wood of the hangman's tree actually served for the nest of a gallows-nightingale. Over every page in the metrical biography of François Villon, poet, pimp, and pickpurse, the extended arm of his native gibbet casts the significant shadow of its fond beckoning hand. In the simultaneous exercise of these three fine arts, relieved by an occasional murder, gilded by many loves and embroidered with many excesses in the way of furtive meat and dishonest drink, he stole and sang his melodious and infamous way through life: arriving at last—the very gallows has forgotten where. Again and once again and yet again did the thief-poet and laureate of all the villainies alive break the faith plighted at his birth to the gibbet, skulk from under its shelter and return to perch on its very branch and begin some fresh tune in its praise: pruning with graceful satisfaction his ruffled plumage and stretching with glad surprise his unhaltered throat; of which no rope seemed able to take fast hold. Are we then to be compelled by the facts and the fates to record that Villon died unchanged after all? that society could not spare him the matter of a twopenny cord? that in the teeth of the nature of things our man-thief, cutthroat, pandar and poet as he was—yielded up his breath under pressure of no human halter and expired without his shoes on? Fond tradition, the child we fear of fond conjecture only, murmurs in an underbreath some consoling hint to the effect that he was ultimately boiled. One may remember with a hopeful but trembling thankfulness that boiling was really in Villon's time the penalty allotted by law to coiners, forgers, or some such classes of the great thief kind. That François Villon was the man to plunge open-mouthed and open-handed into any imaginable or practicable form of thieving or other rascality, no sane student of his works can doubt. Probably then he forged and coined on occasion; assuredly he cut purses and let out his loves on hire; apparently he was not hanged; presumably then he was boiled. Beyond such a flight of inductive conjecture hope dares not spread her rash wing. To believe that after a life so perfect our pandarous and predatory poet came by some ugly and unlucky chance upon a death of incongruous decency, and spoilt the whole lovely pattern of his existence by a winding-up worthy of some virtuous householder or common converted rake, would be too cruel a necessity. There is no proof on either hand. There is a hideous rumour that Villon died decently; there is a probable tradition that he once took shelter in a convent, where the wildest fancy dares not guess what he did or how he fared: but all we can absolutely say is that being mortal he died somehow; and that being the gallows-babe and bird he was, one must suppose that where he dips down out of our sight, he dives into some not uncongenial element, there to suffer or to enjoy a perpetual eclipse.

Of his beautiful life we are happily able to speak with more confidence. Sacred to the gallows from his mother's womb, he was born under the planet Mercury and baptized into the faith once delivered to the Church of Lampsacus. His sponsors were Priapus and Laverna: he was dipped in the font of Venus Cloacina; he emerged in full bud of promise, and broke into full blossom of performance, a thief, pimp, and poet of incomparable excellence. That he was excellent in the first of these qualities or professions, we have the evidence of history; for his excellence in the second we have his own authority; for the third we have the authority of our own senses. How he was born and trained we are not told in any distinct way. It is not given us, with affectionate admiration and devout study, to track and trace the nascent or crescent Villon from cradle to school, from the bit to the birch, and onward to the University of Paris and taking of his degree in klepto-dipso-porno-poetics. That he and all set over him had a hard time of it may be supposed. What his father was biography has not made out; we can only be sure that he was not altogether such another as his son. In the *Grand Testament* our poet, writing under the immediate imminent shadow of the gallows, bequeaths to someone he calls "father" an inexplicable and unmentionable legacy; but the favoured legatee is taken by editors to be merely the father of François, then thirty years old, in some spiritual sense. It is surmised that this charitable man in early years had fed the inner and clothed the outer boy of Villon when bare and lean, in a time of rags and famine, unskilled in the fine arts which were afterwards to imperil and rescue his neck, after supplying him with cakes and ale to chew and gulp for a villainous term of years. Of his mother we have a clearer glimpse: "la pauvre femme!" says her illustrious child, not without probable reason. The poor woman seems to have been very poor, and pious; both seem to have given and received much affection, to no great purpose. How the old bird managed to warm and line the nest for her unfledged gallows-nightingale in his callow days of chirping and picking—how she looked or what she thought when he had grown to the mature stages of singing and stealing—we can but guess. It must be admitted and remembered that he was fond of her and gave her of his best. Her legacy is a hymn to the Virgin, of great and delicate beauty, written expressly to please her, that she might have something of his to use and remember him by. She was hard to please if the legacy did not satisfy her; for there is nothing lovelier extant in that way. Whatever indeed was good in the porno-kleptic poet was very good of its kind, pure from all base metal. His fortitude in prospect of hanging, though very admirable and agreeable to consider, was not perhaps a matter for much praise or surprise: he was hatched and bred in the chinks and cracks of the gibbet-wood, and the halter came naturally to his bibulous and melodious throat. But the freshness and freedom of his repentances, which whatever their practical value might be were at least clear of all hypocrisy or whimpering—his tenderness and kindness and gratitude—his faith and goodwill to his friends, such as they were—ought to be taken into due account and recorded with due credit.

VILLON ("TO MY GOOD MOTHER THAT ME BORE")

The manuscript, in the Rutgers University Library, is a leaf of white paper (watermarked "J. Allen & Sons, Extra Super") folded once to make four pages. The poem is a close translation of the "Ballade que Villon feist à la requeste de sa mère pour prier Nostre Dame," introduced by the concluding eight-line stanza of the "Double Ballade" immediately preceding it in *Le Testament*. Lafourcade (*Le Jeunesse de Swinburne*, II, 104) quoted the first four lines of the "Ballade" proper, but the poem as a whole was not printed, even privately, until it appeared in *The Journal of the Rutgers University Library* in December, 1954.

In the early 1860's Swinburne and Rossetti ("à cette époque mon frère aîné en poésie") planned to translate all of Villon's work. Our knowledge of what the former called his "Villonneries" is neither detailed nor precise, so, except for the fragment of an essay and "The Ballad of Villon and Fat Madge," one cannot be sure how much he accomplished at this time. Years later, however, he once more took up Villon and wrought wonders. "In the last three days" he wrote to Watts in February, 1876 (*Letters*, III, 136),

> I have translated five whole ballads from Villon, and a bit of his text, preserving the order and number of rhymes (only three or four variations in the whole poem), which makes it a considerable feat in metre to find an equal number of corresponding rhymes in English which will fit the original sense as well as (of course) the metres. I think they are at least as well done as my old versions (in which as in DGR's no attempt was made to reproduce the exact metre by adherence to the limited number of rhymes throughout now first observed). . . .

The translation does *not* adhere to "the limited number of rhymes throughout," and for that reason I am inclined to think that the actual translating occurred earlier than 1876, perhaps in the early sixties. It is only fair to point out, however, that Lafourcade, for reasons not given, assigns it to 1877 and that the handwriting of this unique holograph—a fair copy— seems to date from the middle seventies. In any case, Swinburne refrained from publishing it with most of his other renderings of Villon in *Poems and Ballads*, Second Series—partly (no doubt) because it did not meet his standard and partly (perhaps) because of Rossetti's version of the same piece in his *Poems*, 1870.

THE BALLAD OF BULGARIE

The source of my text is a manuscript (by no means a fair copy) in the British Museum. The poem is written on a leaf of blue paper 20.5 by 22.5 cm. (watermarked E Towgood/1874), folded once to make four pages, and on one side of a smaller leaf of white paper.

We know that it was composed early in December, 1876, when passions were inflamed over the Eastern Question. Gladstone (Sir William the Wise) had concentrated his massive energies and formidable rhetoric on the "philo-bulgarian" side. John Bright, Quaker, pacifist, and Member of Parliament for Birmingham, had given him qualified support in several powerful speeches, including one at Birmingham on December 4th. On December 8th a "National Conference on the Eastern Question" was held at the St. James's Hall in opposition to the government's pro-Turkish policy, and Swinburne's reaction to the announcement, forwarded to him by his friend Edward Burne Jones, who stood behind Gladstone, like most other "intellectuals," including Carlyle (Sir Thomas the Bold) and Ruskin (both among the "conveners" of the Conference), can be seen in his letter to Watts on December 8th (*Letters,* III, 228):

> I would give anything by the by for the hand of a great caricaturist at this moment, that I might draw that gallant crusader, the loyal Knight Sir John de Bright (whose very name makes one "drop into poetry," as you see, unawares) in the broad-brimmed basnet of his Plantagenet forefathers, laying his good lance in rest (with "Ha! Beauséant. St. John for Birmingham and Our Blessed Lady of Cotton!") in defence of the Holy Sepulchre against miscreant worshippers of false Mahound. Do you know no comic artist to whom you could suggest the subject and the knightly motto or war-cry (of which I make him a free present) for epigraph?

Within three days the poem had been composed and sent off to the *Pall Mall Gazette,* where it was ignored. As his letters show, Swinburne tried, vainly to get it printed in other papers and even contemplated issuing it as a "fly sheet in the old black-letter ballad fashion" (*Letters,* III, 282), though nothing came of this either.

The poem has never been published, by Swinburne or anyone else. It was privately printed by Gosse and Wise in 1893, with a "Note," unsigned but (according to Wise) written by Gosse: "The following lines were sent by Mr. Swinburne to an evening newspaper in December, 1876, but withheld from publication. They are here printed from the poet's manuscript without the slightest emendation, either in punctuation or any other matter." In his

Bibliography of Swinburne (Bonchurch, XX, 257) Wise quotes a letter from Gosse to himself, written in October, 1893, showing ("And don't let Swinburne know!!") that the printing was done without the author's knowledge. "Despite Sir Edmund's injunction . . . ," he continues, "I did 'let Swinburne know,' to the poet's considerable amusement and surprise."

It is as difficult to disprove Wise's account as to believe it. "Shortly before Christmas 1876," he wrote, "the original manuscript of the *Ballad,* which had then recently been composed, was lent by Swinburne to Sir Edmund Gosse, who took a copy of it, and returned the MS. to the poet. In October 1893 Sir Edmund lent me the copy, in which he had noted all the corrections and alterations of the original, and I printed from it the present pamphlet." Some of this is no doubt true. The first date is certainly wrong. The "holograph manuscript" that he described is, as far as I know, the only one extant and is assuredly the one now in the British Museum, on which the present text is based. It is probably not the "original" manuscript, however, and could scarcely have been the source of their privately printed text of the poem. In line 22 for the manuscript reading "this girdle" they print "the silk"; in one substantial instance the order of the lines in their text differs from that of the British Museum manuscript, in which, though a transposition is indicated, the direction is by no means clear; and, finally, the punctuation of their text is in no sense reconcilable with the statement that they introduced not "the slightest emendation, either in punctuation or any other matter," unless a different manuscript was used. I take it for granted, therefore, that Gosse saw and transcribed another version, and it seems to me likely that the holograph in the British Museum was written down later, in haste and by memory. There is not a tittle of evidence that Swinburne ever knew of the existence of the Gosse-Wise printing of the poem, though, if he had looked, he could have found it described in Wise's *Bibliographical List of the Scarcer Works and Uncollected Writings of Algernon Charles Swinburne,* printed in 1897 (reprinted from *Literary Anecdotes of the Nineteenth Century,* vol. 2, edited by Wise and W. Robertson Nicoll, 1896), not to mention R. J. Lister's *A Catalogue of a Portion of the Library of Edmund Gosse* (1893).

Much of the punctuation in the present text has been contributed by the editor. In the manuscript lines 69-80 come in the following order:

> For the Greek will not fight (which is far from right)
> And the Russian has all to gain
> Which I deeply regret should so happen—but yet
> 'Tis true though it gives me pain
> And I think it were vulgar to cheat a poor Bulgar,
> With offers to help in vain.
> (penultimate)

I don't mind writing—I do mind fighting,
(So spake the bold Sir Bill)
He don't mean outing—he does mean spouting
Like some in Denmark's ill.
We don't mean hitting—we don't mind spitting—
For Turks have swords to kill

Because of Swinburne's inserted direction "(penultimate)," ambiguous though it is, I assume that the intended order (and the order of the earlier manuscript) was that used by Gosse and Wise and have rearranged the lines accordingly. Line 78, which first read "For that's his life's work still," was canceled, and I am far from happy with my transcription of the substitution as "Like some in Denmark's ill." If these words are what Swinburne wrote, they could be strained to yield—with sufficient appropriateness in each case—a reference either to *Hamlet* or to Ruskin, whose home for many years had been (though it was no longer) at 163 Denmark Hill.

THE MARQUIS OF STEAD AND RONDEAUX PARISIENS

The manuscript of "The Marquis of Stead," in the British Museum, consists of two leaves of blue foolscap, one written on both sides, the other on one side only, watermarked 1879. Leaf one, containing the first three stanzas and nearly three dozen canceled lines, was reproduced in facsimile in Gosse and Wise's privately printed "Rondeaux Parisiens" along with a transcription of the three stanzas. Later the second leaf was found, and the three stanzas there, patently a continuation of the poem, were printed in *A Swinburne Library* (p. 235) and in Wise's *Bibliography of Swinburne* (Bonchurch, XX, 398-99). Thus, all the known parts are here, for the first time, printed together. Even as it stands now, however, the poem hardly seems to be complete, and it would be fair to assume that Swinburne never finished it. In my transcription I have added a few indispensable periods and expanded a few abbreviations—most notably in the concluding line of stanzas 3, 4, and 6 (in stanza 5 I supplied the whole line).

Of "Rondeaux Parisiens" there are two manuscripts, both in the British Museum, a first draft and a fair copy; the present text is of course taken from the latter. The earlier manuscript includes the first nine poems of the final version. A tenth, beginning "Believe it we must," was canceled. These drafts, written on both sides of four leaves of the Swinburnian blue foolscap (watermarked 1879), include a great many false starts, canceled words and lines, and even lists of rhyming words and syllables. (On page eight is an early version of the first half of "The Interpreters," untitled and dated at the top "July 16/85.") The fair copy is written, two poems to a page, on one side only of five leaves of the same blue foolscap, also watermarked 1879. After the sixth roundel, at the foot of the page and above the date, Swinburne's signature is heavily marked through.

The "Rondeaux Parisiens" have never been published but were privately printed by Gosse and Wise in 1917, with a preface signed by the latter. Swinburne seems to have offered the poems to James Knowles for publication in the *Nineteenth Century* (*Letters,* V, 128), who, in a note dated September 4, 1885 (*A Swinburne Library,* p. 234), seems to have declined them.

Occasional poems in the strictest sense, "The Marquis of Stead" and "Rondeaux Parisiens" must be read in the context of their own times and causes and some summary of a familiar story may therefore be helpful. In the background are the notorious articles by William Thomas Stead (1849-1912), "The Maiden Tribute of Modern Babylon," in the *Pall Mall Gazette,* of which Stead was editor, in July, 1885.

As a journalist and editor, Stead was a sensationalist, a type still novel enough in the 1880's to call forth Matthew Arnold's description of the *Pall Mall Gazette* as "the New Journalism." ("Yellow journalism," referring to the same thing, dates from 1898.) Before coming to London, he had attracted national attention with a northern newspaper, especially in 1876 with the Eastern Question (his bias was Gladstonian, his keynote the Bulgarian atrocities), and in 1883, after nearly three years of assisting Morley, succeeded him as editor of the *Pall Mall Gazette.* Whenever opportunities arose, he made the most of them, and was, for instance, conspicuous, and even (for those days) flamboyant in the campaign, which he took up like a personal vendetta, to have Chinese Gordon posted to Khartoum.

Stead's next cause was the Criminal Law Amendment Bill, designed to combat juvenile prostitution (by raising the age of consent from thirteen to sixteen) and the White Slave Trade, a measure that had been introduced several times previously and always dropped. In the spring, 1885, Benjamin Scott, aged 75, Chamberlain of the City of London, approached Stead and urged him to intervene. " 'The Bill is practically lost,' " he said, according to Stead's biographer, Frederic Whyte (*The Life of W. T. Stead,* 2 vols., London, 1925, I, 160). " 'You are the only man in the country who can save it.' " His entreaties were seconded by Mrs. Josephine Butler, like himself a well-known social reformer. Stead made up his mind. He called on the Archbishop of Canterbury, Cardinal Manning, and the Bishop of London to assure himself of their approval of his plan of action. "He himself," continues Frederic Whyte (I, 161), "in order to demonstrate that a vicious man could have a girl over thirteen procured for him for vicious purposes, would personate such a man, playing the part in every detail short of actually consummating the crime he would be pretending to wish to commit."

General Booth of the Salvation Army and his son Bramwell Booth, both "close personal friends of his," put him in touch with a woman who, Whyte tells us (I, 162),

> had formerly kept a brothel but who had repented of her ways and had become a Salvationist. This woman, Rebecca Jarrett, was now asked to act as Stead's accomplice and, pretending to have resumed her old habits, to purchase for him, for £5, a girl just over thirteen, ostensibly for vicious purposes. She dreaded the task, but Mrs. Butler, to whom she had owed her own redemption, united her entreaties to Stead's, and at last she consented. She went to a Mrs. Armstrong, the mother of a child called Eliza who had just turned thirteen, and proposed the transaction to her. At first Mrs. Armstrong refused angrily, but the next day she changed her mind and on receiving £3 (there was to be a further payment later) she allowed her daughter to go with Jarrett.
>
> Eliza was brought to Stead and he was free to do with her as he pleased. In pursuance of his project, he now, in his assumed rôle of a vicious man, took her to a house of ill-fame, where she was examined by a woman, Madame Mourez, herself a procuress and also a midwife, and certified by her to be a virgin. She then went to bed, and was left alone for half-an-hour. Stead presently entered the room in which she was lying asleep and she woke up with the startled cry, 'There is a man in the room.' Stead withdrew at once and a Salvation Army officer, a woman, who had accompanied him, proceeded to take Eliza off to a nursing home, where she was again examined, this time by a well-known physician, Dr. Heywood Smith, who certified that she had suffered no injury of any kind. After spending the night at the Nursing Home she was taken next morning to Paris, where the Salvation Army took care of her.

Stead told all (according to some, rather more than all) in a series of four articles called "The Maiden Tribute of Modern Babylon" in five issues of the *Pall Mall Gazette,* Monday to Friday, July 6 to July 10, 1885. The articles are said to have made the *Pall Mall Gazette* "famous 'throughout the entire world'" (Whyte, I, 166), and, as Hugh Kingsmill put it (*After Puritanism,* London, 1931, p. 189), the excitement created "appears to have been at least equal to any manifestation of mass emotion during the Great War." The Bill was passed within a month.

But the story had not ended, for Stead, along with Bramwell Booth, Mme. Mourez, the procuress, and Mme. Combe, "'who had taken charge of Eliza in Paris,'" as well as a Mr. Mussabini, a correspondent who, Stead wrote,

" 'had rendered me valuable services in the under-world with which he had long been familiar' " (Whyte, I, 183), were indicted for the abduction of Eliza Armstrong. Booth and Mme. Combe were acquitted, Mme. Mourez drew six months and died in prison, and Stead, on the technicality of not having obtained the consent of Eliza Armstrong's *father* (rather than her mother), was sentenced for three months. His jury, recommending mercy, recorded their appreciation of his services to the nation but found him "guilty of being deceived" by his "agents" (Whyte, I, 185).

It is not easy to make up one's mind about Stead. No one could fail to approve of the Criminal Law Amendment Bill, and all agree that it would have died once more without this melodramatic mummery. Whether one approves of lying, cheating, kidnapping, a cynical disregard of the feelings and rights of others, of journalism dishonest to the point of deliberate mis-representation, all in the name of a righteous cause, is another matter. Rather, in the case of Stead, it is the same matter. G. B. Shaw, initially so enthusiastic a supporter of Stead that he offered to peddle the articles in the streets, was disillusioned by the revelations of the trial and wrote (in 1922) that nobody ever trusted Stead again "after the discovery that the case of Eliza Armstrong in the Maiden Tribute was a put-up job, and that he himself had put it up" (Whyte, I, 304). Hugh Kingsmill, whose chapter on Stead in *After Puritanism* ought to be read with Whyte's biography, continues this emphasis (pp. 188-89):

> It is impossible to say whether Stead doctored the other facts . . . as sweepingly as he doctored the Eliza episode; but it is quite clear that the facts these articles contain were garnered by someone far too emo-tionally exasperated for exact enquiry into so delicate a matter. When, for example, Stead presents himself to his readers as a debauchee into whose presence this or that procuress ushered defenceless virgins, the only impression produced is that the women concerned were anxious to indulge the illusions of a free-handed gentleman who was not op-posed to their preference for champagne above less expensive wines. Few persons, too, will care to follow Stead in his aspersions on the fair fame of charwomen, a class of his fellow-creatures whom, with the social reformer's characteristic insensibility to the feelings of others, Stead roundly accused of luring unnumbered cooks and housemaids to their doom. Nor does the demon of iniquity, referred to by Stead as "the Minotaur of London," with his two thousand victims, seem much less mythological than the Minotaur of Crete.

It can be taken for granted that the Continental press overlooked no detail. T. J. Wise's "Preface" to his private printing of "Rondeaux Parisiens" calls attention to a chauvinistic series of articles in the *Nouvelle Revue* exposing the "seamy side of social life" in the various European capitals, "La Société de Londres" appearing in 1885. All the articles were collected in a volume issued in the same year—under the name "Le Comte Paul Vasili" (pseudonym of Mme. Juliëtte Adam). Whether Swinburne saw these articles, which were widely circulated and imitated, and so popular that the book quickly ran through many editions, is still not ascertainable. But of his general rage at French journalistic reporting of English vice during the uproar over Stead's "Maiden Tribute" there can be no doubt for the reader of "Rondeaux Parisiens."

1. In the British Museum is another roundel, "To Booth and Stead," which I include here, together with a fragment on the back ("Land of ire") for the sake of convenient reference. Both were printed in *A Swinburne Library* (pp. 235-36):

[1]

To Booth and Stead in rhymes uncouth
Be homage given, and praise be said
By maid and boy, old age and youth
  To Booth and Stead.

The gorge may rise, the cheek wax red,
To hear or read them, what, forsooth,
Concerns it them, if heard and read?

If foul be fair and falsehood truth,
Praise be to creatures born and bred
In cesspools—praise to Stead and Booth,
  To Booth and Stead.

[2]

Land of ire and land of saints—a land of liars and fools and knaves—
Land wherein things foul are fair; things elsewhere loathed excite desire—
Land whose heroes trample women underfoot—the thief's and slave's
  Land of ire.

2. After the first stanza, which includes as many canceled as uncanceled words and lines, the following canceled lines fill the lower third of page one of the manuscript:

  Bedevilled, bemused, and befooled
    (Has ever morality seen a
  Sight sweeter since ink has been shed?)
    As a masculine sort of Marina
  The Marquis of Stead.

Not Shakespeare's own [wd. illeg.] cd bedeck a
Sweet soul by adversity schooled
So well as the touch of Rebecca
Discovers, bemused [?]

The upper third of page two contains these:

Instead of base patricians, wreaking
Their will on victims born and bred—
Lives meant for singing, turned to shrieking
Instead
As Josephine and Jarrett said,
When Butler and Rebecca, squeaking
Alternate, followed where he led
Whom find we now intent on seeking
Truth, flown from haunts whence shame has fled?
The Sire of his incarnate speaking
In Stead

(The last two lines are written in the margin with a directing line pointing under the word "seeking.")

3. Between lines 38 and 39, in the fifth stanza, Swinburne inserted: "Who praise in the name of damn[ation]." Nothing is canceled.

The original tenth roundel, "Believe it we must," canceled in manuscript, as noted above, is printed in *A Swinburne Library* (p. 234) and in Wise's *Bibliography of Swinburne* (Bonchurch, XX, 400-01). I include it here in order to complete the record:

Believe it we must—can affection and loyalty sway
French hearts to think better of England, though leprous with lust
And bleached with hypocrisy? How can we question it? Nay—
Believe it we must.

Gomorrah recoils in amazement and honest disgust.
Is it possible? Look at Jerusalem! Listen! they say
She is like us—and worse! Ah, sister! in whom can we trust?

And Sodom, suppressing a sob and a shudder, gives way
To divine indignation—"Down, down, with her name to the dust!"
A liar self-avowed has avowed it—can true men gainsay?
Believe it we must.

ROUNDEL ["LET US FORGET"]

The poem was published, over Swinburne's name, in the *Scots Observer,* January 25, 1890, page 269, and since then, as far as I know, has never been reprinted or, for that matter, listed in the bibliographies—nor, indeed, even referred to, except for a curt allusion in John Connell's *W. E. Henley* (London, 1949), p. 169. I have found no trace of it in Swinburne's letters, published or unpublished, and the "holograph MS" in the Pierpont Morgan Library that I alluded to so cavalierly in *The Swinburne Letters* (V, 286 n.), though it provided the clue that made possible the resuscitation of this lovely little poem, is not in Swinburne's hand. (The provenance of this manuscript yields no helpful information; the only textual variations are trivial differences in punctuation.)

In short, the poem is something of a puzzle. In view of the date and of what it *says,* however, it can scarcely be coincidence that in the preceding issue of the *Scots Observer* (Jan. 18th, pp. 234-35) was an anonymous attack on Swinburne's arch-enemy, F. J. Furnivall, that, in its partisan violence, would almost have done credit either to Swinburne or to Furnivall himself. (Connell says that it was written by Charles Whibley, and in the Whibley set of the *Scots Observer,* now in the collection of Gordon Ray, it is identified by Whibley's initials.) The article, which mentioned Swinburne only in passing, of course goaded Furnivall to retort—with a post-card, dated January 20th, reading:

> Have received your absurd caricature of me. What a furiously and pervertedly mean-souled cad the writer must be! He attributes all his own low motives to me. Send him up to Barnum's as the champion skunk of Scotland.

If Swinburne's "Roundel"—printed just before Furnivall's note, same page, same column—had been conceived without at least a generalized allusion to his famous quarrel with Furnivall, the editors played an inexcusable trick on him, and they would doubtless have heard from him on the subject. Thus, though I would prefer to speculate, dreamily, that the "Roundel" is an aging poet's nostalgic reminiscence of "A Leave-taking" made many years earlier, I am required by the evidence to assume that it "means" precisely what the context suggests and that Swinburne's reasons for excluding it from either of his two subsequent volumes of poems had more to do with headache than heartache.

The Early English Dramatists

This youthful "review" is reprinted from *Undergraduate Papers,* Volume one, Number one, pages 7-15. Of this luckless little Oxford magazine, organ of an intramural society called Old Mortality, three numbers appeared, the first in December, 1857, the last in the following April. Only six copies of the whole magazine are said to survive. Swinburne's contributions, according to his own deliberate, precise account (*Letters,* V, 235-36), numbered four, according to other evidence, five (Lafourcade, *La Jeunesse de Swinburne,* II, 169-70). Canto One of "Queen Yseult," in the first number, was included with five other cantos in the Bonchurch Edition of Swinburne's works (I, 9-62). "Church Imperialism," to which he owned up, and "Modern Hellenism," to which he did not, were reprinted by Lafourcade (II, 218-23). The other two, this essay and "The Monomaniac's Tragedy," which have never, as far as I know, been reprinted in any form, privately or otherwise, are presented in this volume.

"If ever you do see these worthless rarities," he wrote to T. J. Wise in 1888 (*Letters,* V, 236) about his contributions to this student magazine,

> please remember that they were literally a boy's work—legally an infant's. The article on the dramatists, as far as I remember, was the only thing of any sort of value (except as showing a youngster's honest impulses and sympathies and antipathies)—and that I think I must have shown that before leaving Eton I had plunged as deep as a boy could dive into the line of literature which has always been my favourite.

Swinburne's extravagant commitment to the Elizabethan and Jacobean dramatists is so well known that an extended discussion is not necessary here. The appetite that had been so greedily indulged before he left Eton was far from sated when, thirty years later, he declared, as a sort of credo (*Letters,* IV, 279-80): "My own impression is that every English play in existence down to 1640 must be worth reprinting on extrinsic if not on intrinsic grounds." The last volume he issued was the *Age of Shakespeare,* in September, 1908, a few months before he died, and the first printing of three of the essays collected in *Contemporaries of Shakespeare* (1919) took place only after his death. Of the initial one, in fact, "Christopher Marlowe in Relation to Greene, Peele, and Lodge," we are told that it was "the last prose composition completed by Swinburne before his death" (Bonchurch, XX, 368).

Immature though it is, the present essay seems to me an extraordinary piece of work for a twenty-year-old, worthy in every way of the great critic and poet that its author became. Hindsight is notoriously easy, but the undergraduate who could write in 1857 that Beaumont and Fletcher, "with all their varied and brilliant merit, were the first to mix with the very sources of poetry that faint, false sweetness which enervates the mind and cloys the taste of the reader" or could observe that Webster had gone "deep into the dark places where the sun is silent" was relishing those dramatists with the palate of a connoisseur, rendering his responses with the pen of a poet.

In transcribing this essay I have silently corrected a few typographical errors, expanded such abbreviations as "tho' " and "thro'," and omitted the running heads—"School of Beaumont and Fletcher," "Art of Reticence," "Hero and Leander," "Spiritual and Physical Tragedy," "Characteristics of Style," "Dramatic Completion of Character," "Neglect and Misuse of Criticism," and "Consequences of Dramatic Study."

1. Jonson, "To the Memory of Shakespeare," l.30.
2. He read the paper at a meeting of Old Mortality.
3. Milton, "Of Education."
4. In *Modern Painters,* IV, Pt. V, chap. 19 (1856).
5. Thomson, *The Seasons* ("Winter," l.432).
6. Browning's "Old Pictures in Florence," ll.47-8, 65-8, 161-68.

The Chaotic School

The manuscript consists of twenty-two blue foolscap leaves, none watermarked, written (with seven exceptions, as noted in footnotes 8, 12, 19, 43, 51, and 65) on one side only. These leaves are now owned by Mr. Lowell Kerr, the University of Texas Library, and the Yale University Library, as indicated in this list:

Kerr:	Leaves 1-3, 7-8
Texas:	Leaves 4, 9-11, 13-19, 21-22
Yale:	Leaves 5-6, 12, 20

I hope and believe that I have ordered the pages in proper sequence, but since, as in the case of *La Fille du policeman,* their present disposition is, after all, my own doing, it seems only fair to indicate in the text the beginnings of manuscript pages.

The essay was composed between May 1, 1863, the opening date of the Royal Academy exhibition referred to, and May 28 (or a little later), 1864, the date of publication of Browning's *Dramatis Personae,* which is *not* alluded to (in an essay where nothing is overlooked, no opportunity lost) and which we know Swinburne to have read soon after its publication, probably within a fortnight (*Letters,* I, 100-01). The distance between these two terminal dates can probably be diminished a little. No one, I think, could doubt that the essay was thrown off in a fit of rage. The mere fact that Swinburne, wilfully and dexterously, avoided contact with the Browning poems cherished by himself and all the world shows that his design was to shed (I do not say *draw*) blood.

The provocation seems to have been Browning's indiscretion. They met on June 14, 1863, at a dinner staged by Monckton Milnes, in company with Broad Churchmen, liberal politicians, a "Cingalese in full costume," Froude, Ruskin, and some "fearful" philosophers, among them G. H. Lewes and Herbert Spencer. (Matthew Arnold, himself present, reported these details to his mother two days afterwards, in a letter that attracted some attention, more than three decades later, when it was published, tactlessly, complete with its description of Swinburne as "a sort of pseudo-Shelley.") Nearly every account we read of Swinburne in these days reveals him as a skilled performer delightedly, uninhibitedly dazzling, mesmerizing, and sometimes disgusting the company with his verbal flamboyance. Henry Adams's wonderfully prim, self-depreciatory narrative of his own experience of the "wild Walpurgis-night of Swinburne's talk" in December, 1862, is the most famous, as it is the most artful of them all.

Chez Milnes, as elsewhere, Swinburne regaled the company with recitations, verses that Browning described as "moral mistakes, redeemed by much intellectual ability." Later, Frederick Chapman, of Chapman and Hall, Browning's publisher, asked Browning for an appraisal of Swinburne's abilities and was told " 'that he had genius, and wrote verses in which to my mind there was no good at all' " and that "others present" (presumably at Milnes's dinner) shared this opinion. Whereupon Swinburne lost a prospective publisher and Browning, it seems, lost a friend. Rumor did what it usually does, and on July 7, 1863, Browning, shuffling in an effort to disclaim responsibility, wrote to Milnes, who had apparently asked for an explanation, the astonishing letter from which I have drawn these details (reprinted in *The Swinburne Letters,* I, 84-5). Most things known to Milnes, whose indiscretion verged on infirmity, were soon known to most of Mayfair, Bloomsbury, Westminster, and the Home Counties, as well as the West Riding. He had taken up Swinburne with enthusiasm. In May, June, and July, as James Pope-Hennessy (*Richard Monckton Milnes, The Flight of Youth, 1851-1885,* p. 137) shows, Swinburne not only went to five of Milnes's breakfast parties in Upper Brooke Street and visited the Ruskins at Denmark Hill in his company, he dined there at least once, as we have seen, and in mid-July "brought Whistler to luncheon." To Swinburne this affair would have been a matter of importance. He must have heard. And if my hypothesis is correct, he showed uncharacteristic restraint and prudence in letting his scorn explode (and in masking his hurt) in a manuscript essay that he never published, even partially, and, as far as I know, never once alluded to, even to his intimates.

There is no proof that he ever got wind of Browning's ungenerous lapse and, consequently, no possibility of dating the essay more precisely. We know that he was out of London from late July or early August, 1863, until early in February, 1864. William Bell Scott saw him at Rossetti's soon after his return and, as usual, wrote about him to Lady Trevelyan (*The Swinburne Letters,* I, 100 n.): "Algernon is not much different, only developing some singular conditions of vanity, and otherwise interlarding his discourse with ferocious invectives against Browning." In brief, it seems evident that Swinburne somehow heard of Browning's report to Chapman and that this essay was the result.

It is not necessary to point out that the essay is (to put it mildly) injudicious, but it ought to be noted that Swinburne's estimate of Browning, both before and after this outburst, was of a very different order from what one reads here. In June, 1862, for instance, not only had he called *Sordello* "our greatest modern English poem" but also said that Browning's hand was "as strong as Victor Hugo's own" (Bonchurch, XIII, 164), and in 1875 he introduced into the early part of his long essay on Chapman a remarkable ten-page excursus (Bonchurch, XII, 144-55) on Browning that seems to me still as acute as any appraisal ever written of him and that reads like an affectionate attempt to redress the balance so rudely upset here.

I have transcribed, for the sake of convenience and completeness, two other manuscripts dealing with Browning. The first, from the holograph in the British Museum, was printed in *A Swinburne Library* (pp. 35-36), but with so many errors that, even if it were less relevant to the matter at hand, no apology would be needed for bringing it forward now. It is written, with a great many cancellations, on two small leaves of white paper, 18 by 11.5 cm., with an undated watermark, in a hand that seems to me to belong to the early or middle sixties. It has no title. Wise's printed version not only omits six lines but quite misses the point of the devastating conclusion, and his own final couplet,

> Here lies and stinks a bard who ere he died
> In soul and prayer more foully stank and lied,

must have been in reality merely an extra gibe, an afterthought in a different meter. Swinburne wrote it at the bottom of page two (which ends with line 36, "Easter Day and Christmas Eve") in the right-hand margin, turning the page sideways and writing from bottom to top.

> [This is what I wish my foemen]
> This is what I wish my foemen;
> May none love them, they love no men,

Save some eunuch and a quarter
Saint with sound of English Tartar;
May they ne'er lack heels to nibble,
Ink to splash, or rag to scribble;
May shame flay them to the raw-bones,
And their own verse break their jaw-bones.
May they see their betters, know them,
Lie and lick their feet and loathe 'em;
Keep safe holes to void their spleen in,
Soil the boots they played at cleaning;
Crawl and chafe and rob and quicken
Till in hell their Maker sicken.
Let them howl a thieves' "Te Deum"
Till men spew to hear and see 'em;
Sighing, lying, singing, shamming,
Glad they were not made worth damning.
May they 'twixt their bells and corals
Spice the poisonous page with morals
(Asses' milk that dotage tipples
From such Muse's kiss-creased nipples;)
May they scrawl, crawl, crack their bellows,
Chew pomegranates, spew Sordellos;
Shew with neither blot nor smutch on,
Gules a cart's tail for their scutcheon;
May they take to wife or whore a
New edition of Aurora,
And their mutual moral Muse
Take the windside of the stews;
Yet, to lure the British widgeon,
Lime her twigs with rank religion.
May they dance in one damned lay
Christmas Eve and Easter Day.
May they soil without God's leave
Easter Day and Christmas Eve.
May their souls turn mire, their bodies
Learn what rope, or brand, or rod is;
May their flesh grow here too rotten
For the leanest worm to squat in
When their stench on earth's forgotten;
May they write till earth turn sicker
Of their Hippocrene's soul liquor
May men own who read and gape

Nine such humans make an ape
And their tomb (let no man tarry on
Stone or turf that screen such carrion)
Shew these words the summit crowning—
Traveller, spew; for here lies

The other manuscript, in the Yale Library, is apparently the beginning of a much later essay on Browning. It is written on white paper, and the watermark includes no date. The hand is Swinburnian calligraphy, therefore "late," and from the last sentence of the first paragraph I take it for granted that it was written soon after Browning's death, December 12, 1889, perhaps intended as a sort of counterweight to the "Sequence of Sonnets on the Death of Robert Browning" (Bonchurch, VI, 145-48). The several cancellations are of no interest, but something else is:

(a) Beginning under the word *attempt* in the last sentence of the first paragraph, Swinburne has inserted between the two concluding lines: "lap up the greasy and fetid adulation of the very meanest and dullest of mankind or play a passive part in the vulgar degrading tomfooleries of an Oxford Commemoration."

(b) Under the last line of the same sentence he wrote (quoting from Burke's "Letter to a Member of the National Assembly"):

"The vanity must be omnivorous which can digest such honours"
    humility   "   superchristian   "   enjoy   "   affronts

(c) Near the right margin in the same space is written: *"Pauline* (alone) is hazy."

(d) Between the last two lines of the last sentence, beginning under the words "Mr. Browning" is written: "B's prose is about the worst prose on record—except Walt Whitman's poetry

    Barman & Whitnum
Yankee Dioscuri lucida sidera [word illegible]."

The illegible word is probably "fratres," as in Horace, *Odes*, I.iii.2 ("sic fratres Helenae, lucida sidera").

THE WORK OF ROBERT BROWNING

Time alone, if commonplace and cant may be trusted and accepted as infallible, can determine the quality or distinguish the durable from the perishable part of a great man's work. That time is of all judges the most fallible, the most futile, the most liable to preposterous and irreparable error, it would be no less easy, no less plausible, and no more audacious to assert. Some of the greatest are some of the least familiar names in English literature: the lapse of centuries has done little or nothing to rectify the common estimate of their station and their worth. It may therefore be possible, though we need not assume it to be probable, that the estimate of a great writer taken by his countrymen, we will not say of his own generation, but of the generation succeeding to his own, must not be of necessity inadequate or worthless. And when a writer not only great but unique, incomparable for praise or blame, success or failure, merit or demerit, has come and gone from among us, it is impossible that we should not attempt to anticipate the saner and sounder judgment of the twenty-first century on the value of the legacy he has left us.

No sane or serious student would dream of denying that in the work of most great writers who have done the most as well as the best they could there is a distinct line of cleavage between their triumphs, their successes, and their failures. In the work of Mr. Browning these lines of demarcation are exceptionally evident and obvious.

1. Swinburne canceled the first four words of the title, which originally read:

Caliban in the Clouds
(The Chaotic School)

In transcribing this essay, though I have recorded all the canceled readings that seem to be of interest, I have rejected many more than I have preserved.

2. That is, "Bishop Blougram's Apology" (1855) and *Paracelsus* (1835). Paracelsus's real name was Theophrastus Bombastus von Hohenheim.

3. After "have her" Swinburne canceled: "like the Bastille governor." He was the Marquis de Launay (1740-89), slain in refusing to surrender the Bastille, and his actual words, according to the legend, were "Ah! mes amis, tuez-moi sur le champ, ne me faites pas languir." The ultimate source (since I do not know Swinburne's), including that of Carlyle, who rendered it as "O friends, kill me fast!", is *Histoire de la révolution de 1789,* par Deux Amis de la Liberté (Paris, 1790), II, 37.

4. Imperfectly recollected from the Marquis de Sade's *Justine:*

"Oh! foutre," dit père Ives . . . "elle est dans un état à ne pouvoir rien endurer."

"Tu te fouts de moi," dit Siméon; "jusqu'à ce qu'une putain crève, elle est en état de tout soutenir."

Le gueux la saisit en disant cela . . . (*La Nouvelle Justine, ou les malheurs de la vertu,* 4 vols., Sceaux, 1953, IV, 105).

5. *Sordello,* III.947.

6. Bobadil is in Jonson's *Every Man in His Humour,* Parolles in Shakespeare's *All's Well That Ends Well,* Mascarille in Molière's *L'Etourdi, Le*

Dépit amoureux, and *Les Précieuses ridicules,* and Bessus in Beaumont and Fletcher's *A King and No King.*

7. Perhaps an adaptation of "Some are born great," *Twelfth Night,* II.v.158.

8. I.iii.88. Swinburne's note ("The first two verses of this hideous song . . . ") is written on the back of Leaf 4. For "Nazareth," below, see John 1:46.

9. Alluded to in *The Dunciad,* II. 15 (based on *The Grub-Street Journal,* Nov. 19, 1730). See James Sutherland, ed. *The Dunciad (The Poems of Alexander Pope,* vol. 5, Twickenham Edition, second edition, 1953, pp. 412-17).

10. The quotations are from *A Blot in the 'Scutcheon,* I.2.133, and II.261-64.

11. Cloten is in Shakespeare's *Cymbeline.*

12. These two sentences ("Any man who was by inherited character and tradition . . . tell this by way of news") are written on the back of Leaf 5 of the manuscript. Two small superior crosses in the text indicate its position, and a similar sign precedes and follows the addition.

13. Baron Julius von Haynau (1786-1853), Austrian general notorious for his cruelty when military commander in Italy and Hungary, and Major-General Benjamin Franklin Butler (1818-93), who as military governor in New Orleans in 1862 provoked international protests by his high-handed administration, especially with his notorious Order No. 28: "When any female shall, by word, or gesture, or movement, insult or show contempt for any officer or soldier of the United States, she shall be regarded and held liable to be treated as a woman of the town plying her avocation" (*Dictionary of American Biography*).

14. After "goodness" Swinburne canceled "a laughable."

15. Unidentified.

16. After "incredible" Swinburne canceled "singleness."

17. Browning's "One Word More," l. 131.

18. After "Othello" Swinburne canceled "and Macbeth." After "exist without" he canceled "a caldron and."

19. The words "first . . . admirably too:" are written on the back of Leaf 7 of the manuscript, their insertion being indicated by a small superior cross in the text and by the same sign following and preceding the addition.

20. "Andrea del Sarto," ll. 110-13. These lines may have been transcribed on a separate slip now lost.

21. After "hold water in this world" Swinburne canceled: "If his pebble hits his tutor's window it is not a wholly sufficient excuse that he was shying at an imaginary cat or phantasmal cow. Again." In the next sentence, after "false quantities" he canceled "and accents"; after "school verses;": "if he knows"; after "good intentions to the,": "school purgatory."

22. Richard Redgrave (1804-88), genre and landscape painter. Swinburne is referring to the Academy exhibition of 1863 (which opened May 1): Redgrave's etching "Summer Woods" was Number 968, Whistler's etching "Hungerford Bridge" was Number 969, and his dry-point "The Forge" was Number 972.

23. Blake's "Annotations to Reynolds' Discourse I" (p. 14). The next sentence is, of course, a Swinburnian variation of Augustine's "Salus extra ecclesiam non est," worth mentioning here because in *William Blake* (Bonchurch, XVI, 210 n.) he varied it as "Extra hominem nulla salus."

24. After "definable" Swinburne canceled "and attainable."

25. Before "criminal" Swinburne canceled "liar."

26. The phrase occurs at least eight times in Browning, but the reference here must be to "Cleon," l. 73.

27. Browning's "Through the Metidja to Abd-el-Kadr," l. 39.

28. *Much Ado About Nothing,* V. iv.

29. After "crime in" Swinburne canceled "verse-writing"; after "sight of any,": "poet." At the end of this sentence he canceled: "Such a criminal as Mr. Palmer of Rugeley or as Mr. Hart of the Academy, is Mr. Browning of 'the Metidja'; nay, of the merciless and murderous three he is perhaps the most unpardonable and the most 'pendable.' " (The word "three" is a substitution for "trinity," canceled.)

William Palmer (1824-56) was hanged as a poisoner after a trial that attracted international attention. Solomon Alexander Hart (1806-81), R.A., was professor of painting at the Academy from 1854 to 1863, librarian from 1865 till his death. In 1863 he exhibited three pictures: "Music" (No. 60), "Desdemona's dismay at the unjust accusations of Othello" (No. 329), "Melancthon expounding a text in Luther's Bible to two monks" (No. 662).

30. After "tailor left them." Swinburne canceled "Pedant and tailor."

31. *As You Like It,* V.iv.60.

32. *Sordello,* I. 30.

33. "Bishop Blougram's Apology," l. 14.

34. Like Paracelsus, Machaon was a physician and the son of a physician (see, for example, the *Iliad,* II. 731-32, XI, 512, etc.). Browning alluded, much later, to "Machaon redivivus" in the poem "Doctor—" (1880).

35. Unidentified.

36. *Macbeth,* II.ii.28 (cf. "Childe Roland," l. 100).

37. From the prayer concluding the "Office of Institution" in *The Book of Common Prayer.*

38. *Pippa Passes,* II. 131.

39. Before "polished rocks" (a precise verbal echo of the *Odyssey,* XII, 79) Swinburne canceled "Scylla"; before "muddy whirlpool": "Charybdis."

40. Blake, "On H——y's Friendship," l. 4.

41. *The Duchess of Malfi,* IV.ii.315 (Swinburne canceled "Webster" and substituted "Bosola.")

42. C. J. Wells's *Joseph and His Brethren,* II.iii.683.

43. The final word in Hugo's drama. The three following sentences ("These good separate points . . . such great accidents.") appear alone on the back of Leaf 13 of the manuscript, their insertion being indicated, as usual, by a superior cross in the text and the same sign following and preceding the addition.

44. Ottima, Phene, and Jules are in *Pippa Passes,* Constance and Norbert in *In a Balcony,* Mildred is in *A Blot in the 'Scutcheon,* and Colombe, of course, in *Colombe's Birthday.*

45. *Sordello,* V. 1012-17.

46. After "try at singing" Swinburne canceled "the courtship of curates or married life of county members." The rest of the sentence seems to be a cut at Patmore's *Angel in the House.*

47. Thomas Rymer's *Edgar, or the English Monarch* appeared in 1678, Ambrose Philips's *The Distrest Mother* in 1712, François Ponsard's *Lucrèce* in 1843.

48. "De Gustibus . . . ," l. 36.

49. *Sordello,* V. 43-46.

50. *The Tempest,* II.ii.

51. The words "despite stolen wand and artificial wing" are written on the back of Leaf 17 of the manuscript, their insertion being indicated by two small crosses in the text, one above, the other below the line, and by a cross preceding and another following the addition.

52. After "the voice is" Swinburne canceled: "as before not Ariel's voice, but Caliban's."

53. In "Sir Joshua Praises Michael Angelo," a fragment from the Rossetti MS. The misreading "meekness" for "mildness" was D. G. Rossetti's, in his selections from Blake accompanying Gilchrist's *Life of William Blake* (1863).

54. Musset's "Chanson," ll. 1-5.

55. Gautier's "Barcarolle," ll. 25-30.

56. Fantine's song in Hugo's *Les Misérables,* Vol. I, Bk. vii, chap. 6.

57. Blake's "To the Muses," ll. 2-4.

58. Psalm 139: 9.

59. The next sentence ("What matter whether . . . children of Angelico") is written on the back of Leaf 19 of the manuscript, their insertion being indicated by a superior cross in the text and a similar sign preceding and following the addition.

60. Keats's "Lamia," II.216.

61. From "Le Pas d'armes du roi Jean" in *Ballades* (1828) to "La

Chanson des aventuriers de la mer" in *La Légende des siècles,* First Series (1859). Swinburne wrote and then canceled "chasse du burgrave," replacing it with "tourney of King John."

62. "A Toccata of Galuppi's" and "The Heretic's Tragedy."

63. Ben Jonson's "To the Memory of Shakespeare," l. 30.

64. Before "Blougram" Swinburne canceled "Fra Lippo or a Karshish."

65. *Notre-Dame de Paris,* Bk. One, chap. 7. (By placing the number "2" over lines 1 and 3 and the number "1" over lines 2 and 4, Swinburne indicated that the order of lines 1 and 2 and of 3 and 4 should be reversed, and, moreover, he wrote the last two lines in the wrong order. I have transcribed them here as they appear in the novel.) This long note by Swinburne is written on the back of Leaf 20.

66. That is, "Guitare" in *Les Rayons et les ombres* (1840) and "Le Chant de ceux qui s'en vont sur mer" in *Les Châtiments,* V (1853).

67. Lines 54-55.

68. Dogberry is, of course, in *Much Ado about Nothing.* Hugo's Esmeralda is in *Notre-Dame de Paris,* Marion in *Marion de Lorme,* Catarina in *Angelo,* Gennaro in *Lucrèce Borgia,* and Don César in *Ruy Blas.* Pippa and Phene are in Browning's *Pippa Passes* and Mildred in *A Blot in the 'Scutcheon,* as already noted, Valence is in *Colombe's Birthday,* Luria in *Luria,* and Bluphocks in *Pippa Passes.*

69. *Measure for Measure,* II.ii.107.

70. Unidentified. This astonishingly adaptable phrase must surely be vintage Sade, but a most careful search has failed to turn it up in *Justine, Juliette, La Philosophie dans le boudoir,* or *Aline et Valcour.* Swinburne, I think, would have approved the only source I *can* cite—

> Dans le monde visible, partout un fanal:
> Ce qui existe est bon, le néant c'est le mal!—

which, following his fine example, I composed for the occasion.

71. In "Tu admires, donc tu n'imites pas," *Profils et grimaces* (Paris, 1856).

72. After "smell sweet" Swinburne canceled "the sun to shine, the rain to wet."

FATHER GARASSE

The manuscript, in the British Museum, of this Swinburnian *Dunciad* in miniature consists of four white folio leaves, none watermarked, written in dark ink on one side only. The title is probably not in Swinburne's hand. I do not know the date of composition and have no evidence by which I could challenge T. J. Wise's conjecture (*A Swinburne Library,* p. 223), 1865-66. The essay, printed now for the first time, seems to me an obvious pendant to Swinburne's "Théophile" (Bonchurch, XIII, 397-414; privately printed, 1915), which, according to Gosse, who had seen the manuscript, was "doubtless" written in 1862.

Théophile de Viau (1591-1626) was a Huguenot, poet, libertine, and freethinker who wielded a pretty scurrilous pen. He was certainly capable, and probably had been guilty, of writing licentious verse also, and his free-thinking activities, indiscreet to the point of imprudence, aggressive to the verge of belligerence, had already put him under Jesuit surveillance when the disaster that he seems to have courted came down on his head. In November, 1622, appeared a volume, *Parnasse satyrique,* that, according to one's point of view, could be regarded either as Priapic and blasphemous or as naturalistic and freethinking. Several pieces bore Théophile's name, and it is one of the many ironies in his story that of some of these he was not the author. The second irony is that the book was got up entirely without his consent or even knowledge, so that whatever else he was or was not, had or had not been guilty of, he was innocent of any responsibility for that volume, his name having been appropriated in order to enhance its salability.

For Garasse, a Jesuit priest, the violence of Swinburne's language hardly seems excessive. He was an ass and a buffoon, and the group of *libertins* headed by Théophile knew it and made it known to others and to Garasse himself, on occasion in the midst of his very sermons. In the spring, 1623, Garasse, seeing Théophile's name in the *Parnasse satyrique* and actually mistaking one group of libertines (the compilers of and contributors to the book) for another (his own persecutors), published a tirade called *Doctrine curieuse des beaux esprits de ce temps, ou prétendus tels, contenant plusieurs maximes pernicieuses à l'Estat, à la religion et aux bonnes mœurs, combattue et renversée par le P. François-Garassus, de la compagnie de Jésus,* attacking Théophile and others.

At this point, the story can be further simplified. Théophile brought suit, and Garasse's incoherent attack was suppressed, copies being withdrawn from circulation. Later, however, because of Théophile's gloating, the case was reopened and the sentence reversed. Fleeing Paris in order to escape arrest, Théophile was condemned to death *in absentia,* but was afterwards apprehended and confined in the Conciergerie. Mostly because of Jesuit conniving, he spent two years in prison, after which, for a variety of reasons, his sentence was commuted to banishment for life, though this penalty, too, was lifted just before his death. The final irony of it all (as far as we know) is that Théophile died in the Church. Whether he found peace later as a result of that submission has not yet been revealed.

Four books have dealt with this affair, of which Swinburne, at the time of writing his essay, could have read only one, Charles Nisard's *Les Gladiateurs de la république des lettres aux XVe, XVIe, et XVIIe siècles* (2 vols., Paris, 1860). Charles Garrisson's *Théophile et Paul de Viau, étude historique et littéraire* (Paris and Toulouse, 1899) speculates, ingeniously, that Théophile's troubles had been caused by his indiscreet love for Louis XIII's queen, Anne of Austria, but the idea was dismissed out of hand by Frédéric Lachèvre, *Le Procès du poète, Théophile de Viau* (2 vols., Paris, 1909), as unworthy of serious consideration. He himself explained the persecution in terms of the religious situation in France in the early seventeenth century: Church and State, represented by Garasse, on the one hand, and by Mathieu Molé, Attorney General, on the other, made common cause in guarding common interests. The definitive study, however, is Antoine Adam's *Théophile de Viau et la libre pensée française en 1620* (Paris, 1935), a scrupulous examination of the evidence from which my account here has been drawn.

1. Zoilus, a critic in the 4th century B.C., is remembered for his malignant attacks on Homer's works. Thomas Rymer (1641-1713) formed a memorable and pioneering collection of historical records, *Fœdera,* but is notorious for his attack on *Othello* in "A Short View of Tragedy."

2. George Stephenson (1741-1848), the "inventor and founder of railways" (*D.N.B.*).

3. Carlyle, *The French Revolution,* Book VII, chap. 4.

4. Revelation 14:13.

5. Unidentified.

6. Elie Fréron (1719-76), critic and enemy of Voltaire, and William Gifford (1756-1826), editor of the *Quarterly Review* and putative author of the attack on Keats's "Endymion."

7. Varied from the Erasmian invocation to Socrates.

"CHANGES OF ASPECT" AND "SHORT NOTES"

Both the manuscripts, on which my texts are based, are in the Huntington Library. "Changes of Aspect" consists of twenty-two leaves of blue foolscap, of which three are written on both sides; "Short Notes" consists of two leaves of the same kind of paper, each written on one side only. None of the twenty-four leaves is watermarked. The two pieces were transcribed and edited by Clyde Kenneth Hyder for an article in *PMLA,* LVIII (March, 1943), 223-44, and with Professor Hyder's generous permission I have freely plundered his admirable annotations for use here.

I do not know the date or dates of composition. Both pieces seem to have been written about the same time, and it seems to have been about 1904-06.

As C. K. Hyder pointed out, the date has to be 1897 (when Hallam Tennyson's *Memoir* of his father appeared) or later; it is quite possible (he added) that the remarks on Morris and FitzGerald were set off by passages in Mackail's *Life of William Morris* (1899) and in *More Letters of Edward FitzGerald* (1901). He drew attention also to the violent language leveled at Arnold, Ibsen, Sardou, and G. H. Lewes in Swinburne's essay "Charles Dickens" (Bonchurch, XIV, 57-88) in the *Quarterly Review*, July, 1902, and to the fact that a long paragraph on Blake also appears in Swinburne's 1906 preface to the reissue of *William Blake*, and he has lately drawn my attention to the use of an "axiom" by Blake (see note 2, below) that Swinburne was seeking in September, 1904 (*Letters*, VI, 185). As far as I know, this is the sum total of the evidence. Whenever written, the pieces are, in any case, the work of a disgruntled, *old* man.

1. Swinburne had in mind, of course, his own position on Home Rule for Ireland.

2. Blake, "The Marriage of Heaven and Hell," 19.

3. *Macbeth*, I.iv.7-8.

4. Hallam Tennyson, *Alfred Lord Tennyson, A Memoir* (London, 1897), II, 285.

5. Substituted for "servility"—probably with a glance at Tennyson's "To the Queen" (1851).

6. Substituted for "shameless." After "favour" he canceled: "the pusillanimity which fell silent for nine or ten years under the lash of Lockhart and only (revived) recovered sufficiently articulate expression" [to retort]. . . .

7. Tennyson's "The New Timon and the Poets."

8. Tennyson's poem "The Spiteful Letter" appeared in 1868.

9. Substituted for "disgraces."

10. Tennyson's "Art for Art's Sake" appeared in Hallam Tennyson's *Memoir*, II, 92. Lafourcade (*La Jeunesse de Swinburne*, II, 603-04) cites evidence indicating that the Laureate had Swinburne in mind.

11. Scott, *Rob Roy*, chap. 26 (see *The Swinburne Letters*, II, 302; and VI, 300).

12. *Songs before Sunrise*.

13. After "was" Swinburne canceled: "never much more than a pseudo-Wordsworth." In his essay "Charles Dickens" (Bonchurch, XIV, 85) he refers to Arnold as "a man whose main achievement in creative literature was to make himself by painful painstaking into a sort of pseudo-Wordsworth." Arnold's letter of 1863 describing Swinburne as a "sort of pseudo-Shelley" was published in 1895.

14. "Matthew Arnold's New Poems," *Fortnightly Review*, October, 1867 (Bonchurch, XV, 62-119).

15. Here, Swinburne inserted and then canceled:

" 'a Macpherson, a Moore, a Maginn, and a Mangan.' The would-be Celt—brutal if not bloody, Saxon if not Sane When I incur or at least when I deserve the adulation of such admirers,

> May I—can worse mishap be man's than that?—
> Be born an Arnold, and baptiz'd a Mat. *Note

Note)* Altered from a couplet of Churchill's on a poeticule of the past."

Charles Churchill's couplet is in "The Conference," ll. 271-72:

> May I, (can worse disgrace on manhood fall?)
> Be born a Whitehead, and baptiz'd a Paul.

James Macpherson (1736-96), a Scot, was the improver or inventor and "translator" of "Ossian." The other three were Irish: Thomas Moore (1779-1852), poet and friend of Byron; James Clarence Mangan (1803-49), a poet, and William Maginn (1793-1842), poet, critic, essayist, and writer of fiction, was the original of Thackeray's "Captain Shandon."

16. Unidentified. C. K. Hyder points out that Arnold's criticism of Swinburne's uncle, Lord Ashburnham, for "keeping Celtic manuscripts from students" may have rankled in Swinburne's mind.

17. In Arnold's poem "Haworth Churchyard."

18. "Whose too bold dying song," line 99 in "Haworth Churchyard," referring to Emily Brontë's "No Coward Soul Is Mine."

19. Carlylese.

20. *Pickwick Papers,* chap. 40.

21. Before "Catullus" he canceled "Lucretius and."

22. *Measure for Measure,* V.i.444.

23. "The Lord of Burleigh," ll. 79-80.

24. *The Merchant of Venice,* I.iii.111.

25. Edward George Geoffrey Smith Stanley, fourteenth Earl of Derby (1799-1869), whose translation of the *Iliad* was published in 1864.

26. The remarks on Morris, as C. K. Hyder indicated, *may* have been prompted by his comment, quoted in J. W. Mackail's *Life of William Morris* (2 vols., 1899), that Swinburne's work seemed "to be founded on literature, not on nature" (II, 74).

27. *Antony and Cleopatra,* II.v.85-6.

28. Quoted from Mrs. Anne Benson Procter's preface to *Letters Addressed to Mrs. Basil Montagu and B. W. Procter by Mr. Thomas Carlyle* (privately printed, 1881).

29. Entry under March 6, 1754, in Boswell's *Life.*

30. William Bell Scott, whose posthumously published *Autobiograph-*

ical Notes, edited by William Minto, had made Swinburne paroxysmal. Below, instead of "but left to a brother Scot" Swinburne first wrote: "but left—it must be presumed—an adequate amount of half-crowns and bawhees to discharge this duty to a brother beggarly Scotchman."

31. Two poems—"Dedication" [To William Bell Scott], *Poems and Ballads,* Third Series (Bonchurch, III, 331-32), and "Memorial Verses on the Death of William Bell Scott," *Astrophel and Other Poems* (Bonchurch, VI, 182-85).

32. Most of this paragraph was incorporated into the preface (Bonchurch, XVI, 348-50) added to *William Blake* in 1906. The "Hibernian commentator" was Yeats, in *The Works of William Blake* (1893).

33. "To Edward FitzGerald" ("I chanced upon a new book yesterday"). Swinburne may also have had in mind here an allusion to himself in *More Letters of Edward FitzGerald* (1901), p. 186.

34. From "Fabian Fitzdottrel" in Jonson's *The Devil Is an Ass.*

35. "Half-thinking, sensual France, a natural Slave" comes from the original first stanza, later dropped, of Coleridge's "Ode to Tranquillity."

36. Substituted for "Aeschylus and Sophocles."

37. "To Walt Whitman in America" (Bonchurch, II, 184-88).

38. Beaumarchais, *Le Mariage de Figaro,* V.iii. The "English Longfellow" is, of course, Martin Tupper (1810-89), author of *Proverbial Philosophy.*

39. Judges 5:20.

40. Laurence Eusden (1688-1730), poet laureate from 1718. Swinburne, first writing "Blackmore," perhaps had in mind one of Pope's gibes, "And Eusden eke out Blackmore's endless line" (*The Dunciad,* I, 104). Henry James Pye (1745-1813), poet laureate from 1790, was to Byron as Eusden was to Pope ("English Bards and Scotch Reviewers," ll. 103-05, "The Vision of Judgment," l. 736). Of Pybus I know nothing except that he seems like a combination of the two. C. K. Hyder pointed out that "Charles James Pybus was the author of *The Sovereign; a Poem* (London, 1800) and other works." He is said to have been satirized by "Caroline Petty Party" (pseudonym of Elizabeth Cobbold) in *The Mince Pie; an heroic epistle humbly addressed to the sovereign dainty of a British Feast* (1800).

41. Pope's "Epistle to Dr. Arbuthnot," l. 308 (cf. ll. 169-70).

42. "Burial of the Dead," *Book of Common Prayer.*

43. Romans, 4:6.

44. Swinburne first wrote "genius."

45. Alfred Bunn (1796-1860), theatrical manager and translator of operas; Edward Fitzball (1792-1873), dramatist; and G. W. M. Reynolds (1814-79), author of sensational novels and translator.

46. Instead of "scribbler" Swinburne first wrote: "Margites who knew

so many things and knew them all so badly towards the dead and yet." (Plato, "Alcibiades," ii. See *Hesiod, The Homeric Hymns and Homerica,* translated by Hugh G. Evelyn-White, Loeb Classical Library, pp. 536-39.)

47. Dante Gabriel Rossetti.

THE MONOMANIAC'S TRAGEDY

This *jeu d'esprit,* earliest in date of the Swinburnian hoaxes, first appeared in the second number, February-March, 1858, of *Undergraduate Papers,* of which some account was given in the discussion, above, of "The Early English Dramatists." Thirty years later, it was dismissed by Swinburne (*Letters,* V, 235) as a "boyish bit of burlesque," but it seems to me well worth rescuing. The mock-review is clearly directed against "spasmodic" poetry, of which the best description, survey, and discussion is in Jerome H. Buckley's *The Victorian Temper* (Cambridge, Mass., 1951), pp. 41-65. The question is, *what* spasmodic poetry? Lafourcade (*La Jeunesse de Swinburne,* II, 165-66) cast his net wide enough to contain the "works" of Alexander Smith and Sydney Dobell, mentioning, as an afterthought, Tennyson's "Maud" and the poems of Mrs. Browning, all of which, though not inaccurate, is not very helpful. I think it is possible to be more precise.

The "principal" spasmodic poems are Philip James Bailey's *Festus* (1839; 1845, etc.), Sydney Dobell's *Balder* (1853), and Alexander Smith's "A Life Drama," published in his *Poems* (1853). All three derive ultimately from Goethe's *Faust,* a lineage suggested in the very title of Bailey's poem, and if I were concerned here with the genealogy of the "school," I would try to trace it through Shelley's "Queen Mab," some of Byron's dramas, especially "Manfred," "Cain," and "Heaven and Earth," Carlyle's *Sartor Resartus,* Mrs. Browning's "A Drama of Exile," Browning's "Paracelsus." Happily, however, since Swinburne was not writing literary history, my duty here is not— to use a word any one of the Spasmodics would have been proud of—so cataleptogenic.

Swinburne's satire is, as Lafourcade pointed out, general, but his debt is particular and his creditor was William Edmondstoune Aytoun, whose *Firmilian, A "Spasmodic" Tragedy,* purportedly by T. Percy Jones, appeared in 1854, a direct parody, preface and all, and a wonderfully funny one, of Dobell's *Balder.* Like the hero of Wheldrake's *Monomaniac's Tragedy,* who finds he must become a thief and murderer in order to write *Iscariot, a Tragedy,* Aytoun's Firmilian, in order to "paint the mental spasms that tortured Cain," the subject of *his* song, recognizes that "What we write Must be the reflex of the thing we know." He soliloquizes (scene vi):

O shame, Firmilian, on thy coward soul!
What! thou, the poet!—thou, whose mission 'tis
To send vibration down the chord of time,
Until its junction with eternity—
Thou, who hast dared and pondered and endured,
Gathering by piecemeal all the noble thoughts
And fierce sensations of the mind—as one
Who in a garden culls the wholesome rose,
And binds it with the deadly nightshade up;
Flowers not akin, and yet, by contrast kind—
Thou, for a touch of what these mundane fools
Whine of as pity, to forego thine aim,
And never feel the gnawing of remorse,
Like the Promethean vulture on the spleen,
That shall instruct thee to give future voice
To the unuttered agonies of Cain!
Thou, to compare, with that high consequence
The breath of some poor thousand knights and knaves,
Who soaring in the welkin shall expire!
Shame, shame, Firmilian! on thy weakness, shame!

He blows up the Cathedral of St. Nicholas and hurls his friend and benefactor Haverillo off the summit of the Pillar of St. Simeon Stylites, as Balder
had threatened to hurl his friend Dr. Paul from the ramparts of a ruin. And
just as clearly the little idyl "Keeping Cattle," from *The Monomaniac's
Tragedy,* was suggested partly by the song of Sancho, the Costermonger
(scene x):

Down in the garden behind the wall,
Merrily grows the bright-green leek;
The old sow grunts as the acorns fall,
The wind blows heavy, the little pigs squeak.
One for the litter, three for the teat—
Hark to their music, Juanna my sweet!

and partly by the Chorus of Ignes Fatui (scene xv):

Follow, follow, follow!
Over hill and over hollow;
It is ours to lead the way,
When a sinner's footsteps stray—
Cheering him with light and song,
On his doubtful path along.
Hark, hark! the watch-dogs bark.
There's a crash, and a splash, and a blind man's cry,
But the poet looks tranquilly up at the sky!

For the most part, it is distinctly more agreeable to read about than to read spasmodic poetry, though a line like the one addressed to Lucifer in the second scene of *Festus*—"You look as if you lived on buttered thunder" —does much to compensate for one's lost innocence. The violent themes, rendered (and rent) in hysterical language, the neurotic, warped sensibilities, the exposed, exacerbated ganglions, the unabashed, unremitting solipsism, the *absolute* humorlessness of the main characters can be fused into art only by a first-rate poet, a lord of language, a Tennyson, who, in "Maud," surely the only *good* spasmodic poem in existence, has turned these very qualities to account, or by a Carlyle, an early Victorian Ezekiel, standing "in the centre of Immensities, the conflux of Eternities," struggling towards "the impalpable Inane."

Certainly, Mrs. Browning does not bring it off, and, even without specific verbal echoes or any other evidence, it is easy to believe that Wheldrake's *Eve, a Mystery* owed something to her "Drama of Exile," a tableau on the expulsion from Eden:

> *Eve:* . . . But now it is no choice of mine to die—
> My heart throbs from me.
> *Adam:* Call it straightway back.

Or, a little later, her question put to Adam:

> Shall I be mother of the coming life?
> Hear the steep generations, how they fall
> Adown the visionary stairs of Time,
> Like supernatural thunders—far yet near;
> Sowing their fiery echoes through the hills.
> Am I a cloud to these—mother to these?

Or Christ, after admonishing Adam and Eve, when "gradually transfigured . . . into humanity and suffering":

> Eternity stands alway fronting God;
> A stern colossal image, with blind eyes
> And grand dim lips that murmur evermore
> God, God, God! While the rush of life and death,
> The roar of act and thought, of evil and good,
> The avalanches of the ruining worlds
> Tolling down space—the new world's genesis
> Budding in fire—the gradual humming growth
> Of the ancient atoms and first forms of earth,
> The slow procession of the swathing seas
> And firmamental waters,—and the noise
> Of the broad, fluent strata of pure airs,—
> All these flow onward in the intervals

Of that reiterated sound of—God!
Which WORD, innumerous angels straightway lift
Wide on celestial altitudes of song
And choral adoration, and then drop
The burden softly, shutting the last notes
In silver wings.

Or the Chorus, addressing Adam and Eve:

Live, work on, O Earthy!
By the Actual's tension,
Speed the arrow worthy
Of a pure ascension.
From the low earth round you
Reach the heights above you;
From the stripes that wound you
Seek the loves that love you!
God's divinest burneth plain
Through the crystal diaphone
Of our loves that love you.

A good year before his Wheldrake critique, Swinburne had declared Mrs. Browning to be the "greatest woman that ever lived, except Sappho and Deborah" (*Letters,* I, 10), and in 1875 he told John Nichol, his own close friend and Dobell's, that in his "boyhood and first youth" he had worshiped Dobell's "name and his work without any admixture of criticism or reason" (*Letters,* III, 29). The bones must have been "ploughed over in the sepulchres of time" before he created Wheldrake, however, though in any case one would be inclined to believe that it was Dobell's fervid republicanism rather than his perfervid poetry that had made Swinburne glow. "What am I," asks Vittorio Santo, disguised as a monk, addressing Rome, the Eternal City, in the first scene of Dobell's poem "The Roman,"

That I am tortured to supernal uses,
Who have not died; and see the sights of angels
With mortal eyes? Unhand me, mother! why
Must I, so many years removed from death,
Be young and have no youth?

And Wheldrake's language, in spite of being a mishmash of keepsake verse, Marlowe, Shakespeare, Webster, Milton, Shelley, Byron, Keats, Tennyson, Arnold, Emily Brontë, Carlyle, and what you will, is not pinnacled dimmer in the intense inane than Balder's. "Be exhaled, O Power," he says, apostrophizing the "Invisible":

let me behold the sudden stars
Meet in omnipotent havoc that results
To utter space and ebbs and flows and ebbs
In vast conflux and infinite recoil
Systole and diastole, till lo!
A universe that like our mortal lot
Panteth to death, and in the hopeless sight
We leap to final flames; or now at last
Unveil thyself and save us! Come forth strong
To judgement! Justify the shows of things,
And heal HER and this world!

Or, looking up and seeing the clouds:

You while full heavens!
You crowded heavens that mine eyes left but now
Shining and void and azure!—
                 ah! ah! ah!
Ah! ah! ah! ah! ah! ah! ah! ah! ah! ah!
By Satan! this is well. What! am I judged?
You ponderous and slow-moving ministers,
Are you already met?

And twenty-five lines later:

              Mine eyes do pierce
The lower ostentations of your brief
And temporary royalty to reach
A Paramount Supreme.

In my transcription I have silently corrected a few misprints and expanded a few abbreviations.

1. With echoes of Marlowe's *Tamburlaine the Great*, Part One, V.ii.76 ff.

2. *Twelfth Night*, III.iv.31.

3. Webster, *The White Devil*, V.iii.32.

4. The whole passage contains echoes, probably deliberate, of *Othello*, V.ii.

5. Cf. Arnold, "Balder Dead," l. 340.

6. That is, Hortense de Beauharnais, mother of Napoleon III; the "Flemish sailor" was the Dutch Admiral Verhuel, whom gossip (not unfounded) nominated as his father.

7. Louis Veuillot (1813-83), violent ultramontane editor and propagandist.

FÉLICIEN COSSU

The manuscript in the British Museum, on which my text is based, consists of two double sheets of paper (and part of a third), the first leaf of which has as a watermark the figure of Britannia and the second the maker's name, E Towgood, and the date 1860. Folios 2 and 4 therefore carry the date, and are each the same piece of paper as folios 1 and 3, respectively. Folio 5 is one of the sheets of paper torn in half and then in half again, so that half of Britannia appears. The text was printed privately by T. J. Wise in 1915, with a preface by Gosse, but has not otherwise appeared in print.

The only reference to "Félicien Cossu" in Swinburne's letters is on August 18, 1862 (*Letters*, I, 58), but three months earlier he had carefully planted in the *Spectator* an allusion to his creation, a footnote stating that the poem "After Death" was taken "from the *Recueil de Chants Bretons,* edited by Félicien Cossu, première série (no more published), p. 89, Paris, 1858." He continued this campaign of authentication, presumably against the day when he would need it, or, if not, at least as a means of conditioning (not to say brainwashing) Hutton, the editor of the *Spectator,* into accepting for publication these two by-blows of his buried self, "Félicien Cossu" and "Ernest Clouët." In his first article on *Les Misérables,* June 21, 1862, he had alluded casually to the latter, and now, in the second, on July 26th, he artlessly pushes forward his other bantling. Swinburne is here speaking of Hugo's tendency to separate rigidly rather than to blend, like Shakespeare and Molière, the humorous and the serious. "In his *Pochades et Paradoxes,*" he observes, as urbanely as if he were offering the testimony of Sainte-Beuve or Matthew Arnold (Bonchurch XIII, 166-67),

> Félicien Cossu has remarked acutely enough on this difference, which he accepts as the generic point of difference between two styles and two centuries. "Que la fatalité frappe sur les Molière," the critic says, in his sharp, affected way, "on n'entendra point les pleurs, mais on verra le sang; que la fatalité frappe sur un homme de nos jours, et qu'elle lui fasse même la plus mince entaille, cela gémira, pleurera, maudira, hurlera, demeura à faire hausser les épaules à l'infini. Il n'y a plus de cocus depuis que le réalisme commence à s'apitoyer sur les mains."

And three more references are introduced later in so offhand a fashion that even the suspicions of an alerted editor would have been lulled.

Swinburne's third article on *Les Misérables* keeps up the pretense, and, perhaps recognizing his final opportunity, he alludes now to both Cossu and Clouët, shifting the point of view all but imperceptibly from his own passionate celebration of Hugo's famous doxology of generation, "Foliis ac

Frondibus," that luxuriant, multisonant sublimation of sense into spirit, in order to attribute to these creatures of his fancy a magnificent distillation of the ideas if not the very language of Sade and Whitman (Bonchurch XIII, 176-77):

> In this chapter of the garden the mere words have caught up (so to speak) and given back some sense of the vast, vigorous growth and death of things, of all those physical glories, all that mystical side of sensuous nature, handled so grandly in the great Pagan-renaissance poem of the *Petites Épopées*. At every step or stroke which opens up or cuts out some new point of insight, we know again the strong and cunning handiwork of the man who wrote *Le Satyre*. There is a whole season, the body and soul of it, "done into print"; the soft or sharp sound of wind, the smell of sap, "the hunger before the conception of spring, and the travail before the birth of summer, endless desire translating itself into endless production, the surplus of pain poured out to compound the excess of pleasure," whatever that may be, "a power and quality reminding him," the author of *Les Amours Étiques*, "of those words of an American poet," happily unknown to us, but quoted by the reviewer in legible if questionable English, "who has sung, in a cadence luminous and vibrating, 'the lusts of the leaves, the famine of the flowers, the appetite of the youth of the year'; all the tremulous odour and rumour of a season filled to the lips with luxury and life; justice done to every bird and blade and insect that has to complete spring." Reserving our opinion of those writing formulas peculiar to MM. Cossu and Clouet (or Clouët, is it?) and their school, we may allow this; that "there never was such a rush and overflow (*élancement et débordement*) of dumb natural beauty into human language." In the second book of the fifth part it appears to M. Cossu that "we get the wrong side of this curious great gift. One feels," that is, those endowed with the nerves and the perceptions of the writer feel, "in the throat and nostrils and hair that horrible pungent poison"; much as the actual thing might make one "sicken and sneeze and shudder all in a breath." Charity would recommend, would even implore, M. Cossu to abstain from the reperusal of this part of the book.

Hugo, Sade, Whitman! who but Swinburne could have brought it off? A new note in English prose is sounding, a voice that attained its full, if limited, power and range a few years later in the unfamiliar harmonies and dissonances of Walter Pater, whom one can easily picture coming for the first time upon these strange cadences, dwelling on them as in a revery, gasping, as old Marshal Blücher is said to have gasped on first beholding Paris, "Was für plündern!" And Swinburne, never really sure of his own commitment, seems hardly to have resisted when Pater rose beside the Isis and advanced, like the grim usurper in the sacred grove of Diana Nemorensis, to wrest his priesthood from him.

Swinburne's tone betrays, I think, not frivolity for its own sake but frivolity arising from uneasiness. Oscillating between the two poles of Hugo and Sade and far from comfortable at either extremity, he seems unable to resist either or to adapt himself to either. The invention of Cossu and Clouët was his solution, a temporary equilibrium, and thus we get the self-conscious parrying—"whatever that may be," "happily unknown to us," "legible if questionable English"—and also the cunning ribaldry of his re-translation of "rush and overflow" into "élancement et débordement," words that appear significantly in another (though still generative) sense in Sade.

Yet the essay on Cossu was certainly written before Swinburne had read Sade, to whom, we know, he was first exposed in the middle of August, 1862; the letter that establishes this shows also that Cossu had been completed some time earlier (*Letters,* I, 53-59). I suppose it was written before his first reference to it in the *Spectator,* May 24, 1862 (though a similar supposition regarding "Ernest Clouët" could be shown up as inaccurate), and I would surmise the date to be the summer or autumn, 1861. The truth is, however, that we know so little about Swinburne in the very early sixties that conjecture is otiose.

It remains only to be said that the French verses attributed to Félicien Cossu, competent and original though they are, are the verses of a man who has read, and read it well, the poetry of Gautier and Baudelaire but who, born and baptized in the church of Victor Hugo, remained in it for confirmation. Nothing would be easier than to cite a "source" for a great many lines and passages in these poems, but I have contained my enthusiasm and called attention to only a few similar passages, enough, I hope, to put the matter beyond doubt.

1. There are many cancellations in this short poem, but none in the third line, where the howler is Swinburnian, not editorial.

2. This line first read: "Plume d'oiseau malade—pied d'un ange."

3. The matter-of-fact opening is Hugolian:

"C'est la date choisie au fond de ta pensée ("Nox," l. 1, in *Les Châtiments*)

"C'est la nuit; la nuit noire, assoupie et profonde" (*Les Châtiments,* I.xiv.1)

4. Another version of the fifteen lines beginning here (with line 15) is in the Library of Congress, written on the back of the leaf (watermark undated) containing the concluding twelve lines of "Messaline au cirque." I record the most interesting variants:

l. 18: "La jeunesse a le front chauve et l'enfer aux yeux." (In the British Museum manuscript this line first read: "L'enfer emplit de feu ces lèvres et ces yeux.")

l. 26: "Et la volupté veut du sang pour s'apaiser."

l. 28: "C'est le débordement de l'âme des latrines."

5. (a) "Et la nature, au fond des siècles et des nuits,
Accouplant Rabelais à Dante plein d'ennuis,
Et l'Ugolin sinistre au Grandgousier difforme,
Près de l'immense deuil montre le rire énorme"
("A André Chénier," ll. 21-24,
in *Les Contemplations,* I.v)

(b)   "Dans les cachots profonds,
Les bourreaux s'accouplaient à des martyres mortes"
("Au Lion d'Androclès," ll. 18-19,
in *La Légende des siècles,* VIII)

6. *Sic.* Line 36, below, first read: "Semble un démon plaqué sur la moule d'un ange."

7. A manuscript of this poem in the Library of Congress is watermarked 1863. In line 3, *ossements* (correctly spelled in the Library of Congress manuscript) was written without the letter *t*.

8. A separate manuscript of this poem, "Messaline au cirque," written on blue foolscap without a dated watermark, is in the Library of Congress. The only departures from the text here are in punctuation and in line 25 the word *tendus* instead of *brisés*. (In the British Museum text there are several cancellations, but the only one of interest is in line 33, which first read "Eclaboussé de sang par l'arène infernale.") In certain specific ways the poem seems to show the influence of the description of Dürer's "Melancholia" in the concluding section of Gautier's poem "Melancholia," and also of such poems as "Les Vendeurs du temple" (especially the section beginning "Des hommes vivent là" and the conclusion), "À un Jeune Tribun," "Magdalena," "La Mort dans la vie" (notably Section 6), and, most of all, "Le Lion du cirque." Precisely, Swinburne seems to have learned from Gautier, as well as from D. G. Rossetti, the hard, sharp outline, the precise positioning, of the drawing, a quality not at all characteristic of Hugo but perfectly distinct in much of Gautier's poetry and very conspicuous in his art criticism, where (I believe) there can be no doubt of his influence on Swinburne. And I suspect that with more day-by-day knowledge of Swinburne in these dimly lit years one could make out a case for the effect on him of the Roman pictures ("The Christian Martyrs," "Age of Augustus," "Ave, Caesar") of Gérôme, both directly and (once more) via Gautier.

For the rest, anyone who will read a few hundred lines of Hugo, that world without end, will see who fashioned Swinburne behind and before.

An almost random sampling of *Les Châtiments* (1853), *Les Contemplations* (1856), and *La Légende des siècles* (first series, 1859) would probably serve the turn, but a few carefully chosen specimens will serve it more efficiently and I therefore suggest "L'Égout de Rome" in *Les Châtiments* (VII. iv) and, in *La Légende des siècles,* the poem "Au Lion d'Androclès" (VIII), the description of the "ancien manoir de Corbus" in "Eviradnus" (XV. iii. 513-88).

9. "Pourquoi ce choix? pourquoi cet attendrissement
   Immense du profond et divin firmament?
   Pourquoi tout l'univers penché sur une tête?
   Pourquoi l'aube donnant à la femme une fête?
   Pourquoi ces chants? Pourquoi ces palpitations
   Des flots dans plus de joie et dans plus de rayons?
   Pourquoi partout l'ivresse et la hâte d'éclore,
   Et les antres heureux de s'ouvrir à l'aurore,
   Et plus d'encens sur terre et plus de flamme aux cieux?"
                     ("Le Sacre de la femme," ll. 191-199,
                        in *La Légende des siècles,* II. i)

10. *Sic.* Two lines below, *Stryge* is, as Gosse has pointed out, a Hugolian word. It appears frequently in *Notre-Dame de Paris,* and I have noted it in "Le Poète" (l. 26) in *Les Contemplations,* III.xxviii, in "Eviradnus" (ll. 15, 756) and in "Ratbert" (l. 169) in *La Légende des siècles* (XV. i and xii, and XVIII.i).

11. "Messaline en riant se mettait toute nue
    Et sur le lit publique, lascive, se couchait."
               ("Au Lion d'Androclès," ll. 28-29,
                 in *La Légende des siècles,* VIII)

12. (a) "O temps miraculeux! ô gaîtés homériques!
    O rires de l'Europe et des deux Amériques!
    Croûtes qui larmoyez! bons dieux mal accrochés
    Qui saignez dans vos coins! madones qui louchez!
    Phénomènes vivants! ô choses inouïes!
    Candeurs! énormités au jour épanouies!
    Le goudron déclaré fétide par le suif,
    Judas flairant Shylock et criant: c'est un juif!
    L'arsenic indigné dénonçant la morphine,
    La hotte injuriant la borne, Messaline
    Reprochant à Goton son regard effronté,
    Et Dupin accusant Sauzet de lâcheté!
                     ("Eblouissements," ll. 1-12,
                        in *Les Châtiments,* VI. v)

(b) Sur ce, les charlatans prêchent leur auditoire
    D'idiots, de mouchards, de grecs, de philistins,
    Et de gens plein d'esprit détroussant les crétins;
    La Bourse rit; la hausse offre aux badauds ses prismes;
    La douce hypocrisie éclate en aphorismes;
    C'est bien, nous gagnons gros et nous sommes contents;
    Et ce sont, Juvénal, les maximes du temps.
    Quelque sous-diacre, éclos dans je ne sais quel bouge,
    Trouva ces vérités en balayant Montrouge,
    Si bien qu'aujourd'hui fiers et rois des temps nouveaux,
    Messieurs les aigresfins et messieurs les dévots
    Déclarent, s'éclairant aux lueurs de leur cierge,
    Jeanne d'Arc courtisane et Messaline vierge.

                 ("A Juvénal," ll. 80-92,
             in *Les Châtiments*, VI. xiii)

13. *Sic.* As in "Caprice," above, Swinburne chose rhythm over grammar.

ERNEST CLOUËT

The source of my text is the manuscript in the British Museum, nine leaves of blue foolscap, written on one side only, of which numbers 2, 5, 6, and 9 are watermarked 1862. Certainly not a fair copy, this is probably the first draft, as the cancellations and interlinear additions would seem to indicate. Swinburne never refers to this work in his letters. The watermark, however, proves, at least, that this version (and no other holograph is known or suspected) was written on this paper in 1862 or later, and since Swinburne referred to Clouët in passing in his review of Parts II and III of Hugo's *Les Misérables* in the *Spectator,* June 21, 1862 (Bonchurch, XIII, 162), we can take it for granted that he had something of the sort in mind as early as that date.

The actual composition was somewhat later, for in the final paragraph he refers explicitly to "Jean Valjean in the great sewer," and Part V of *Les Misérables,* in which this episode occurs, was published June 30, 1862, in both the Brussels and Paris editions. It is also clear from other allusions that Swinburne had this section of the novel in mind: "the odour of all these moral drains and sewers"; "chiffonniers . . . qui tiennent dans leur hotte l'avenir encore tout ruisselant des fanges du passé" from Hugo's "une hotte de chiffonnier . . . fit l'admiration des connaisseurs" (Pléiade edition, p. 1292) and "Il se redressa . . . tout ruisselant de fange" (p. 1322); "he plunges ear-deep into some unspeakable quagmire" from Hugo's "Il n'avait plus que la tête hors de l'eau" in the chapter called "Le Fontis" (p. 1322); "il y a dans ces latrines quelque chose de Dieu" from Hugo's "Il . . . y resta quelque temps, l'âme abîmée dans on ne sait quelle parole de Dieu" (p. 1322) or, equally, of Jean Valjean's entering the sewers, "La pupille se dilate dans la nuit et finit par y trouver du jour, de même que l'âme se dilate dans le malheur et finit par y trouver Dieu" (p. 1303); "portefaix flamboyante de l'idéal" from Hugo's "portefaix de Rome" (p. 1288).

I believe, though I cannot prove it or even produce a real clue outside the actual text, that the language here shows the direct influence of the Marquis de Sade, an influence that would necessarily put the date in or after the second half of August. The only shred of evidence that can be adduced is negative: it is probably significant, though in no sense conclusive, that Swinburne did not refer to this piece, along with the allusion to "Cossu," in his letter to Milnes on August 18th. It seems to me obvious, for instance, that Swinburne is trifling with Sade (as well as with his readers) in the passage "Ouvrir à coups de ciseaux la matrice noire des siècles frémissants pour en dégager, foetus radieux, la régénération humaine; eventrer le sphinx impitoyable, éviscerer Dieu." In my zeal, I have gone so far as to compile a little anthology of Sadique eviscerations—surely choiceness of subject matter cannot be further refined—and yet am forced to conclude, once more, that with Swinburne the farther you go, the more Hugo. His fine flourish was certainly suggested not by surgery in Sade but by Hugo's description of the birth of time and matter at the beginning of *La Légende des siècles:*

> Ouverture du monde! instant prodigieux! . . .
> On sentait tressaillir sous leurs groupes confus
> La terre, inépuisable et suprême matrice . . .
>
> ("Le Sacre de la femme," ll. 67, 80-81)

and by the revery of Jupiter later on (*La Légende des siècles,* XXII):

> On voyait dans ses yeux le monde commencé;
> Et dans l'un le présent, dans l'autre le passé;
> Dans le troisième errait l'avenir comme un songe . . .
> Son pouce et son index faisaient dans les ténèbres
> S'ouvrir ou se fermer les ciseaux d'Atropos;
> La radieuse paix naissait de son repos. . . .
>
> ("Le Satyre," ll. 149-68)

All we know about the date, then, is that the piece was composed after June, 1862. It was sent for publication in the *Spectator,* but here again we have no way of knowing when. The manuscript bears the notation "Proof to Mr. Swinburne," and the very galley-proofs are in the British Museum; but Richard Holt Hutton, the editor, performed a little preventive surgery of his own, so that Swinburne's joke, though apparently never detected as a hoax, died a-borning. "Les Abimes are still in type," Hutton wrote primly (*A Swinburne Library*, p. 225),

> but I cannot say I think they will appear. The subject seems to me to deserve no more criticism than a Holywell Street publication, nor could I speak of it in The Spectator without more real disgust than your article inspires. There is a tone of raillery about it which I think one should hardly use to pure obscenity. I confess your tone on Art is a little unintelligible to me. What is Poetry and Art? Are they all "flowers"? Are they all to be judged by smell and sight? I ask not in prejudice, but because I really wish to get at the theory of a man who seems to me to have some narrow theory imprisoning a very subtle and keen sense of the poetical within unnatural limits. You write as if Art and Poetry consisted of pictorial qualities. Can you hold to anything so narrow? . . .

This letter, according to T. J. Wise, was dated "December 16th, 1862," but W. D. Paden ("Swinburne, the *Spectator* in 1862, and Walter Bagehot," *Six Studies in Nineteenth-Century English Literature and Thought,* Univ. of Kansas Humanistic Studies, No. 35, pp. 91-115) has pointed out, first, that the letter bears *no* date, and, second, that it must have been written after September 16th, since it alludes to a letter of that date. (The last seven sentences refer, of course, not to Clouët but to Swinburne's essay on Baudelaire, which appeared in the *Spectator,* September 6, 1862.) Thus, Hutton's letter being undatable, the most definite statement possible about the time of composition of this piece, unless I have overlooked some clue, is that it was probably written in the summer or very early autumn, 1862.

It was privately printed by T. J. Wise, with an introduction by Gosse, in 1916.

1. This sketch of Borel seems to have been based on Baudelaire's essay "Petrus Borel," posthumously collected in *L'Art romantique* (1868) but first published in *Revue fantaisiste,* July 15, 1861.

2. Published in 1829.

3. Aside from its obvious debt to Hugo, this piece of bravura must owe something to Baudelaire's *Les Fleurs du mal,* especially "Une Charogne."

La Soeur de la Reine

I

This fragment of manuscript, now in the Library of Congress, comprises ten leaves of Swinburne's familiar blue foolscap, written, in dark ink, on both sides, making up, therefore, twenty pages in all. Of these leaves numbers two, three, five, and six are watermarked E TOWGOOD/1861; number eight is the same, except that the date is 1862.

Swinburne had sketched the outlines of this drama as early as January, 1861, when he dashed off this summary in a letter to a friend (*Letters,* I, 42):

> A twin sister of Queen Victoria, kidnapped on her birth by consent of the late Sir R. Peel and Lord Chancellor Eldon for political reasons—to remove a rival candidate for the throne—grows up a common prostitute—is discovered in The Haymarket by the *Lor Maire* on a profligate excursion—informed of her origin claims her rights—is confronted with queen—queen swoons—the proofs of her birth bought and destroyed—the Abp of Canterbury solemnly perjures himself to the effect that she is an impostor—finally consumed by an ill-requited attachment to Lord John Russell, the heroine charcoals herself to death.

Although this drama has never been printed, even privately, it has not wanted admirers or an audience. Julian Osgood Field (1849?-1925), expatriate American, swindler, scoundrel, and man about town, of whom Sir Osbert Sitwell wrote with such scorn and indignation in *Great Morning,* left an account of it that is certainly in the main authentic, though no doubt untrustworthy in details. Slippery, dishonest, charming, plausible, like his friend Charles Augustus Howell, of whom he seems a sort of replica done in darker colors—Field was a rascal, Howell a rogue—he was the pseudonymous "Sigma" of a book called *Personalia* (1903) and the anonymous author of several others, including *Things I Shouldn't Tell* (1924), *Uncensored Recollections* (1924), and *More Uncensored Recollections* (1926), of which the titles admirably suggest the tone and quality. In 1866 or 1867 he met Swinburne at Howell's house in Brixton, where he heard a good deal about the unpublished novel now known as *Lesbia Brandon.* In 1869, aged 19, he matriculated at Merton College, Oxford, and, according to Osbert Sitwell (*Great Morning,* p. 179), Swinburne "stayed with him on several occasions"—a statement that must be viewed skeptically in the absence of corroborative evidence. Jowett is said to have "thought highly" of him, Sitwell adds, and one supposes that during some of Swinburne's visits to the Master of Balliol, Field, like many another worshipful undergraduate, was summoned to meet the great poet. At all events, here, though Field did not reveal how he came by it, is his version of "La Sœur de la reine" from *Things I Shouldn't Tell* (Philadelphia and London, 1925, pp. 137-38):

> All Swinburne's friends will remember his very funny unpublished, in fact, unwritten, parody of Victor Hugo—the play, *La Princesse*

Katy, which the little bard used to recite to his intimates. As most people know, fine as Hugo's plays in verse are, his plays in prose are absolute trash—like much of his poetry—not quite perhaps so grotesquely ridiculous as old Dumas's *Richard Darlington* and *Halifax,* but very nearly. *La Princesse Katy* is a very clever parody of the great Victor. There was no special plot, but Princesse Katy, although only a barmaid, is the rightful Queen of England, Queen Victoria being illegitimate! The two advisers of Her Majesty are "Sir Peel" and "Sir Russell." Sir Peel is described as "young, beautiful and debauched"; and Sir Russell (they are both, by the way, madly in love with Queen Victoria) says in a soliloquy—"I am not young, I am not beautiful, but I can be profligate and I will!" Sir Peel serenades the Queen at Windsor and here are the opening words:

> "Ce qu'il faut chercher sur la terre
>   Nuit et jour,
> Ce n'est pas la vertu sévère,
>   C'est l'Amour!"

Poor Princess Katy has a most terrible adventure in a hansom cab, quite unfit for publication, and the curtain rises on the scene to discover *Quelques jeunes Aldermans très gris.* The last act is in Queen Victoria's bedroom. She has just been confined of the Heir Apparent and Sir Locock is with her. Her Majesty dismisses him. She is agitated: she has heard of Princess Katy and knows she is the rightful Queen. What is to be done? Obviously destroy Katy. So she sends for the Public Hangman and tells him he must do away with this dangerous young lady. He, *gentilhomme quand même,* refuses to do so vile a deed, but falls on his knees before the Sovereign as he murmurs that he cannot obey her. Then says Victoria, "Levez-vous, Sir Calcraft, Pair d'Angleterre!" But the glorious fellow rises proudly and puts aside the tempting honour—"Pardon, Madame: je ne suis que le bourreau de Londres!"

W. H. Mallock, another admirer, in his *Memoirs of Life and Literature* (1920) recorded his recollections of it in a tableau that I, for one, would not willingly let die, and this time we do not have to rely on supposition. As an undergraduate at Balliol, Swinburne's old college, Mallock had the good fortune to see him there more than once in the early seventies, and on one occasion, probably in December, 1871, he dined in the Master's Lodge with Jowett and Swinburne. No one reading his account of that memorable evening could be surprised that he was stirred with a sense of wonder. "Here at last," he wrote, "I realized the veritable genius who had made the

English language a new instrument of passion. Here at last was the singer for whose songs my ears were shells which still murmured with such lines as I had first furtively read by the gaslight of the Brighton theater." A few days later, Mallock tells us, just after an undergraduate luncheon, he again saw Swinburne plain, but this time with a difference, old in a new state, another yet the same, not Hyperion but the satyr:

> He was, as I presently gathered, about to begin an account of a his-
> torical drama by himself . . .—a sort of parody of what Victor Hugo
> might have written had he dramatized English events at the opening
> of the reign of Queen Victoria. The first act, he said, showed England
> on the verge of a revolution, which was due to the frightful orgies of
> the Queen at "Buckingham's Palace." The Queen, with unblushing
> effrontery, had taken to herself a lover, in the person of Lord John
> Russell, who had for his rival "Sir Peel." Sir Peel was represented as
> pleading his own cause in a passionate scene, which wound up as
> follows: "Why do you love Lord John Russell, and why do you not
> love me? I know why you love Lord John Russell. He is young, he is
> beautiful, he is profligate. I cannot be young, I cannot be beautiful,
> but I will be profligate." Then followed the stage direction, "Exit for
> ze Haysmarket." In a later act it appeared that the Queen and Lord John
> Russell had between them given the world a daughter, who, having
> been left to her own devices, or, in other words, to the streets, reap-
> pears as "Miss Kitty," and is accorded some respectable rank. Under
> these conditions she becomes the object of much princely devotion; but
> the moral hypocrisy of England has branded her as a public scandal.
> With regard to her so-called depravities nobody entertains a doubt, but
> one princely admirer, of broader mind than the rest, declares that in
> spite of these she is really the embodiment of everything that is divine
> in women. "She may," he says, "have done everything which might
> have made a Messalina blush, but whenever she looked at the sky she
> murmured 'God' and whenever she looked at a flower she murmured
> 'mother.' "

Only the portions of the manuscript printed here, Act Two (probably complete) and Act Four (probably incomplete), are known to me, but much more was composed and very likely still exists somewhere. Other accounts make it clear beyond doubt that a theme, or a variation, of first importance has been lost. Georges Lafourcade (*La Jeunesse de Swinburne,* II, 375), for instance, who saw a "fragment" of this drama, quoted a portion that does not appear here. "Swinburne nous peint cette fois John Russell," he says, "faisant une scène de jalousie, au sujet du poète Wordsworth, à la Reine, qui se défend ainsi:

Ah, mon Dieu! Faut-il être fou pour avoir de telles jalousies. Ce pauvre cher M. Wordsworth, c'était le meilleur des hommes; il venait tous les soirs m'apprendre le clavecin; tu n'iras pas me dire que ce n'était point dans ses devoirs de poète lauréat?

We know from other sources, however, that the Queen protests too much, for John Bailey (1864-1931), a critic and reviewer who picked up much town talk and literary chit-chat, heard in 1917 from an old Arts Club acquaintance of Swinburne's about an "invention" of the poet's in which Queen Victoria confessed in French "to the Duchess of Kent her unfortunate lapse from virtue":

> Ce n'était pas un prince; ce n'était pas un milord, ni même *Sir R. Peel*. C'était un misérable du peuple, en nomme [sic] *Wordsworth*, qui m'a récité des vers de son *Excursion* d'une sensualité si chaleureuse qu'ils m'ont ébranlée—et je suis tombée.

And Swinburne himself, recalling these galliantics in 1880 (*Letters*, IV, 168), though, like the author of *Things I Shouldn't Tell*, he momentarily fused (or confused) "La Fille du policeman" and "La Sœur de la reine," leaves no doubt that Wordsworth's name too peals in the "kyrielle" of the Queen's lovers. "Albert the Good," he wrote, "then better known as 'le prince prolétaire' . . . ,"

> reproached the Queen with the early weakness which had led her into a criminal connection with Mr. Wordsworth, who had scandalously abused his privileged position as Laureate to seduce her by means of recitations "de cette poésie fiévreuse et palpitante de sensualité—cette excursion, comme il l'appelait, à bride lâchée, à travers les champs fiévreux de l'amour illégitime—de la passion sans frein."
> . . . When Lord John Russell, who had supplanted him in the royal favour, reminded her Majesty of this first liaison, she could only reply (see historical MS. *penes me*) "Combien de fois, mon Jack bienaimé,—toi qui me le reproches—ne t'ai-je pas entendu roucouler à mes pieds sa chanson érotique de Betty-Foy!" These things will be known some day.

On Swinburne the inevitable effect of either the Queen or *The Excursion* was levitation; with the two combined he was of course a *pater ecstaticus*. We have a sample of what he could do with and to the poem in a wicked comparison, tossed off to divert William Michael Rossetti (*Letters*, II, 95), between Wordsworth's prosy old "gray-haired Wanderer" and the equally somniferous Marquis de Sade, both of whom drone on and on till sense and shame and right and wrong are drowned. With the Queen he was perhaps

more a child of his time, no more able than others to resist the alluring
speculations that to this day humanize and rejuvenate certain senior citizens
in our greater universities, that have nourished the growth, chapter by chapter, of the John Brown Society. More than two decades after the fragmentary
piece printed here, Swinburne, rising splendidly to the occasion, delighted
Georgiana Jones with the first act of a tragic drama ("Sir Brown: drame en
7 actes et 49 tableaux") based on Queen Victoria's *More Leaves from the
Journal of a Life in the Highlands,* published in 1884. Here is the entire
sketch (*Letters,* V, 54-5):

"LA MORT DU MARI."

The scene is at Osborne's House, Ile de Wigth. The Queen is discovered impatiently expectant of news, seated in her own apartment.
"Entre Brown, Grand costume de Higlander. Il l'embrasse.

La Reine) C'est fini?

Brown)   Tu l'as dit. Mais embrasse-moi donc aussi, toi, ma reine!

La Reine) Mon Johny! Mon Jack adoré! Je vais donc enfin être
toute à toi!

Brown)   Et tes enfants, Victoria?

La Reine) Et la Tour de Londres?

Brown)   (avec un méchant sourire). En effet—c'est un séjour
malsain, à ce qu'on dit, pour les Princes de Galles."

Till the last act, the shadow of the scaffold and the axe—the recol-
lection that George II. at the instigation of Strafford, Bolingbroke, and
the elder Pitt, had his son beheaded in the Tower for a reflection on
the character of Nell Gwyn—prevents the Prince of Wales from aveng-
ing his father: till the end (as aforesaid) of the last act, when Brown,
stabbed to the heart, expires at the feet of his accomplice, who is spared
on condition of taking a vow to appear no more in public—and the
Prince exclaims as the curtain falls—

"Dors en paix, ô mon père! Tu m'avais donné la vie—je te donne
la vengeance!"

One inference, though there is nothing like proof of it in anything we
know, is, if not inescapable, at least irresistible. Mallock's too-brief and ill-
remembered synopsis does not even mention Wordsworth, but it is remarkable, in his account, that Kitty is the Queen's daughter, not her sister,
and this being true, at least in one redaction, one can't help surmising that
Wordsworth rather than Lord John Russell, the Laureate rather than the
statesman, the poet rather than the Prime Minister, must have fathered the
Princess Kitty. Mallock's last line really leaves one no alternative.

II

In this rapid improvisation, tossed off solely to amuse his friends, Swinburne's French was as fluent as his fancy, his grammar as uncontainable as his wit. Idiom and orthography, therefore, sometimes burst under the pressure. There are very few cancellations, however, and of these I record all that merit preservation, ignoring half a dozen of no conceivable interest.

1. Here, Swinburne canceled: "qui me creuse le corps et l'âme, qui me ride, qui me dessèche."

2. Doubtless a deliberate echo of the song of François I in *Le Roi s'amuse*, IV,ii, which became in *Rigoletto* one of the most familiar of all arias.

3. Part of this seems to be a parody of Mary's lovemaking with Fabiani in Hugo's *Marie Tudor*, II,i. And there can be no doubt that her imperious offer of Fabiani's head to the executioner (II,ix) inspired the scene, described by Julian Osgood Field, in which Victoria consigns the Princess Kitty to Calcraft, the Public Hangman.

4. Before "Mausprick" Swinburne canceled "Prickwell."

5. Here, and in the three instances following, Swinburne substituted "Kitty" for "Mary."

6. Before "John!" Swinburne canceled: "C'est lui! c'est mon amant."

7. Sir Francis Burdett (1770-1844) and, below, Sydney Smith (1771-1845), though he was a canon, not a dean, are the themes of these freewheeling improvisations.

8. After the stage direction Swinburne canceled: "Tu m'aimes! tu m'aimes bien! tu m'aimes!"

LA FILLE DU POLICEMAN

I

"La Fille du policeman" was written in 1860 and 1861, a period when we know very little about the author. Swinburne's sole reference to it, except for a glancing allusion years later, occurs in late January, 1861, in a letter to William Bell Scott:

> Item—nearly completed my French novel by way of relaxation—don't talk of French horrors till you have read the hideous disclosures of English society contained therein! Rape, perjury, murder, opium, suicide, treason, Jesuitry, are the mildest ingredients. The atrocious conduct public and private of Prince Albert is branded with deserved and scathing indignation. As for the clergy. . . .

The only other contemporary allusion is a famous two-edged description by Meredith that, for a full century now, has invested it with an astonishing coterie glamour: "Swinburne read me the other day his French novel . . . : the funniest rampingest satire on French novelists dealing with English themes that you can imagine," he wrote to a friend. "One chapter, 'Ce qui peut se passer dans un Cab Safety,' where Lord Whitestick, Bishop of Londres, ravishes the heroine, is quite marvelous. But he is not subtle; and I don't see any internal centre from which springs anything that he does." This hapless last sentence has long dogged Swinburne criticism and damned Swinburne, but it has had its day. No one who *knows* Swinburne's poetry and his prose, critical or fictional or burlesque, including the present piece, could judiciously maintain, that, whatever their shortcomings, they lack subtlety or a radiant center.

Meredith's remarks have kept it alive, but Georges Lafourcade alone among Swinburnians has concerned himself with "La Fille du policeman"—with a few remarks in his general ordering of Swinburne's early works in *La Jeunesse de Swinburne* (II, 373-74), with a popular account in an article, "Swinburne romancier, ou La Fille du policeman," *Minotaure,* VII (1935), 62-65. Suggesting that the target of this "parody on the worst class of French novels" was general rather than particular, he specified a novel by Dumas *père* and certain dramas (*Richard Darlington, Catherine Howard, Kean*) as probably falling within range of Swinburne's fire. As far as these titles are concerned, my own impression is that they prove nothing but the vanity of human wishes, though Lafourcade cites two other names that deserve more attention, Paul Féval's drama *Les Mystères de Londres* (1844) and, in a footnote in *Minotaure,* Petrus Borel's novel *Madame Putiphar* (1839). Of the former of these not much need, or can, be said. Swinburne, who read everything and forgot nothing, may well have known it, but tempting as the possibility is, it remains merely an assumption. What is more to the point is that the wretched play, for all its flacon of laudanum, its password "Newgate et Treadmill," its poor but noble Irish heroine who loves above her station, its caricatured names (Lady Bloomberry, Lord Brompton, Paddy O'Chrane, Handcuffs, the policeman), contains nothing but the paraphernalia of melodrama, nothing that need have been drawn upon for "La Fille du policeman." One wonders languidly what the object would be in burlesquing so abject a thing. With equal insouciance I would put on record an English imitation of Eugène Sue's *Les Mystères de Paris*—George M. W. Reynolds' *Mysteries of London* (1845-46), affirming only that I have read it and I live.

"La Fille du policeman" is, as far as I know, unique. The closest comparison I could make to it is that hauntingly brilliant bad joke *L'Histoire d'O,* published a few years ago, by "Pauline Réage," but in spirit and technique both "La Fille du policeman" and "La Sœur de la reine" must have something in common with the "Irish Court Scenes" that so titillated the initiate a century ago. Maurice Kingsley, in his essay "Personal Traits of Henry Kingsley," prefacing an edition of the novel *Leighton Court* (New York, 1895), writes that his uncle

> was the only man, I believe, who ever knew by heart the famous "Irish Court Scenes"—naughtiest and most humorous of tales—unpublished of course, but handed down from generation to generation of the faithful. Most delightful was an interview between his late Majesty George the Fourth and an itinerant showman, which ended up with, "No, George the Fourth, you shall not have my Rumptifoozle!"

A different case can be made for *Madame Putiphar*, a novel that Swinburne described in 1879 as a "very queer and grim work of crude and impudent tragic genius" (*Letters*, IV, 118), which seems a fair appraisal. We cannot be sure when he first read Borel. The earliest date that can be affirmed is the summer, 1862, when, as C. K. Hyder (*Swinburne's Literary Career and Fame*, pp. 10-11) has demonstrated, he set in motion an elaborate campaign of artful, seemingly casual allusion—in cunningness of conception and thoroughness of groundwork worthy of the latter-day master-forger from whom, by an unhappy irony, his name can never be divorced—in order to establish the authenticity of his two wonderful hoaxes, "Félicien Cossu" and "Ernest Clouët." In the latter of these essays Swinburne's familiarity with Borel's life and works is indubitable.

As for *Madame Putiphar*, it seems to me as hard to take it seriously as a whole as it is to forget some of its parts, and since it has never been discussed in detail by a Swinburnian, a quick summary might be helpful. The title refers to Madame de Pompadour—Louis XV appears briefly as Pharaon —who is not even a major character, but the story concerns the love of Déborah, the daughter of the Earl and Countess Cockermouth, herself daughter of Sir Meadowbanks, for Patrick Fitz-Whyte, poor but worthy. As Lady Cockermouth tells him (I, 35): "Déborah, c'est ma fille! c'est la comtesse Cockermouth! Et toi, Pat, tu n'es qu'un lourdaud!" Lord Cockermouth and his valet, mistaking her in the dark for her lover, attack and wound Déborah, whereupon Patrick flees to Paris. There he is welcomed by Monseigneur Arthur-Richard Dillon, a Frenchman of Irish extraction, Archbishop of Narbonne (as in real life), who ought to have been "*in partibus infidelium*, archevêque de l'Opera" (I, 89).

Patrick is struck by all the luxury of the archiepiscopal surroundings: "Ce qui surtout lui jetoit du désordre dans les idées, c'étoient ces parures féminines étalées au milieu des aumuces, des mitres et des rochets, c'étoit une mantille jetée sur une crosse, et des jupons mêlés avec un pallium; il trouvoit bien une solution à ce problème, mais comme elle entachoit la chasteté de monseigneur Dillon, sa candeur ne pouvait l'admettre" (I, 90-91). Through the good offices of the Archbishop, he enters the musketeers and the colonel of the regiment, Monsieur de Gave de Villepastour pursues Déborah, who has long since joined and married Patrick in Paris, through interminably multiplied episodes. Patrick's virtue, meanwhile, is assailed by Madame Putiphar (I, 181-82):

> Elle soulevoit, elle entr'ouvroit comme par étourderie son peignoir, et complaisamment laissoit voir à Patrick ses épaules potelées, ses beaux seins, sa belle poitrine et ses jambes blanches, jeunes et gracieuses de formes, qui depuis vingt ans faisoient les délices de Pharaon.
>
> A ce spectacle Patrick en apparence demeuroit assez froid; cependant ses regards subitement enflammés s'arretoient parfois amoureusement sur ces eloquentes nudités; et la Putiphar, qui devinoit son émotion, souffloit sur cet embrasement par les poses les plus excitantes et l'abandon le plus coupable. Il y avoit en lui un combat violent entre sa fougue et sa raison, entre son appétit et son devoir. Il comprenoit parfaitement toutes les invitations tacites de la Putiphar; ses sens y répondaient, son sang bouilloit, il trembloit de fièvre. Comme une main invisible le penchoit sur elle ainsi qu'on se penche sur une fleur pour en aspirer le parfum. Lorsque, l'esprit éperdu, il se sentoit sur le point de se jeter sur ce corps revissant de de lui appliquer de longs baisers, ses mains s'agrippoient au canapé, et il se retenoit avec violence.

A vision of Déborah coming into his mind, he begins to examine the pictures and the painted panels. Later, he sings her Irish ballads, and, after resisting her renewed blandishments through several pages, protests his fidelity to Déborah and reads aloud from a volume of *La Nouvelle Héloïse* that he picks up (I, 198): "La femme d'un charbonnier est plus estimable que la maîtresse d'un roi."

Both Déborah and Patrick are imprisoned, and their son Vengeance is born in prison. Ultimately, hundreds of pages later, Déborah, with the aid of her godfather, Sir John Chatsworth, to whom she had smuggled a letter, escapes from a Mediterranean fastness, secludes herself, now a wealthy lady, on the Irish estate inherited from her maternal grandfather, and rears her son. When he is grown up, they go to France, and he seeks out and challenges M. le marquis de Gave de Villepastour and is of course himself slain. On the surrender of the Bastille, Patrick is discovered and Déborah summoned. What she finds, instead of the bonny, openhearted Irish lad for whom she had forsaken all, to whose memory she had devoted her life and thoughts during years of apparent widowhood, is a repulsive, stinking, almost nude emaciated body and bushy, matted beard, a beast babbling unintelligibly in Erse, recognizable (finally) only by the ring, on a fleshless finger, that she had given him, years before at Cockermouth Castle. Approaching, she tells him who she is, but, hopelessly insane, comprehending nothing, he pushes her violently away. She falls to her knees in supplication and then, over-whelmed—"Rentrant subitement en soi-même avec la vitesse d'une épée qui rentre dans le fourreau"—she collapses and dies, and with this powerful, horrible, moving scene, which, along with a few others, more than compensate one for the supreme silliness of much else, the novel comes to an end.

There is much here that Swinburne may have turned to account in a general sense, nothing that can be established or even comfortably put forward, though if we had all the parts of his burlesque, such a judgment might have to be modified. Bishop Whitestick may well be a composite of Borel's voluptuous archbishop and his false-hearted, false-tongued, false-faced colonel, and it is not hard to see how Borel's misanthropic republicanism (in Baudelaire's phrase) would have fascinated Swinburne, especially in the early sixties. Moreover, the novel not only is filled with the Anglo-Saxon words that fit so uneasily, so comically, in the French prose, with the names that, as Wordsworth put it, in a roughly comparable context, appear to "license some unruliness of mind," but also has its share of the orthographic and typographic delights on which Swinburne was to ring so many changes —Lord Cokermouth, cokney, and, most awe-inspiring of all, "Saint hearted milk-soup," as the Earl calls the Countess (I, 55).

Still, due allowances having been made, with Swinburne it is nearly always safest to assume that to Victor belong the spoils, and there can be no doubt of it here. One need look no further than at the opening sentences of *Notre-Dame de Paris* (1831) or at the preface to *La Légende des siècles*, First Series, which Swinburne read in December, 1859, just after its publication, pronouncing it "the grandest book that has been published . . . for years," to see that his prose is vintage Hugo:

Les personnes qui voudront bien jeter un coup d'œil sur ce livre ne s'en feraient pas une idée précise, si elles y voyaient autre chose qu'un commencement.

Ce livre est-il donc un fragment? Non. Il existe à part. Il a, comme on le verra, son exposition, son milieu et sa fin.

Mais, en même temps, il est, pour ainsi dire, la première page, d'un autre livre.

Un commencement peut-il être un tout? Sans doute. Un péristyle est un édifice. . . .

Il existe solitairement et forme un tout; il existe solidairement et fait partie d'un ensemble.

Cet ensemble, que sera-t-il? . . .

Quant à ces deux volumes pris en eux-mêmes, l'auteur n'a qu'un mot à en dire: le genre humain . . . a deux aspects: l'aspect historique et l'aspect légendaire. Le second n'est pas moins vrai que le premier; le premier n'est pas moins conjectural que le second.

And there is more. Hugo cannot have been far from his mind, or his heart, when he composed, and if "sources" exist for "La Fille du policeman," they are not among those works of Dumas that happen to have an English setting, not in such subliterary confections as those of Paul Féval, nor even, I believe, in a novel like *Madame Putiphar,* profoundly as it may have infiltrated his sensibility. The source is the one claimed for "La Sœur de la reine"—the dramas of Hugo, principally, his *Cromwell* (1827), *Marie Tudor* (1833), and *Ruy Blas* (1838).

In a sense, there is no need to turn to Swinburne for burlesque. *Cromwell* itself reads so much like a burlesque of French writers dealing with England that one wants to exclaim "Aut Algernonus, aut Diabolus!" The play is notoriously a sitting duck, partly because of its splendid howlers (the first Earl of Rochester confounded with his son, the poet, a boy of eleven at the time, for instance), and much of it is (or was designed to be) deliberately comic. And though one realizes that Hugo's aim, as announced in the now-classic preface, was to show the multiplicity of Cromwell, it is one thing to understand all, another to pardon. From the opening scene, in which Lord Ormond, plotting the overthrow of Cromwell ("Nous comptons dans nos rangs le gardien de la tour, Barksthead"), attempts to persuade Lord Broghill to join the conspiracy, to the curtain line, many pages and five long acts later, Cromwell's wistful "Quand donc serai-je roi?", nearly everything that can be found in the other "sources"—and more of it—can be found here.

The orthographic embellishments vary from edition to edition, each with its special achievements: Thurloe, Thurloë, Turloë, Thurloé; Fletwood, Flewood; Whitelocke, Whiteloque; White-Hall, Wite-Hall, etc. Address and titles take on an almost independent existence: "Ecoutez, Lord Wilmot, comte de Rochester." "Oui?—Wilmot Rochester ou Buckingham Williers?" muses Cromwell. "Mais enfin, je préférerais, moi, Notre hôtel de Cock-Pit, à ce palais de roi," exclaims Élizabeth Bourchier, milady protectrice. The Protector, himself the archetypal "prince prolétaire," has a scene (III, v) with his favorite daughter, Lady Francis, that, despite the different ending, can hardly fail to remind one of Albert's revelation to Sir Boggs:

> LADY FRANCIS (*l'embrassant d'un air de joie*).
> De grâce, dites-moi, serait-il vrai, mon père?
> Vous relevez le trône?
> CROMWELL.
> On le dit.

LADY FRANCIS.
                              Jour prospère!
L'Angleterre, milord, vous devra son bonheur.
                    CROMWELL.
Ce fut toujours mon but.
                    LADY FRANCIS.
                         Ah! mon père et seigneur!
Que votre bonne sœur, milord, sera contente!
Nous allons donc revoir, après huit ans d'attente,
Notre Charles Stuart!
                    CROMWELL (*etonné*).
                         Quoi!
                    LADY FRANCIS.
                    Que vous êtes bon!
                    CROMWELL.
Ce n'est pas un Stuart.
                    LADY FRANCIS (*surprise*).
                         Quoi donc? Est-ce un Bourbon?
Mais ils n'ont pas de droits au trône d'Angleterre.
                    CROMWELL.
Je le pense de même.
                    LADY FRANCIS.
                         Au sceptre héréditaire
Qui donc ose toucher?
                    CROMWELL (*à part*).
                         Que répondre en effet?
Mon nom me pèse à dire, et me semble un forfait.
                    (*Haut*).
Ma Francis, d'autres temps veulent une autre race.
N'auriez-vous pu penser, pour remplir cette place?
                    LADY FRANCIS.
A qui donc?
                    CROMWELL (*avec douceur*).
               Par exemple,—a ton père? à Cromwell?

Marie Tudor, only a quarter the length of Cromwell, has much of the same, and it will suffice here to call attention to a single scene—the showdown between Queen Mary, on the one hand, jeopardizing crown and risking revolution in her reckless passion for the (fictional) adventurer Fabiani, and, on the other, Simon Renard, emissary of her fiancé, Philip of Spain, here described (I,ii):

La reine le hait, ce Simon Renard, mai elle le craint, et ne peut rien contre lui. Il a déjà détruit deux ou trois favoris. C'est son instinct de détruire les favoris. Il nettoie le palais de temps en temps. Un homme subtil et très malicieux, qui sait tout ce qui se passe, et qui creuse toujours deux ou trois étages d'intrigues souterraines sous tous les événéments.

Bishop Whitestick himself, confronting a helpless Victoria with his ultimatum—sharing the throne with Albert or revolution and exile—is not more imperious than the man who forces Mary Tudor to consent to the execution of her scoundrelly lover, as shown in these excerpts from the great scene (III,ix):

SIMON RENARD.

Il faut que votre majesté prenne un parti sur-le-champ, madame. Le peuple veut la mort de cet homme. Londres est en feu. La Tour est investie. L'émeute est formidable. . . . Qu'ordonne votre majesté? . . .

LA REINE.

Pardieu, milords, vous tremblez tous autour de moi, il me semble! Sur mon âme, faut-il que ce soit une femme qui vous enseigne votre métier de gentilshommes! A cheval, milords, à cheval! Ese-ce que la canaille vous intimide? Est-ce que les épées ont peur des bâtons?

SIMON RENARD.

Ne laissez pas les choses aller plus loin. Cédez, madame, pendant qu'il en est temps encore. Vous pouvez encore dire la canaille, dans une heure vous seriez oblïgée de dire le peuple.

(*Les cris redoublent, le bruit se rapproche.*)

LA REINE.

Dans une heure!

SIMON RENARD (*allant à la galerie et revenant*).

Dans un quart d'heure, madame. Voici que la première enceinte de la Tour est forcée. Encore un peu, le peuple est ici. . . .

LA REINE.

Mais savez-vous qu'il est infâme qu'il y en ait pas un de vous qui bouge, messieurs? Mais, au nom du ciel, défendez-moi donc! . . . Je vous jure qu'il est faux que Fabiani ait voulu assassiner la reine.

LORD CLINTON.

Il y a une autre reine qu'il a voulu assassiner, c'est l'Angleterre. . . .

SIMON RENARD.

Choisissez, madame:

Il désigne d'une main la porte du cachot.

—ou cette tête au peuple,

Il désigne de l'autre main la couronne que porte la reine.

—ou cette couronne à madame Élizabeth.

It remains now to say a brief word about a drama of a very different kidney, *Ruy Blas,* magnificently (and at long last) revived by the Comédie Française a few years ago. Once more the focus narrows to an ultimatum delivered to a helpless queen (V,iii)—Dona Maria, Queen of Spain, in love with the so-called Don César, really Ruy Blas, liveried lackey of Don Salluste, presumably exiled by the Queen. On Don Salluste's sudden, dramatic re-appearance, he confronts the Queen and Ruy Blas with the chilling announcement, "Madame de Neubourg n'est plus reine d'Espagne," and it is impossible not to recall Swinburne's "On ne disait plus la reine; on disait Mistress Cobourg." When Don Salluste throws in the Queen's face

> Vous m'avez pour femme offert votre suivant,
> Moi, je vous ai donné mon laquais comme amant,

it is again impossible to resist recalling Lord Chops's equally cruel "Tu m'as pris la femme, mon bon, je te prends la maîtresse; épouse pour épouse, c'est assez raisonnable." In an earlier scene (III, v), Don Salluste (whose haughty command, "Ruy Blas, fermez la porte—ouvrez cette fenêtre," is the opening line of the play) cynically reasserts his power over Ruy Blas, now first minister and savior of Spain, though still a valet, with the command, "Faites-moi le plaisir de fermer la croisée," and we can be sure that Swinburne had this scornful challenge in mind with Bishop Whitestick's brutal display of power to John Bright, merchant, in a similar context: "Ouvrez la fenêtre, Sir Bright, dit l'impérieux prélat."

Swinburne had lived with these dramas so intimately—as he lived with so much literature—that their clichés leapt naturally from his pen and were transformed gaily into something very funny indeed. Even in Academia, however, the question of sources is always a question, never an answer, and, fascinating and illuminating as it is to ask it here, what is of ultimate significance is that deeper involvement so sensitively hinted at by Lafourcade: "Dans cette récréation, dans cette fantaisie, sa verve, son irrévérence, sa sensualité, son imagination et (qui sait?) son cœur peut-être ont joué librement" (*Minotaure,* p. 62). The tragic vision of the greatest of Hugo's works, *Notre-Dame de Paris,* concluding with the horrible death scenes of Esmeralda and her mother, of Claude Frollo, and the ghastly sacramental "Mariage de Quasimodo" ("Quand on voulut le détacher du squelette qu'il embrassait, il tomba en poussière") is no grimmer than the cutting down by Lord Chops of his own son ("Tiens, c'est drôle. . . . C'est là mon gaillard à moi. Et du plat de son sabre il souffleta la joue morte de Paddy") or Hervey's final view of Nelli beside the mocking, always triumphant Whitestick, before they both die at his feet. The comic vision of "La Fille du policeman" is not different in any essential respect from the tragic vision—not only of *Madame Putiphar*

but—of *Le Roi s'amuse, Hernani, Ruy Blas,* not different in any essential
respect from Swinburne's *Poems and Ballads* read, as I think it must be read,
as a whole poem, not different from the grandest of all his works, *Atalanta
in Calydon.*

II

The manuscripts of the extant portions of "La Fille du policeman" known
to me are in three places, the British Museum; the Huntington Library; and
the Mitchell Library, Sydney, Australia; with one small exception my text is
based directly on them. For the few pages from the Mitchell Library I have
relied on the transcription privately printed in 1963 in Bethesda, Maryland,
by John S. Mayfield, who based his text on photostats.

I will not attempt a detailed description of these manuscripts. One's
sense of proportion boggles. Swinburne's merry foolishness would collapse
under the weight of so much solemnity. Yet, because of the peculiar nature
of my text, a certain amount of description is indispensable. Except for the
initial six chapters (roughly, two-fifths) of this burlesque novel, the separate
parts do not fall into place naturally or even easily, and my editorial conscience requires me to make it possible for him who can to catch me out and
rearrange the parts to suit himself. For this reason, I have risked the charge
of pedantry, here, of all places, where the possibility ought never to arise,
so that the skeptical reader who does not like mine can construct his own text.

The parts of the manuscript in the British Museum have been designated
A, those in the Huntington Library B, those in the Mitchell Library C. I
have indicated in square brackets in the text exactly where each new page
begins.

The British Museum manuscript consists of fifty-four pages written on
twenty-three leaves of foolscap (and on one small white leaf, measuring
about 23 cm. by 18 cm., written in brown ink on one side only—page 49 of
the present text). Of the twenty-three foolscap leaves the first eight are
blue, the remainder white. None of the paper is watermarked. The ink, for
the most part, is brown, though some is black and some light blue. Leaf
number one, folded, contains pages 1, 38, and 39; number five, pages 5,
33, 34, and 35; number eight, pages 8, 36, and 37; and these instances will
doubtless serve to show why, if some description may be necessary, more
would be overwhelming.

The Huntington Library manuscript consists of ten quarto pages. Eight
of these (pages 41-48) make up the chapter called "Les écoliers britanniques,"
which is probably complete. The other two (here, pages 33-34) are certainly,
and most excitingly, the only known surviving pages of the famous chapter

—Meredith called it "marvelous"—"Ce qui peut se passer dans un cab-safety." I have not been privileged to stub my toe upon an Etruscan tomb in the Roman *campagna* or to dive to the sea floor of the Grecian Isles for shipwrecked treasures. I have braved neither African desert nor Central American jungle to search for abandoned temples, nor have I penetrated ancient caves near Jerusalem and found morsels of crumbling scrolls. I have never deciphered a forgotten language, never recovered a precious fragment of the *Anglo-Saxon Chronicle* from the binding of a modern book or established the priority of a first edition, first issue, or even exposed a twentieth-century forgery. But the shock of recognition that I experienced in divining the identity of this fragment of a supposedly lost masterpiece is uniquely mine, and I shall not forget it easily.

The Mitchell Library manuscript, according to information passed along to me by Mr. Mayfield, comprises ten octavo pages. Of these, pages 35-40 make up the chapter called "Le Prince prolétaire," although, as Mayfield has pointed out, there is "evidently a hiatus in the manuscript" between pages 38 and 39. Another crux is more perplexing, and because of the difficulty Mayfield excised a short passage of eight lines (five sentences), relegating it to a "Note" at the end of his pamphlet. These lines, he realized, could not possibly belong where they appear in the text as printed, and, with the evidence available to him, the difficulty was insurmountable.

With more evidence to hand, I have chosen another course. It seems to me certain not only that the excised lines belong where they occur in the manuscript but also that the entire four pages (here, pages 50-53) beginning with these troublesome five sentences (from "C'est ce qu'ont affirmé les journaux anglais" to "il attendait en frémissant les suites de cette émeute") have nothing at all to do with the chapter "Le Prince prolétaire," with which they happen to be grouped, but, instead, conclude the chapter called "L'époux de la reine," of which the title page is in the British Museum. (In solving this problem—if I have solved it—I may have stumbled upon another one even more complicated: the possibility that we have here two versions of the same chapter. All the evidence known to me appears in these pages, however, and I can discover no grounds for pushing the matter beyond the mere speculation.)

The difficulties of description do not end here. On yet another page (now in the British Museum) Swinburne drew up parallel lists of chapter titles, all of which, in both columns, are, or seem to be, canceled, some a good deal more vigorously than others, and one can only assume that these titles represent intentions rather than achievements. At the head of the page is written a word that has remained illegible, beneath which, heavily scored through, are the words "Arthur et Philip." In transcribing these two lists I have retained all the cancellations that I could decipher.

[1]

1. Le Cabaret des
2. Les Jésuites Protestants.
3. Un La concile Tribune du Peuple.
4. Ce qui peut se passer dans un cab-safety
5. Où Nelli dit son fait à un
5. Où l'on voit que les tartuffes sont de toute couleur
6. Chez La Reine chez elle.
7. Le bal de La soutane et l'épée.
8. Chez Le peuple chez lui.
9. L'enlèvement.
10. Le prince prolétaire.
11. Les écoliers d'Egford.
12. Ce qui se passait à Buckingham-Palace.
13. La torture selon les maîtres de
12. Ce qu'on fait des enfants La torture
13. Le père et la fille.
14. Fustigation Flagellation d'Arthur
12. Les bas-fonds de Piccadilly.

13. La torture.   14. Le père et la fille.   15.   L'émeute.
16. La trahison   17. Les deux enfants.   18. Sang pour sang.
19. L'époux de la reine 20. La Révolution manquée.

[2]

1. Un tribun des bas-fonds.
2. Les jésuites protestants.
3. Ce qui peut se passer dans un cab-safety.
4. 3. La reine chez elle.
5. 4. Le peuple chez lui.
6. 5. L'enlèvement.
7. 6. Le prince prolétaire.
8. 7. Où l'on voit que les tartuffes sont de toute couleur.
9. 8. Les écoliers anglais britanniques.
10. 9. La torture
9. L'émeute de la reine
10. Ce qui peut se passer dans un cab-safety.
11. 11. Le père et la fille.
12. L'émeute. Le père et la fille.
13. 12. La trahison.
14. Sang pour sang.
15. L'époux de la reine.
14. 13. Révolution manquée.

There are, of course, many, many cancellations in this manuscript, but, in order not to pile even more weight on a joke already overburdened, I have refrained from transcribing them, except the changes in chapter titles and in one other instance. Editorially, I have corrected or supplied a few accents, expanded several contractions, and occasionally adjusted a misspelling, though of course I have not tampered with *objets d'art* like "blugdeon," "Brigth," "Suothwark," "Hyde's-Park." Composing hastily, Swinburne, as often as not, jauntily refused to be bothered by gender and number in his past participles, and, though I feel pedantic, not to say disloyal, in mentioning it, he really did write such things as "le droit reconnue," "la poivre," "belles groupes," "un boucle," "son part," "chevau-legers," "homage," "qu'il accord," for which I am too pusillanimous to assume the responsibility.

III

1. Swinburne canceled two titles here—"Un tribun des bas-fonds" and "Les jésuites protestants."

2. Guillaume Dubois (1656-1723), cardinal and (in 1722) prime minister.

3. *It Is Never Too Late to Mend* (1856), which Reade followed up with a pamphlet "Proofs of Its Prison Revelations" in 1859. In the prison in Reade's novel the treadmill had been replaced by the crank.

4. That is, Anthony Ashley Cooper, 7th Earl of Shaftesbury (1801-85).

5. Canceled: "La reine chez elle."

6. St. Dominique de Guzman (1170-1221)—in the war against the Albigensians.

7. The joke is clear enough, but not the significance of the name "Challs."

8. " 'I cannot,' said Bright, in the Free Trade Hall, Manchester, October 18, 1847, 'boast of blood and ancestry. My ancestry were people who followed an honourable industry—such as I myself should have preferred always to follow, such as you follow now, and such as your forefathers followed. My sympathies are naturally with the class with which I am connected, and I would infinitely prefer to raise the class of which I am one, than by any means whatever to creep above or out of it' " (quoted in R. Barry O'Brien, *John Bright, A Monograph,* London, 1910, pp. 19-20).

9. Daniel O'Connell (1775-1847), Irish leader and catalytic agent in politics.

10. Cobden refused a baronetcy in 1860.

11. One would expect "laiteux" here, but Swinburne did not write it.

12. Canceled: "L'enlèvement."

13. As noted in the introduction, I have separated these two pages from

their fellows in the Huntington Library on the assumption that they are (regrettably) the only surviving fragment of the most famous of all chapters of this novel.

14. [*p. 35*(C)]. The title is preceded by the roman number "x," as is, also, "L'époux de la reine" (see below, note 20).

15. The rest of the sentence and the few lines following (ending with "articula le lord mayor épouvanté) are written on the lower third of the seventh page—here, [*p. 40*(C)]—of the Mitchell Library manuscript.

16. Clearly, a hiatus in the manuscript.

17. See note 15, above.

18. [*p. 41*(B)].

19. After "Swutchin," of which the first spelling seems to have been "Switchin" (in this instance only), Swinburne canceled "Tickletail."

20. [*p. 49*(A)]. At the top of this page Swinburne wrote and then canceled (except for the numeral): "x. Ce qui peut se passer dans un cabsafety." Above the cancellation he wrote "L'émeute," then lined through the noun and added, above, the title as given. For further details, see the note, p. 241.

21. Apparently, a hasty translation of *pinchbeck,* for which Littré gives *peinchebec.* The more normal word would be *similor.*

22. [*p. 54*(A)]. Canceled: "Trahison."

23. Probably (but not necessarily) a hiatus in the manuscript here.

24. [*p. 67*(A)].

INDEX

(An asterisk indicates actual quotation from the work cited in the index.)

Adam, Antoine: *Théophile de Viau et la libre pensée française en 1620*, 209

Adam, Juliette: author of articles in *Nouvelle Revue*, 194

Adams, Henry: describes Swinburne's conversation at Milnes's in 1862, 199

Æschylus: FitzGerald's and Browning's versions of *Agamemnon* outrages, 74; 67, 71, 212

Albert, Prince, Prince Consort: called "le prince prolétaire" in "Ernest Clouët," 98; confused reference by Swinburne to, in "La Sœur de la reine," 229; disposed of by Queen and John Brown in "La Mort du Mari," 230

Alexandre VI (Borgia), Pope, 123

Alfieri, Vittorio, 67

American Philosophical Society, xv

American poetry: inferiority of, 76

Anne of Austria, 209

Aphaca, 8, 180

Armstrong, Eliza: taken by Stead to brothel, 192

Armstrong, Mrs.: agrees to procuring of daughter for Stead, 192

Arnold, Matthew: as poet-critic, x; censured and praised, 68-72; translations of *Iliad* in "On Translating Homer," 71-72; influence of Wordsworth on, 72; "Merope" bloodless and spiritless, 72, 80; denounced as trimmer, 75; blind to glory of Dickens, Shakespeare, Shelley, Coleridge, Tennyson, Hugo, 77; one of worst of critics, 78; censures "the New Journalism," 191; describes Swinburne as "pseudo-Shelley," 199, 210; described by him as "pseudo-Wordsworth," 210; "Haworth Churchyard" censured, 211; contemptuous allusion to in canceled couplet, 211; criticism of Lord Ashburnham perhaps resented, 211; 216, "Balder Dead," 217; 218

Arts Club, 229

Ashburnham, Bertram, 4th Earl of: Arnold's criticism of, perhaps resented, 211

Augustine, 205

Aytoun, William Edmondstoune: *Firmilian* parody of Dobell's "Balder" and starting point of "The Monomaniac's Tragedy," 213-14

Bailey, John: "La Sœur de la reine" in *John Bailey, 1864-1931, Letters and Diaries*, 229

Bailey, Philip James: *Festus*, 215*; Wheldrake's *Eve* seemed parody of, 83

Barnum, P. T., 202

Baudelaire, Charles: essay on Borel first printed in *Revue fantaisiste*, 225; collected posthumously in *L'Art romantique*, 225; apparently drawn on by Swinburne, 225; probable influence of *Les Fleurs du mal* on passage by Swinburne, 225; Hutton discusses Swinburne's essay on, 225; 60, 220, 235

Beauharnais, Hortense de, 86, 217

Beaumarchais, Pierre Augustin Caron: *Le Mariage de Figaro*, 76*, 212

Beaumont and Fletcher: compared with contemporaries, 31-32; Bessus in *A King and No King*, 43, 204; 198

Benson, Edward White, Archbishop of Canterbury: approves plan for Criminal Law Amendment Bill, 191

Beyle, Henri. *See* Stendhal

Bible: Judges, 76*, 212; Psalms, 58*, 206; John, 13*, 44*, 204; Romans, 76*, 212; Revelation, 62*, 209

Blackmore, Sir Richard: allusion to in *Dunciad*, 212

Blake, William: "Annotations to Reynolds' Discourse I," 49*, 205; "The Marriage of Heaven and Hell," 65*, 210; "On H---y's Friendship," 52*, 205; "Sir Joshua Praises Michael Angelo," 56*, 206; "To the Muses," 58*, 206; Yeats denounced as "Hibernian commentator" on, 73

Blücher, Gebhard Leberecht von, 219

Boileau-Despréaux, Nicolas, 60

Bolingbroke, 1st Viscount, 72

Book of Common Prayer, 51*, 76*, 205, 212

Booth, Bramwell: in "The Marquis of Stead," 21; assists Stead's plan for Criminal Law Amendment Bill, 192; Eliza Armstrong case and, 192-93

245